The Road to El Cielo

Gorgas Science Foundation, Inc.
Treasures of Nature Series

The Treasures of Nature Series is produced by
Gorgas Science Foundation, Inc. (GSF), and
reflects its continuing commitment to the
production of education films, books, field
guides, and laboratory manuals.

Gorgas Science Foundation, Inc.
80 Fort Brown
Brownsville, Texas 78520

MEXICO'S FOREST IN THE CLOUDS

The Road to El Cielo

Fred and Marie S. Webster

Foreword by Paul S. Martin

Drawings by Nancy McGowan

UNIVERSITY OF TEXAS PRESS

Austin

Requests for permission to reproduce material from this work
should be sent to Permissions, University of Texas Press,
P.O. Box 7819, Austin, TX 78713-7819.
http://utpress.utexas.edu/index.php/rp-form

ⓧ The paper used in this book meets the minimum
requirements of ANSI/NISO Z39.48-1992 (R1997)
(Permanence of Paper).

Library of Congress Cataloging-in-Publication Data

Webster, Fred, date
The road to El Cielo : Mexico's forest in the clouds /
Fred and Marie S.Webster ; foreword by Paul S. Martin ;
drawings by Nancy McGowan. — 1st ed.
p.   cm.— (Treasures of nature series)
ISBN 978-0-292-79140-4 (cloth : alk. paper)
1. Reserva de la Biosfera El Cielo (Mexico)—History.
2. Biological diversity conversation—Mexico—
Reserva de la Biosfera El Cielo. 3.Webster, Fred,
1915– 4.Webster, Marie S., 1930– I.Webster, Marie S.,
1930– II. Title. III. Series.

QH77.M6 W43 2001
508.72'12—dc21
2001027792

ISBN 978-0-292-74490-5 (paperback)

This book is dedicated to the memory of John William Francis "Frank" Harrison of Rancho del Cielo, Tamaulipas, Mexico, and John H. Hunter and Barbara T. Warburton of Brownsville, Texas, without whose friendship and cooperation over many years this volume would not have been possible.

Foreword

Paul S. Martin

The 1,500-mile boundary separating Mexico and the United States is unique. This border sees more change, more contrast between neighbors, than any other of its length. Language, religion, ethnicity, government and legal systems, and biota—all differ to varying degrees, and these differences lead some *norteamericanos* to be surprised by the warm hospitality that they receive from the people in rural Mexico.

Not everyone cares for surprises. I have known sophisticated, highly trained, and widely traveled biologists, with a deep interest in the rich ecology of the Mexican Plateau, to be so phobic that they simply would not be pried loose from the United States to explore Mexico, unless it was within the confines of a resort like Cancún. This was before the current period of violence along the border stemming from the drug wars, which has, of course, only increased the apprehensions of the apprehensive.

In contrast, Fred and Marie Webster are venturesome. In this book we learn that in about 250 miles—half a day's drive south of Brownsville, Texas, and not far south of the Tropic of Cancer—one arrives within a few miles of a lush temperate broadleaf forest, the cloud forest surrounding Rancho del Cielo. Those last few miles, from the pavement to the field station, are an adventure all their own.

On the jolting "road" to El Cielo, the Websters introduce us to Brownsville businessman John Hunter, who loved to put four-wheel-drive vehicles to the test. Following a serendipitous breakdown on a foggy night in the mountains, with only fireflies for illumination, daylight revealed to him a forest that rivaled the green mansions that we read about in William H. Hudson's famous novel of that title.

Rancho del Cielo is located in the middle of a fascinating montane vegetation gradient straddling the Sierra de Guatemala, an offset of the Sierra Madre Oriental. On the east side, tropical lowland forests, those not cleared for tomatoes or sugarcane, support palms, strangler figs, and dozens of other species of tropical trees. On the west side of the sierra is thorn scrub of the Chihuahuan Desert, with creosote bush, cholla, prickly pear cactus, and arborescent yucca. In the mountains between the tropical lowlands and the desert are moist forests of sweetgum, podocarpus, magnolia, redbud, and many species of oak. Numerous epiphytes drape the tree branches, and numerous animals, including lungless salamanders, live in the epiphytes. Here, just south of the Tropic of Cancer and growing within forty miles of each other, are six climatically and biotically distinct plant formations, diversity to match what one finds in the entire state of Texas. Nestled between the lowlands and the desert, the cloud forest of El Cielo is a cathedral with sacred music provided by solitaires and singing quail, a gift of the gods for birders, botanists, and those choking on city life.

This book tells of the Websters' many adventures at Rancho del Cielo. For example, Marie, along with an ornithological companion, ran a breeding-bird census fifteen years after the first in 1949–1950 by Byron E. Harrell. We learn how Frank Harrison, the Canadian who had lived alone in the cloud forest since 1935, eventually assumed the unofficial role of a field station manager, until his tragic murder. Frank's knowledge, aid, and enthusiasm proved crucial to the completion of numerous biological research projects, theses, and dissertations, my own included.

We learn how John Hunter patiently brokered a land transfer of Frank Harrison's property at Rancho del Cielo to the Gorgas Science Foundation, then at a small Texas junior college, to the lasting benefit of its students. Given the convolutions of both Texan and Mexican laws and politics, it was an amazing achievement. Additional land on tropical slopes too rough to cultivate was added with the financial aid of George M. Sutton, who pioneered ornithological research in the region. The Sutton reserve attracts cracid game birds, brocket deer, and jaguar.

I have barely scratched the surface here. In 1985 the Mexican government designated the Gómez Farías region as a biosphere reserve. Subsequent research by Mexican ecologists and their students has yielded a rich corpus of new information on the biota of the region and its management (to appear in a book in Spanish being edited by Gerardo Ramos Sánchez of the Universidad Autónoma de Tamaulipas, with contributions from dozens of authors on the natural history of the El Cielo Biosphere Reserve). No regional biosphere reserve could exist without friends and supporters in the republic of Mexico; here those people include Enrique Beltrán and Efraim Hernández X., both active in preservation efforts beginning in the 1950s, followed by G. Halfstetter and the French ecologist Henri Puig, who has written a book on El Cielo's remarkable forest.

As Fred and Marie Webster reveal, the exploitation of forest resources, especially lumbering, accompanied by hurricanes, drought, and wildfire,

has taken its toll. Yet we do not know what happened to the Tamauli-
pan cloud forest a thousand years ago when sizable parts of lowland rain
forest throughout the New World tropics yielded to heavy use by prehis-
toric agriculturalists. Archaeological remains abound around Rancho del
Cielo. Perhaps ecologists underestimate the capacity of the tropical forests
to rebound from severe disturbance, as the temperate forests in the eastern United States have. With the interest of Mexican ecologists and the
Universidad de Tamaulipas, one hopes for some solutions to that daunting
conundrum, unresolved during the twentieth century: how to balance the
needs of humans with those of nature. The Websters' fascinating story takes
us up the pounding road to heaven's ranch, Rancho del Cielo.

Acknowledgments

In writing *The Road to El Cielo,* we drew material from many sources: research papers, personal journals, historical accounts, and letters from individuals. Our thanks go to all who contributed in various ways.

We wish to recognize a number of individuals who were most influential in providing background material, moral support, or critical evaluation of the manuscript:

Nancy McGowan, our superb illustrator and fellow Mexico traveler; Paul S. Martin, whose critical reading of the manuscript was most helpful and whose earlier research in the Gómez Farías region was the source of much of our information; Lawrence V. Lof, who persuaded us to do this book, assisted us in many ways, and pointed out necessary alterations to the manuscript; Marshall C. Johnston, who first told us of Frank Harrison and Rancho del Cielo and who reviewed the manuscript with a critical eye.

William Bishel, our supportive editor; Shannon Davies, whose early editorial assistance and encouragement kept us on track; Sharon L. Casteel, who had the unenviable task of converting the typed copy to computer disk; Sterling Evans, whose painstaking perusal of the manuscript and insightful suggestions were most helpful.

Robert and Mabel Deshayes, companions and co-workers on many Mexico adventures; Alfred Richardson, incomparable friend and confidant — very much a part of our Mexico experience; the faculty, staff, and students of the Gorgas Science Society, whose assistance and companionship at Rancho del Cielo over a span of many years will always be treasured.

Byron Eugene Harrell, whose study of the birds of the cloud forest at Rancho del Cielo ignited our interest in the region; the late George Miksch Sutton, who loved El Cielo as few men have, and whose writings on Mexico inspired our own efforts.

Special recognition is due our friends in Mexico: Laura Alcalá Vargas, whose tireless efforts were largely responsible for the creation of El Cielo Biosphere Reserve; Andres M. Sada, who experienced the wonders of El Cielo in our company and saw the value of preserving its environment; and all the officials and other citizens of Mexico who helped bring the dream to reality.

There are other special people, but none more special than Dr. James George, a major backer of the Rancho del Cielo biological station, who reviewed the manuscript, and Charlotte Boyle, our most ardent advocate, who was eager to promote the manuscript when it was yet in first draft.

The Road to El Cielo

Prologue

THE Sierra de Guatemala etched a wavy margin along the western sky, sun-bathed browns and greens against December morning blue. The mountain was clean and remote, untouchable from the lowland course of the Pan-American Highway. We wondered what made this range different from others in northeastern Mexico.

Marshall Johnston stirred in the back seat. "You can just see the cloud forest from here, below the higher ridge."

"Oh. Yes." We were polite, if not enthusiastic.

"Frank Harrison's place is up there, behind one of the peaks."

The name, Frank Harrison, was unfamiliar. At the moment the terrain held our attention. We were fascinated by the tropical lushness of the landscape since crossing the Río Guayalejo and twisting down Galeana Canyon. It was a blessed relief from the dry scrub we had traversed since leaving Ciudad Victoria. The thatched roofs, banana and papaya trees, people on foot, people on burros, wandering domestic fowl and swine, and the ever-pervasive smell of wood smoke, this was Mexico as we remembered it. Now our destination, Xilitla, far to the south, was less a figment of anticipation.

Marshall leaned forward. "They're collecting donations to buy land before the forest is gone."

"Oh? How is that?" Marie, my wife, is quick to sense a crisis.

We looked away to the mountain again, across a sea of cane to forested slopes.

"The lumber people are taking timber out."

We waited for more. Marshall could leave a subject dangling indefinitely; we were ready to settle the matter.

"Who wants to buy the land?"

"Irby. And scientists who've investigated up there."

Mention of L. Irby Davis reminded us again of Xilitla; we were to meet Irby there before the day was over. But Marshall had more to say. The land they wanted to buy and preserve was unique: the northernmost tropical cloud forest in America, an oak-sweetgum forest with temperate as well as southern affinities. We learned that much before Marshall leaned back, pleased at our partial enlightenment.

We thought the topic was closed until, a few miles later, we crossed the Río Sabinas. A dirt road branched off to the right.

"San Gerardo," Marshall announced as a tiny settlement appeared and vanished. "That's the road to Gómez Farías, last stop before Rancho del Cielo . . ."

"Frank Harrison's place," he added when we seemed more interested in a strangler fig that was suffocating its sabal palm host.

The conversation had proceeded somewhat as reconstructed here. That was December 26, 1954, and at the time we had no reason to record our remarks in transit. We do recall, in particular, that Marshall Johnston was the first to bring our attention to Frank Harrison and his beloved mountain retreat. Marshall, then a student at the University of Texas in Austin, had been to Rancho del Cielo with Irby Davis—the premier interpreter of tropical birdsong—on a recording expedition.

Ironically, Marshall's comments were of only passing interest. Marie and I were impatient to reach the mountain village of Xilitla in San Luis Potosí state, where we would participate in our second Christmas bird count with Irby Davis and friends. This time we hoped to add the Emerald Toucanet to our bird life-list. The Sierra de Guatemala faded quickly from view and memory.

About ten years later we would again cross the Río Sabinas; this time we would turn right at San Gerardo and head for Gómez Farías, and from there to Frank Harrison's Rancho del Cielo, birds again high on the agenda. We could not have known that we soon would be engaged in much more than birdwatching, but the struggle to save the cloud forest was—again— just over the horizon.

I

JOHN HUNTER was responsible for getting us to Rancho del Cielo and the cloud forest. John owned a cabin on Frank Harrison's property. A trip from his Brownsville, Texas, home to the mountain was John's idea of the ultimate adventure and delight. It was, we would learn, an experience that he shared with many friends and kin over the years, for John Hunter was generous to a fault.

Actually, it was John's wife, Caroline, who—quite innocently, we are certain—started us on a pilgrimage that would span three decades. Or should we credit circumstance, a chain of events fashioned by pure chance, or providential design?

Whatever the guiding force, we can start with my father, Fred S. Webster, Senior, and Caroline's father, Ira Webster, who were first cousins. Both men had acquired a penchant for tracing the family tree, which diversion eventually brought them together. Exact dates are lost in the passage of time, but it is likely that Frank Harrison had not yet discovered Rancho del Cielo when their first meeting occurred.

Long after both fathers had passed on, Caroline played her part. She needed to research our genealogical files further, and to that end she visited us in Austin. The family business resolved, talk turned to more current topics. No doubt we mentioned that we "did" birds and had been to Xilitla in pursuit of the hobby. The subject of Mexico now laid on the table, the conversation may have proceeded thusly:

"John has found a wonderful place in Mexico that you would enjoy." Caroline's smile was genuinely cordial, a mirror of John's hospitable nature, we would discover. She spoke slowly and deliberately, holding but not commanding attention. "John calls it 'the mountain.'" She paused for a moment and regarded us intently, but I suspected that she was looking beyond us. "The fruit trees are wonderful. Frank Harrison can grow just about anything. We have an article about his gloxinias—that's how John learned about Frank."

We let the matter drop there. Mention of Mexico had aroused our interest, but from my perspective, Mexico was for birds, not for fruit trees or gloxinias—or "the mountain."

Azure-crowned Hummingbird

Some time later (it may have been several years) we received a letter from Caroline, dated July 6, 1963.

> We now own a cabin on the mountain in Mexico that I told you about. My twin sister Elizabeth lives in Victoria—just about seventy miles this side of the place where we turn off to go up to the mountain. She lost her husband a year ago and her son is running the box factory and looking after their cattle and other interests there. Sonny has just fixed up a 4-wheel-drive jeep so that he can get up to the cabin when his jeep is needed. We would like for you to plan a trip down there sometime. Sonny would be glad to take you up and you are welcome to use our cabin.

It was becoming obvious that Frank Harrison and Rancho del Cielo would not go away. Marie, being the more adventurous, embraced the idea of a jeep ride into alien territory to see a mountain forest. Maybe it was the age differential (I being fifteen years the senior), but I was more cautious about committing to a lark in the wilderness. Besides, I had not outgrown the conviction that birds were the principal excuse for human residence on planet Earth. It was this quirk in my character, however, that eventually led us up the mountain. John Hunter was to administer the finishing stroke in the scenario.

A letter from John, dated April 8, 1964, read in part: "I was down at the mountain last weekend and talked to Frank about when would be the best time for you to come down. . . . Under separate cover I am sending you a copy of a thesis which Byron Harrell wrote on the birds of the Rancho del Cielo forest. I'm sure you will find this interesting." (Harrell, from the University of Minnesota, had studied the cloud forest birds in 1949 and 1950.)

Indeed, the thesis was interesting. I had long been under the misconception that in order to enjoy a suitable menu of tropical avifauna, one must journey at least as far south as Xilitla. Harrell's thesis completely refuted this tenet, for only 500 airline miles south of our home in Austin, Texas, one could find such exotic species as macaws, trogons, motmots, and woodcreepers. Harrell's list was both impressive and compelling.

John green-inked a footnote to his letter: "Be sure to bring anyone with you that you might want to, there is plenty of room." In time, we would follow his suggestion, and with unexpected results.

In the meantime, the next phase in a total breakdown of resistance to the idea of a mountain vacation was a nagging curiosity as to what, exactly, made this cloud forest so special. Marshall Johnston had dropped a few hints (which we had failed to pursue) on our trip to Xilitla. Now, a decade later, we turned to Byron Harrell for answers.

The introductory comments to Harrell's thesis proved invaluable. The Sierra de Guatemala, as we learned on a second and now intent perusal of the manuscript, is a disjunct segment of the Sierra Madre Oriental, the mountain system that extends north-south off the east coast of Mexico. Our particular range is about 90 miles removed from the gulf beaches, a karst limestone formation defined on the north by the gorge of the Río Guayalejo and on the south by the Chamal Valley—an intervening distance of some 34 miles. The nearest familiar reference point is Ciudad Victoria, capital of the state of Tamaulipas, about 38 highway miles north of the Río Guayalejo highway bridge.

The remarkable ecological diversity of the sierra progresses both altitudinally and on an east-west line for a distance of fewer than 20 miles. On its eastern front, the range is bordered by a wide swath of tropical deciduous forest that encroaches on its lower reaches and also is found in the Chamal Valley to the south—that is, where field crops and orchards have not replaced the native vegetation. The Río Sabinas, originating mainly in a deep *nacimiento* (source, spring) at the eastern base of the front, snakes through the lowlands, traced by its gallery forest of Montezuma bald cypress and other tree giants.

Progressing up the mountainside, tropical deciduous growth merges with and eventually yields to another forest type, tropical semievergreen and evergreen. The latter, in turn, is supplanted by oak-sweetgum cloud forest. All three forest types reach their northernmost limits within the Sierra de Guatemala. The oak-sweetgum forest generally occupies a narrow shelf of irregular surface features along and atop the lower (easternmost) ridge. Its characteristic vegetation dominates at elevations between about 2,950 and 4,600 feet but is confined on the west by a higher second ridge clothed in humid pine-oak forest.

Several factors contribute to the uniqueness of the region, climate and geology being of utmost importance. In summer months, the eastern mountain face, rising abruptly from the valley of the Río Sabinas, provides lift for moisture-bearing trade winds from the Gulf of Mexico, while above and to the west of the cloud forest, peaks reaching 7,000 feet or more tend to block further advance of rain clouds, thus concentrating heavier precipitation amounts to the eastern slopes; rainfall in the cloud forest during this period may exceed 100 inches. This geological configuration leaves the back (or west) side of the mountain in the rain shadow; the dominant plant community here is a relatively dry oak-pine woodland.

Of particular interest to naturalists are the plant associations, tropical and temperate species found in a bewildering mix. We noted that bird populations, too, represented many ecological niches. One fact, especially, intrigued us: most of Harrell's study had been conducted during the breeding season, leaving huge seasonal gaps for some lucky birders to fill.

The Hunter house on West St. Charles in Brownsville was to be our home while in transit for years to come. Although the sojourn was usually of the one-night-stand variety, we always felt that we belonged; it was an oasis of acceptance in unfamiliar territory, a cool refuge on a hot summer afternoon for the Mexico traveler. The structure was aging, yet clean and neat, framed in tropical foliage. Alamanda blossoms beguiled the passerby on summer days, and in season, avocados and limes dropped their abundance on fermenting earth.

The house stood resolutely in a neighborhood that had aged less gracefully, but it was conveniently distant from downtown Brownsville and its frantic mix of tourists and local shoppers from Matamoros across the Río Grande. And it was only a short distance from the "Valley's Oldest and Largest Refrigeration House," the firm of John H. and Earl Hunter on Elizabeth Street.

Inside the house on West St. Charles one sensed the vitality and charm of its occupants. The sturdy furniture reflected John's character as well as physical attributes, and the African violets constantly in bloom against the dining-room windows were Caroline in floral elegance. Not visible to the casual visitor, closets bulging with items no longer in use recalled family years. Quite conspicuous, on the other hand, were the bookshelves that lined the entry hallway with volumes accumulated and assimilated over time.

We experienced our first impression of the house on West St. Charles on an afternoon in early May, but it was John Hunter's Jeep station wagon, parked on the lawn by the front porch, that elicited our attention. It was backed up to the porch side—obviously an impromptu loading zone, as attested by the amount of baggage crammed behind the seats of the vehicle. Having endured 350 miles of hot pavement to reach this moment, we had not placed additional travel foremost on our wish list, so we were relieved when John assured us that departure was set for some time on the following day.

John's greeting was in a booming voice with a slight quaver. He was impressive at six feet and four inches and 300 pounds or more, a bulk supported with the aid of a walking cane. Caroline was quite short by comparison, prim and self-composed, pleasantly round-faced with peaches-and-cream complexion and beautiful white hair pulled up in a bun.

Besides a comfortable bed and private bath, the Hunter hospitality always included a most satisfying evening meal. Thereafter, and the supper dishes being put to rest, we would relax in the living room for a session of conversation and enlightenment. John graciously and enthusiastically provided most of the latter from a limitless reservoir of experience and acquired knowledge, particularly of historical matters and particularly those of Mexico.

Of primary interest to us at the outset was the nature of John Hunter's involvement at Rancho del Cielo and the circumstances that had led him there. To appreciate fully the situation into which we were being drawn, it was necessary to penetrate the veil of decades past, back to the moment of Frank Harrison's discovery (while on a hunting expedition into the Sierra de Guatemala) of a small homestead, long abandoned and slowly yielding to second-growth forest. Call it mystical experience or practical consideration, the outcome was that Frank Harrison soon forsook his Chamal Valley home and its amenities (such as they were in a malarial lowland environment) to chop out a new life in the wilderness.

For Harrison, the climate at Rancho del Cielo was good for body and soul. He found it ideally suited to varied horticultural practices, not just for sustenance but also for the pleasure of working with such ornamentals as gloxinia, tuberous begonia, amaryllis, and others.

Harrison came to Rancho del Cielo in 1935. By 1940 his gardening commentary had appeared in at least one trade journal. It is not clear if it was his writing that first apprised the natural-science fraternity of the existence of a virgin forest ripe for investigation of its floristic components and related animal elements. It may have been Everts Storms, Harrison's good friend who resided at Pano Ayuctle (Pumpkin Ford) down on the Río Sabinas, who passed the word; Don Evaristo (Everts) was hosting researchers as early as the 1940s. Or it may have been the local people at Rancho Rinconada, downstream from the Storms place, who spoke of the forest in the clouds to members of the John B. Semple expedition in 1938. Irby Davis, an earlier traveler in the region, recalled hearing of a hermit living on the mountain, before he was aware that Frank Harrison existed.

No scientific exploration of the area occurred before the Pan-American Highway, connecting Laredo, Texas, with Mexico City, was opened to traffic in the early 1930s. Until that momentous achievement, the valley of the Río Sabinas was served by oxcart trail, while the Sierra de Guatemala loomed remote and mysterious westward, its ramparts challenged only by occasional foot travelers and beasts of burden as they sought to cross to the settlement of La Joya de Salas on the back side of the mountain.

On April 9, 1948, a three-man party—Paul S. Martin, Ernest P. Edwards, and Roger P. Hurd—on a collecting expedition to Mexico climbed the slope from Pano Ayuctle to Rancho del Cielo. This "discovery of undisturbed cloud forest" encouraged Martin to develop a regional study of the area, subsequently published as *A Biogeography of Reptiles and Amphibians in the Gómez Farías Region, Tamaulipas, Mexico* (Miscellaneous Publication 101, Museum of Zoology, University of Michigan, 1958). Other parties soon followed, eager to investigate the plant and animal life of the region. Byron Harrell first visited Rancho del Cielo on April 2, 1949.

If Frank Harrison's writings did not lure scientists to the cloud forest, they definitely aroused the curiosity of John Hunter and some other Texans in deep South Texas. Possibly the first of these to learn of Frank Harrison and Rancho del Cielo was Fred Blesse of Brownsville.

We have heard conflicting accounts regarding Blesse's first contact with Frank Harrison—one, that Blesse had a chance meeting with Paul Martin and Byron Harrell at the Río Frío (near Gómez Farías) sometime in 1948. But there is no doubt that Fred Blesse was John Hunter's link to Rancho del Cielo.

It was a magazine article that started John on his quest for the land of eternal youth, to paraphrase his pronouncement after visiting the mountain. The article, "Achimenes in Mexico," appeared in the January-February 1954 issue of the *Gloxinian;* the author was "Pancho (William Frank Harrison, Mexico)." In his account, Pancho described the native achimenes species but devoted more space to such a graphic exposition of the environment (climate, geology, the plants in his orchard) as to pique the interest of any nature-oriented person. The exact location of his wonderland was not given, but it was "about 35 miles south of the Tropic of Cancer." From this clue and the description of the region, John knew that Pancho's place must be tucked away in some portion of the Sierra Madre Oriental that he had passed in his travels. But he must know more. Who in Brownsville had ever heard of William Frank Harrison? Persistent inquiries led to Fred Blesse and an invitation to visit Rancho del Cielo.

Blesse had first gone to Rancho del Cielo in 1952, the cloud forest having become accessible to vehicular traffic by a one-lane logging road from Gómez Farías. On July 15, 1953, he entered into an agreement with Frank Harrison whereby he, Blesse, would rent two hectares (about five acres) of land at the ranch for ten years from date, at $5 per year, paid in advance. Blesse then built a cabin on the land.

John Hunter was a guest at Blesse's cabin in November 1954; it was the beginning of John's love affair with the mountain. That would not have been so for a man who cringed at adversity, for the journey up the mountain proved to be an adventure worthy of the John Hunter tradition. The climb was attempted at night. Daunting enough by day, night passage added an element of mystery—and terror to the faint-hearted. The roadbed seemed not so rugged as jeep headlights sheered over the higher rocks and left the depressions in shadow, but therein lay the hazard for the careless driver. The way tunneled through choking greenery except where canyon walls dropped off from the too-meager shoulder into—mercifully—total blackness.

As was his custom, Blesse stopped at the foot of the first steep climb to listen for trucks. It was defensive strategy. Descending vehicles had the right-of-way; those going up must pull over for passing or back down, usually the latter; it was not a maneuver to be undertaken at night. On this occasion, there were no trucks on the road, but some time later, on the most treacherous grade up, the jeep stalled out. Details are lacking here. We do know that Lucas Romero, Frank Harrison's part-time helper, was present and was able to talk a lumber truck's crew into pulling the jeep. The tow made it to the junction with the ranch road and some distance beyond, but the truck (doubtless one of the World War II discards operating on the mountain) was unable to get the jeep up the last steep incline. From that point, the trip to Blesse's cabin was completed on foot. On the following morning, the jeep's engine was removed, and Frank Harrison, Lucas, and another local man carried it on poles to the junction with the main road, from where a lumber truck took the party to town, presumably Ciudad Mante.

We have no doubt that for John this rude introduction to the mountain was soon mellowed by the charm of the forest. It may be, too, that the physical challenges of the trip energized him, for he seemed always to thrive on meeting problems, and with a devilish sort of pleasure. Whatever, the mountain had claimed a life convert. John could not have known that the Blesse cabin would eventually be the Hunter cabin, but he was determined to maintain a presence at Rancho del Cielo. In January 1955, John returned to the mountain with a nephew, Bob Hunter, of Brownsville; the following summer, Bob and Gordon McInnis built a cabin on leased land within an easy stone's throw of Blesse's cabin.

Fred Blesse surrendered his lease in 1959 but sold his cabin to a friend, Fred Welch. Welch arranged to rent the land for fifteen years for a fee of 10 pesos annually, beginning November 19, 1959.

When John Hunter finally moved to provide a mountain base for himself, it was not to be at Rancho del Cielo but at neighboring San Pablo. San Pablo had been the property of Paul Gellrich, who had shared Rancho del Cielo with Frank Harrison in the early years. John had given Frank money to buy Paul's clearing at San Pablo and had taken photographs of possible cabin sites when Fred Welch decided to sell his interests at Rancho del Cielo. The San Pablo project was quickly abandoned, and in the spring of 1962 John and his brother, Earl Hunter, bought the former Blesse cabin.

Thicket Tinamou

2

OUR first trip with John Hunter lacked what would become the typical early morning start of later years. Around 3 A.M. John would throw open our bedroom door and flip the light switch, invariably beating our travel alarm to the punch. This untimely introduction to the morning was tempered somewhat by Caroline's breakfast offering of orange juice, bacon, eggs, toast, and coffee, after which we boarded the Jeep as soon as expedient and headed for the International Bridge and an uncertain fate at the *aduana* (customhouse) in Matamoros.

In May 1964 we were denied, also, the experience of helping to load ("pack" is a better word) John's Jeep. Since residency at Rancho del Cielo was entirely self-sustaining, one furnished all bedding, utensils, food, drink, and anything else that would be needed for a prolonged stay. If these items were not already stockpiled at the cabin, they must be provided. In addition, John maintained his "short list" of items that were in short supply; these, plus perishables, were assured of space in the Jeep. Eggs and meat were always procured in Brownsville. Eggs were meticulously snuggled into army surplus ammo boxes, the meat preserved with dry ice.

John's packing technique was an art form, with the result that every centimeter of space was utilized, and miraculously, there always seemed room to cram in anything that might have been overlooked. On our first expedition, not only was the Jeep packed to the hilt, but a mattress and a water-heater tank were also secured to the roof.

At mid-afternoon on May 2, 1964, we headed for Matamoros—John, ourselves, and John's friend Leon. The officials at Mexico customs may have raised eyebrows at our overstuffed vehicle and its overhead load, but John was a veteran at making the border crossing, and we cleared customs without argument. One way to avoid baggage search, John had instructed us, was to pack personal items in a duffel bag rather than a suitcase; we have been ever grateful for this useful stratagem.

We passed the night at the house of Caroline's sister, on the outskirts of Ciudad Victoria and 200 miles into our adventure. Elizabeth McCollum was taller, on the slender side, with more narrow facial conformation, dark hair, and hazel eyes. Mac, her late husband, had had business interests on the mountain, although they did not directly affect Rancho del Cielo.

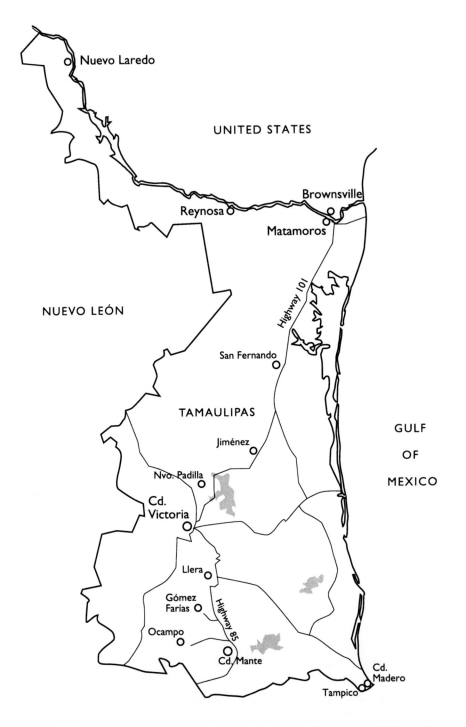

Nuevo Laredo

UNITED STATES

Brownsville

Reynosa

Matamoros

NUEVO LEÓN

Highway 101

San Fernando

TAMAULIPAS

Jiménez

Nvo. Padilla

GULF

OF

MEXICO

Cd.
Victoria

Llera

Gómez
Farías

Highway 85

Ocampo

Cd. Mante

Cd.
Madero

Tampico

The road from Brownsville to Gómez Farías, in the southern part of Tamaulipas.

We had reached Ciudad Victoria after dark, so the light of morning brought revelation of a sort. The Sierra Madre Oriental, a roller-coaster mass of unbroken green, crowded the western horizon, brooding over the city confined in a depression at its foot and seemingly aloof from the humanity that, like ants, constantly moved through a maze of narrow passages lined by pastel-tinted walls. For whatever imaginings the sierra might evoke, vibrant, teeming life flowed on a lower plane, intent on its own agenda.

This portion of the Sierra Madre held no real interest for us; we knew there was no cloud forest here. Rather, semiarid lowlands graduated to semiarid mountain slope, topped off in semiarid oak forest. We were impatient for birds of a tropical cloud forest.

We had checked out the birdlife in Elizabeth's citrus orchard after breakfast. The aroma of orange blossoms was pleasing, but the birds were all familiar Texas species. Obviously, it was time to move on. First, John advised, we were due a foray into town; our mission: to buy fresh produce at the market.

As the morning progressed, rising wind blew hot puffs of dust copiously along narrow streets, and shadows blended into substance. The sierra had pulled a veil of haze across its flanks and appeared to retreat from reality. Not so the market, athrob with activity, saturated with sound and smell. A typical market, one that you would expect in a typical Mexican city, it was geared to local trade rather than tourism, with an expansive roofed area of open stalls, vegetables stacked, meat hanging, and a labyrinth of small shops with garish merchandise.

Most impressive was John Hunter's shopping pace; despite his physical size and limitations, we found it difficult to keep at his heels. Thanks to John's market-harvesting technique, we were out of the city well before noon, when shops close for a two-hour siesta.

Elizabeth had been added to our party, in addition to various fruits and vegetables, of which we remember only the tomatoes, and that for good reason.

How many times were we to take the old Pan-American Highway south from Ciudad Victoria! Never having the time to experience the fascinating life of the dry, scrubby thorn forest, yet anticipating the lushness of the forest in the clouds. Always teased by the mountains, which, though persistently filling the western horizon, shunned intimacy. Always alert on the serpentine stretch of highway up and down from the Mesa de Llera. For a few moments wonder would override stress as the road maneuvered to align "Gunsight," the precise positioning of three ancient volcanic plugs that rise unexpectedly from the valley floor beyond. Then came the hairpin turns, and gawking at roadside debris where trucks had gone out of control.

Finally, we reached a gentle descent to the Río Guayalejo, northern boundary of the Sierra de Guatemala. We were a dozen miles south of the Tropic of Cancer, but thorn forest had not yet given way to more luxuriant growth; however, as we wound through verdant foothills down to the valley of the Río Sabinas the change was dramatic: remnant patches of tropical deciduous forest competed with cultivated fields and orchards that encroached up the hillsides. Small stick-and-wattle houses with thatched roofs squatted at random; roadside stands displayed fruit, juices, honey.

The trip was coming into clear focus at last. What John had been telling us along the way, of the history, the people, the natural features of the land, was becoming reality. We could see it and hear it and smell it.

The terrain flattened out. The village of El Encino, at highway mile 55, gave access to the Río Sabinas, still several miles to the west, by a dirt road that cut the town in half. To reach Rancho del Cielo by the longer route, John explained, one turned here, continuing to a low-water crossing at the Sabinas, a steady and laborious climb to cloud forest level, the lumber yard at Julilo where the pines begin, then some four miles through forest to Frank Harrison's place. This route pulsed with recent and not-so-recent events. We would hear much of the people, their exploits and shattered dreams—and we would be drawn inexorably into the ongoing drama. But today it was to be the short route to Rancho del Cielo, through Gómez Farías.

Past El Encino the highway set a rather straight and level course through the river valley. Two miles from El Encino, John pointed to a dirt road on the right, a lonely trail vanishing toward the river. "That goes to Pano Ayuctle, Everts Storms' place," John said. "He's gone now, drowned in the river. Heart attack. That was a great loss to Frank."

We recalled names from the literature and word of mouth. It hadn't been too many years ago that Don Evaristo was hosting eager young naturalists. Frank Harrison would make frequent trips down the treacherous short trail to Pano Ayuctle, on the way to market with produce from his garden, to return with supplies for the ranch.

We were beginning to feel that John's mountain—Frank Harrison's mountain—was more than just a chunk of real estate; it was an obsession. It seemed, at the moment, quite beguiling, discreetly removed and untouched by human events, sprawled along the western horizon beyond sugarcane fields. On later trips, the range most often would be clothed in thunderheads, which rolled up its flanks in daily summertime ritual. In May 1964, however, the mountain merely shimmered in a clinging haze; the rainy season was yet to come, and the humid lowlands broiled under the sun's absolute rule.

We were distracted from our mountain musings by flashes of color at roadside, lavender-blue flower clusters of the jacaranda tree, bright scarlet of the royal poinciana; the two seemed to vie for favor. Neither species was native to Mexico, John informed us, a fact that failed to diminish our appreciation.

"Much of this area was palm bottom a while back."

We had noticed isolated trees or small patches of *Sabal mexicana* but had assumed they were planted exotics. I was beginning to understand that we actually had little concept of this area's appearance a hundred or more years ago. Was there any tract of palm jungle remaining? Where was the tropical deciduous forest? If the view from the highway was any indication, cultivated field, orchard, and pasture were supplanting native vegetation in the Sabinas Valley. We suspected that much land had been put to the plow even since we passed here en route to Xilitla years before. The coming of the Pan-American Highway had been a boon for the people but a scourge to the native flora and fauna.

Actually, as John pointed out, things had gone downhill long before the 1930s. Although Indian tribes in this region of northeastern Mexico had successfully resisted the Spanish for two centuries after the fall of the Aztec empire, they were unable to turn back a force led by José de Escandón in January 1747. Spanish colonization meant new farming practices and herds of livestock.

We had reached the bridge across the Río Sabinas. This would be our first and only glimpse of the river from the highway. The water ran clear and cool under a canopy of huge cypress trees, fed by a distant spring that took water from the bowels of the mountain. It was called gallery forest, the columns of trees that lined the river banks and rose, like a gallery, above the adjoining land.

Not far beyond the bridge, John slowed the Jeep and turned right. We were at San Gerardo, little more than a wide place in the road, but the only highway access to Gómez Farías; only 12 kilometers, the sign read. Ciudad Victoria was 67 miles to the north. This would be our last highway reading, and a farewell to smooth road surfaces. At first glance the dirt road ahead did not appear threatening, and it pointed straight toward the mountains, but it would have to climb soon, for our altimeter read just 400 feet above sea level.

About five miles later, after enduring a washboard road through a landscape given over to crops and pasture, we did start to ascend. It was here that we had our introduction to apparently undisturbed tropical deciduous forest.

The forest presented an almost impenetrable understory of trees and shrubs, with taller trees protruding randomly above the canopy, as though squeezed from the press. Lianas and epiphytes added to the confusion of plant species, and we caught glimpses of that large and spiny terrestrial bromeliad *Bromelia pinguin* (wild pineapple), which in places covered the forest floor and discouraged foot traffic by human and beast alike. As for the trees, we recognized none of them in passing, although we had learned some of them by name in searching the literature. We had been fascinated by such odd names as eardrop tree (*Enterolobium cyclocarpum*), apes-earring (*Pithecellobium dulce*), and strangler fig (*Ficus cotinifolia*). The last species sprouts when a seed is deposited in the crotch of a host tree; it sends roots to the ground and eventually strangles the host. We remembered, also, that the tropical deciduous forest has various species of the genera *Acacia, Cassia,* and *Leucaena.* The presence of many compound-leaved and thorny species reminded us of the nearby thorn forest; here, too, most plants have a reduced leaf surface to offset the usual hot and dry spring season.

One tree caught our attention for its smooth trunk and coppery orange outer bark, which seemed to be peeling off. "That's the chaca tree," John told us. It was a *Bursera* species, similar to the gumbo limbo of Florida. The peeling bark frustrated epiphytic growth.

"Naked Indian," John added. We knew he was referring to the tree. There was a so-called naked Indian back home, the Texas madrone. Reddish, smooth-barked trees commonly evoke such a comparison.

Overall, the forest had a wilted appearance. New leaves had emerged in March and April, yet the rainy season might be weeks away. Somehow, the forest adjusts to this annual waiting game.

The few bird calls that reached us over the groanings of the Jeep tantalized us, but the only birds in evidence were those disturbed by our approach; of course, these quickly vanished into their leafy haunts. Nor did we dare request a bird stop; we were climbing steadily now, and it was the noon hour, not the ideal time for bird or birder.

A vista opened below to our right: the lowlands, a mosaic of field and orchard and remnant patches of woodland, all steaming under the sun. Shortly, a sign at roadside proclaimed, "Bienvenidos a Gómez Farías"—a simple welcome.

The village seemed to begin at this point, laid out along this, the main and only street, following the crest of a ridge—a hogback lava formation, as attested by dark-hued rocks stacked casually in the form of barrier walls at roadside. We were informed that the street ran unpaved for about three miles before dead-ending.

Gómez Farías was Mexico removed from the tourist influence. Most of the village crowned the ridge, a few abodes clinging to either slope. Small houses of unpainted lumber or just wattle and mud were distributed in no apparent order. Dooryards were aflame with color, hibiscus, rose, bougainvillea in luxuriant bloom; mango trees towered over stands of banana and papaya. From open doorways, women in long-skirted print dresses glanced at us without expression, while barefooted children waved and yelled greetings. Less moved by our passage, dogs, pigs, and chickens gave right-of-way grudgingly. We had the feeling that we were the main event of the day in Gómez Farías, and indeed, there was no evidence of other visitors from the outside world.

We arrived shortly at the plaza, a raised square sporting a bandstand and an ancient ceiba tree (*Ceiba pentandra*). A few small commercial edifices and the municipal building gathered around the plaza, which was obviously the focal point of the community; however, at this time of day, little seemed to be in focus. Few people were on the street, a deficiency we could understand given the heat and humidity. A small, very road-worn and driverless bus crowded the plaza wall, waiting to carry townspeople south to Ciudad Mante at some appointed hour.

John paused at the plaza long enough for the dust to settle, and we tried in that moment to absorb the flavor of the town. We recalled what we had been told of the history of Gómez Farías and the surrounding region. Tamaulipas was very late in being conquered and incorporated into the Spanish colonial system. By the middle of the eighteenth century, few indigenous people remained in the southern part of the state; they had fled, died of disease, or been killed in the continuing struggle between the colonial world to the south and nomadic tribes to the north. Beginning in 1747, the forces of Count José de Escandón subdued the hostile elements in the region and parceled out the land for settlement; people were brought in and towns established all the way to the Río Grande.

The town of Gómez Farías, at first called Joya de San José, was established in 1836 by families from central Mexico, mestizos, persons of mixed Spanish and Indian blood. (Spanish women were slow in coming to the New World.) Small tracts of land were parceled out to 40 recipients. In 1870, the government of Tamaulipas granted a village charter, creating a free municipal government. The village was now called the Villa de Gómez Farías, in honor of the then president of Mexico. The Municipio de Gómez Farías, the encompassing entity, roughly comprises the Sierra de Guatemala.

Gómez Farías was one of few settlements in the region, isolated, with heavily forested lowlands adjacent. Only in the 1890s did development start in the lowlands. It was during that period that settlers from the United States were encouraged to come and cultivate the land.

We left the plaza with no regrets, although a sign on one of the buildings, in familiar red and white, proclaiming "tome Coca Cola," was impossible to ignore. We refrained from comment; John was now intent on putting the town behind us.

We had enjoyed a relatively smooth road surface through town as far as the plaza, but beyond that the red dirt became rock-infested. That was only the beginning. Before the road curved upward to the right—soon to dead-end—John took a left turn, downhill. This was the inauspicious gateway to the mountain settlements and Rancho del Cielo. Now, as the Jeep crawled downslope, we overlooked a valley wedged between the Gómez Farías ridge and the serrated mountain front, where woodland was ever yielding to cultivated fields and a scattering of farm dwellings. It was an idyllic scene when viewed with detached interest, but we were not suddenly suffused with inner calm; rather, a nervous excitement mounted as we realized that we were now fully committed to the adventure.

Descending rapidly, Jeep and passengers bounced past the community spring, largely deserted at midday, and rolled onto a flat stretch. We had reached bottom. This spot was destined to become known, to some of us, as

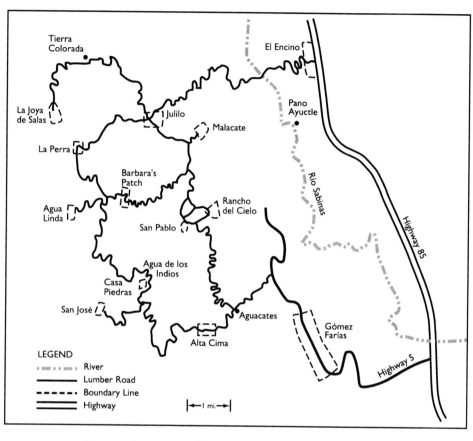

The northern part of the municipality of Gómez Farías.

LEGEND

· · · · · · · · River

——— Lumber Road

- - - - Boundary Line

═══ Highway

|←— 1 mi. —→|

Tierra Colorada

El Encino

La Joya de Salas

Pano Ayuctle

Julilo

Malacate

La Perra

Río Sabinas

Barbara's Patch

Rancho del Cielo

Highway 85

Agua Linda

San Pablo

Agua de los Indios

Casa Piedras

San José

Aguacates

Gómez Farías

Alta Cima

Highway 5

Lucas's Bottom, for the house of Lucas Romero, Frank Harrison's helper, sat no more than a stone's throw beyond the road. We paused while John looked toward the house.

Now at a standstill, we felt the full impact of the heat. It was surely more than 100 degrees, with no breeze. A haze filled the valley basin and distorted the features of the mountainside ahead.

Lucas was not to be seen. He would have heard the Jeep and come out, John reasoned; probably he was at the ranch. A middle-aged woman appeared at the door of the house: Lucas's mother-in-law, a troublemaker. She was reputed to be a *bruja* (witch). John grunted and shifted gears to four-wheel drive.

We had dropped from 1,000 feet of elevation in Gómez Farías to probably less than 500 feet at Lucas's Bottom. Now it would be all uphill, I thought with some misgivings as the Jeep lurched forward. We climbed slowly, penetrating, almost imperceptibly, the mouth of a long canyon. We had left all evidence of human activity, embraced by bushes that crowded the roadside, shaded by trees that intertwined branches overhead. A dry, boulder-strewn ravine on our right awaited the rainy season. There were birds, unseen, teasing us with snatches of song. We knew the hoarse croaking of the Elegant Trogon, but other sounds were foreign to our ears and usually fragmented by the grinding, crunching efforts of the Jeep. A morpho butterfly, large and blue, appeared alongside, then moved ahead effortlessly, buoyantly, catching splashes of sunlight on iridescent wings.

Birds and butterflies were but minor distractions from the trials of the trip. The roadbed had deteriorated badly. The Jeep's progress was never straightaway; tires nudged through drifts of loose rock, slipping and sliding as John struggled to keep on a general heading; meantime, the Jeep's underparts slammed bottom with disturbing regularity. As passengers, we were bouncing up and down, lurching backward and forward, and weaving sideways, seemingly all at the same time. Marie and I were in the back seat, Elizabeth wedged snugly between us. Confined as we were, we absorbed one another's bodily shocks, an exercise for which we were ill-suited. Marie, in particular, must have felt mistreated. She was slender, at five feet ten inches, while I carried more padding, at about 180 pounds on a six-foot-two frame. But Marie would have been the last to complain; she has a strong German disposition and red hair (well, auburn), from the Scotch influence.

"We do have springs?" Marie's voice rolled with the motion of the Jeep. Oddly, she was laughing.

I hoped John had not heard. "We started out with springs," I tried to whisper. "I haven't seen any drop off."

My remark received what it deserved: no response. I made no further attempt to make light of the situation.

I was so absorbed with my own concerns that it never occurred to me that Marie was enjoying every moment of the trip, from John's generous pontificating to the sights and sounds and smells of the countryside; this I learned at a later date. Rough roads were no novelty to Marie. Her father had been a beekeeper, and as a child she had ridden with him as he trucked the back roads and pastures of the southwest Texas brush country, tending his bee yards. I, on the other hand, had a strictly urban background and expected highways and byways (at least by the year 1964) to show some semblance of a paved surface.

I was increasingly apprehensive. We had no precedent for this experience, and I had been too naive to question the possibility of conquering a substandard mountain mule trail in an overloaded Jeep station wagon.

"You just relax," Elizabeth said. "Yield to the motion."

I glanced at her; she was smiling faintly. Elizabeth had been here before, but this was a different trip, I reasoned. If she had sought to reassure me, her words had little effect other than to discourage further comments on my part.

In reality, we were traveling more than a mule trail. This was the main, and only, route to the settlement of Alta Cima, in a wide valley on the edge of the cloud forest, and a few mountain villages beyond. Understandably, however, most traffic was by foot. Lumber company trucks of World War II origin (British vehicles used in Burma) patrolled the one-lane mountain roads almost uncontested, and then only sporadically. Few outsiders dared drive beyond Gómez Farías, and for good reason: there were no watering places or gas pumps on the forest network.

Exploitation of the forest for lumbering purposes had necessitated access by road, a convenience we took for granted, unaware of the labor involved in sculpting a trail through the wilderness. In a sense, the project is never completed, for upkeep remains a seasonal problem. The degree of maintenance usually depends on the amount of rainwater flooding down the right-of-way. Often, smaller, filler rocks are washed away during summer downpours, leaving solid rock mounds too high for a vehicle to pass over and too wide to maneuver around. To reduce a mound to acceptable size, workers build a fire over the rock, then chip away at the heated surface with sledgehammers. Over the years, only main arteries have been maintained, while many logging spurs quickly disappeared under second-growth vegetation.

We had gained little elevation when we came to an abrupt right-angle turn in the road. John stopped the Jeep, engine still running. A cliff loomed ahead, its sheer face softened by a mass of greenery. Access into the upper canyon was blocked here by a steep hillside that, like a dam, lay horizontally between the ramparts. Accordingly, the road bent to the right and took off uphill at a severe slant before curving out of view. John turned halfway toward the back seat.

"Fred Blesse always stopped here for a cigarette, to listen for trucks coming down. They have the right-of-way."

Leon leaned from the front passenger window. "I don't hear anything, John."

Leon had been uncharacteristically quiet since we left Gómez Farías. Earlier, we had been entertained (or at least kept awake) by Leon's chatter, which filled the gaps between John's informative comments.

"Well, the motor's running, Leon," Elizabeth said.

John turned the ignition key. I groaned inwardly, convinced that the Jeep would refuse to start again. But we did enjoy a few moments of relative silence, discounting the incessant buzz of insects.

"What is this?" Marie was pointing out her window.

Being on the right side of the road, I had been contemplating the steep grade ahead. On Marie's side, the canyon wall dropped precipitously to road level. At that point, a troughlike concrete structure had been placed against the rock. It was a *pila,* or water reservoir, John told us. Although no longer in use as such, it had once been a waystation in a pipeline system that took water from a spring, high in the mountain, to Gómez Farías. To one side of the pila, resting on a concrete block, was a rusting 60-gallon tin with a portion of the side cut out. Inside, we could discern a figure of the Virgin Mary and spent candle stubs. Cut flowers, now wilting, had been arranged about the tin.

We expressed curiosity. It was John's turn again.

"That's a shrine. People light a candle and pray for a safe trip."

"Up," I added.

"Or give thanks for a safe trip down," Elizabeth suggested.

Leon dropped the bomb. "This is where the truck went over?"

"Right here." John seemed to dismiss the matter.

"How many did you say were killed?" Leon persisted.

"Well, I don't know if they ever said."

"The shrine could be a memorial then," Marie said.

It was not difficult to visualize an ancient truck, bouncing down the grade, failing to make the turn at Blesse's corner and dropping into the ravine opposite the pila. We were respectfully silent as John started the Jeep.

From Blesse's corner the road cut across the canyon as described, with the downside on our right as we climbed. At the top of the grade it turned sharply left while inclining laterally at a precarious angle. Here John made the widest turn possible, successfully keeping four wheels to the road surface. Elizabeth and I converged on Marie in the process.

From this point to the Aguacates junction we could breathe easier, for the most part. At times we were hugging the mountainside with the canyon dropping off to our left. No one had thought to install a guard rail or other safety feature; there was just the one lane and little, if any, shoulder. Marie could look over into the canyon, the bottom of which was impossible to discern through the foliage of tree, bush, and vine.

We were now in the tropical semievergreen and evergreen forest that completely clothed both steep canyon slopes. Again, the tree species were mostly unfamiliar. Now there were no chacas, whose absence alone told us that we had left the tropical deciduous zone. Had we looked more closely we would have noticed that trees were taller here, with larger leaves, and more than half were evergreen species. Thorny species were all but absent; epiphytes and lianas were common.

A list of the trees shows mostly tropical genera. A few names were familiar to us: Mexican buckeye (*Ungnadia speciosa*), hackberry (*Celtis monoica*), oak (*Quercus germana*), and orchid tree (*Bauhinia mexicana*).

We were able to identify a few of the flowering plants, notably two vines, Mexican flame vine (*Senecio confusus*), with its bright reddish orange daisy-like flowers, and the delicate, pendant clusters of purple wreath (*Petrea volubilis*). Other familiar plants were a *Heliconia* species, scarlet hamelia (*Hamelia patens*), cestrum (*Cestrum nocturnum*), and shrimp plant (*Justicia brandegeana*).

FRED AND MARIE S. WEBSTER

One plant that John troubled to caution us about was mala mujer (*Cnidoscolus urens*), or "bad woman," a rank nettle with large hand-shaped leaves. Both leaf and stalk bear stinging hairs that can cause lingering infection if not treated promptly. We learned to wipe with moist towelettes at the merest contact with this plant. Eventually we would meet mal hombre (*Urera caracasana*), also equipped with stinging hairs but much less invasive and toxic, a comparison Marie thought fitting.

Mala mujer is a disturbance plant, likely to appear in any forest opening. In addition, it crowded the roadside and threatened to enter through the Jeep windows. The plant did have one redeeming quality: hummingbirds were attracted to the white flower clusters.

We reached a section of the road that was relatively smooth and, we thought, level. As to the latter assumption, John assured us that if he put the Jeep in neutral it would roll back downhill. We did not press him on the matter, but he did stop to let us admire the view.

From this elevation, we could look back on Gómez Farías, the Sierra Chiquita (a foothill just north of the village), and mesas beyond the Sabinas Valley. It was a pleasantly green vista, merely dappled with human handiwork.

"On a clear day you can see Sombrero," John said. His reference was to Bernal de Horcasitas, a huge volcanic plug, a tapering dome rising abruptly from the lowlands to the southeast and likened to a hat placed on a flat surface. Today the far horizon was too obscured by smoke haze to display one of John's favorite annotative subjects.

Looking back on a scene that we had traversed but which now appeared quite unfamiliar, I felt a stranger in alien territory. The world we knew was somewhere beyond Gómez Farías and the farthest horizon. Even as the thought crossed my mind like a foreboding shadow, we noticed movement up the road: a small group of local people, a man leading a pack burro, trailed by a woman and young girl on foot.

"Buenas tardes." The man turned his head slightly toward us, then quickly looked away. The others stared straight ahead, the woman gently prodding the girl. Two emaciated dogs gave the Jeep suspicious glances and a wide berth, slinking on the far side of the humans. As the party vanished around the bend, we were startled by the sudden appearance of a tiny woman, quite elderly and stooped, walking resolutely along the margin of the road. The brown, wrinkled face did not turn toward us, but seemed to contemplate the hem of a faded skirt, from which bare feet extended at each step.

"They should let her ride the burro," Leon said. "She won't have any skin left on her feet."

"They're tough, Leon," Elizabeth said. "Walking is *the* way of life. As for me, I'd have a hard time even with shoes."

I looked back down the road; the old woman was not to be seen. Had she been there at all, really, or had time skipped ahead a moment? Whatever, the incident reinforced my feeling of estrangement from the familiar.

There was little time for brooding; I was jarred back to reality as the Jeep lurched ahead once more.

The depth of the gorge on our left had gradually decreased until, now, we were traveling on the floor of the canyon. The green-flanked cliff towered directly ahead, beyond which open sky spread in an ever-expanding arc. It was apparent that we were nearing the head of the canyon. Even as I savored the thought, John halted the Jeep, engine still running. It was then that I noticed the road branching off to the right.

We were at Los Aguacates junction. Ahead, beyond the canyon, was the village of Alta Cima; to the right—somewhere—was Rancho del Cielo. John leaned back, half facing us. He had words to share, but I suspected, also, that he was pausing to marshal energy for the challenge ahead. Sweat beaded on his forehead.

We were at the site of the first Anglo settlement on the mountain, John explained. Murdock C. Cameron, a Scotch Canadian who had been a medic with the Royal Canadian Mounted Police, and his French-Canadian wife had come to Mexico in the 1890s seeking a healthy environment for the doctor, who had lost a lung while working above the Arctic circle. The Camerons had first lived in Ciudad Victoria, where Dr. Cameron was said to have opened a pharmacy and served as company doctor of the Texas-Mexican Railroad. After several years they had come to the Gómez Farías region. Some sources state that they resided in Gómez Farías for a few years before settling at the Aguacates. (The word *aguacate,* or avocado, comes from the Nahuatl Indian word *ahuacatl.*)

The Cameron residence at the Aguacates had been a cabin about 40 feet square. Presumably the timber was hand-hewn on the site, as were the split-oak shakes for the roof. Now, many decades later, there was no readily visible sign that anyone had lived here. Wooded slopes reached down to bare roadbed, erasing all but memories. The only reminder of the Camerons' brief sojourn at the Aguacates are a few avocado trees—unless, by chance, the curious visitor should probe about the adjacent woodland to find the foundations of the Cameron house.

Considering the difficult terrain, it is not surprising that after two years, the family moved up to the broad, flat valley now known as Ejido Alta Cima.

The next leg of our journey was the so-called Aguacates grade, which would take us to Frank Harrison's red gate in the cloud forest. We have traveled this route dozens of times over the years, and I can say with all sincerity that my respect for this stretch of road has never diminished.

One may find a degree of detachment from the tensions of the Aguacates grade by forcing attention on the flowering plants along the way, or by pondering strange bird calls. Fending off advances of mala mujer certainly offers a diversion. But always underlying the total experience is an awareness of the relentless struggle of people and machines against the mountain, the grinding, whirring, crunching of vehicles, the constant jostling of riders.

Riding with John at the wheel, we learned, added a degree of excitement to any trip. John knew the mountain roads, and he was confidently optimistic, but diabetes and arthritis, combined with oversized shoes, made his footwork suspect. Neither footwork nor mechanical trouble slowed us on this occasion. Our main hazard, beyond the physical beating, proved to be an errant sack of tomatoes, quite ripe; dislodged from a precarious perch by an especially strenuous maneuver of the Jeep, the sack emptied its contents on us in the back seat.

Eventually the Aguacates grade was conquered and we paused at Frank's gate. The red gate consisted of four rough-hewn poles of reddish hue positioned through holes in posts to either side of the road. In order to proceed, one merely pulled the poles out of one supporting post and laid them aside. Leon and I shared the task, replacing the poles when the Jeep had passed through the gap.

The gate was intended to discourage Frank's cattle from venturing down the Aguacates. To bypass the barrier, an animal would have to work through rocks and heavy forest.

We had been too preoccupied with the mechanics of the trip to notice a gradual change in the composition of the forest as we neared the crest of the Aguacates. Now, at Frank's gate, we realized that at long last we were in cloud forest. To reach Rancho del Cielo, we would travel on a northerly heading, subject to the contours of the cloud forest corridor.

Momentarily, my mind wandered to literature I had read, information I had tried to assimilate regarding the geological and climatic conditions that support cloud forest so near the Tropic of Cancer. This forest type is not extensive; it starts as a narrow strip about twelve miles north of Rancho del Cielo but broadens considerably near the southern terminus of the range. In the vicinity of Rancho del Cielo, cloud forest probably is no more than two and a half miles in width.

It is said that the Sierra de Guatemala is composed of three north-south running ridges. The easternmost ridge (home to the cloud forest) is most clearly defined from about the latitude of Pano Ayuctle or El Encino southward. Along this front, gulf moisture crossing the coastal lowlands on easterly winds meets with the least opposition, the Sierra Chiquita being a minor and apparently insignificant deterrent. This foothill (about 2,300 feet in elevation and just north of Gómez Farías) is an anticlinal formation, with folds of rock strata inclining downward on both sides from a central axis.

Topographic maps show a remarkable consistency in the contour lines of the first ridge on its north-south alignment. The second ridge westward shows considerable irregularity but can still be delineated. As for a third or westernmost ridge, peaks and canyons destroy any continuity.

Timewise, we had reached a halfway point in our journey from Gómez Farías. We had traveled a little over three miles from the plaza to the Aguacates, and from that point a little over a mile to Frank's gate. Each portion of the trip had taken about 30 minutes. The stretch from the gate to Rancho del Cielo was close to three miles, which, John assured us, normally required somewhat less than an hour; that is, if we avoided mechanical breakdown and the road was not blocked by fallen trees.

The road from the gate to the ranch was rough and rocky in places, particularly as we neared the ranch, but after the Aguacates experience we were prone to tolerance. There were occasional smooth stretches of red clay surface, spoiled only by deep truck ruts, which stored water for days after a rain.

We could rejoice that we had reached the cloud forest, the northernmost tropical cloud forest in the hemisphere. This was the wilderness that had been home to Frank Harrison since 1935. This was the magnet that had drawn scientists of various disciplines to investigate and record diverse ecological subjects.

Two features of this wonderland impressed us most: trees and rocks. Trees were tall and straight for the most part, older trunks wrapped in epiphytic growth—lichen, moss, fern, bromeliad, orchid. Tank bromeliads, supporting microcommunities of living organisms, clung to the trunk or perched on larger branches. Ground cover was sparse where the canopy was most dense but thrived in disturbed areas or where rock outcrops created permanent openings. In places, second-growth saplings reached skyward like so many toothpicks, with little chance in the competition for sunlight.

Rocks were everywhere, weathered and gray, adorned with lichen, moss, and fern not yet revived by summer rain. Rocks protruded from a leaf-littered surface as house-sized boulders; smaller rocks cluttered the forest floor at random. Although the latter appeared to rest on the surface, we would discover later that most were anchored in the subterranean mass. What we would not discern from a moving vehicle were the numerous fissures, which in some instances appear bottomless.

Frank Harrison had expressed it graphically in an early writing: "This part of the mountain must have been the discards after the rest of the world was made. It is just a jumble of loose rocks . . . no creek or any signs of any streams, just holes, caves and sunken spots amongst the rocks. It can rain all night, and sometimes it does, 7 or 8 inches in a terrible thunderstorm that shakes the house and the very mountain itself, and the next morning you will not get your feet wet walking in the forest."

In Frank Harrison's words, the foregoing applied to "this part of the mountain," not to the entire range. His statement was puzzling until we learned more of the geology of the region. The Sierra de Guatemala is composed mostly of El Abra limestone of the Cretaceous period, but there is a striking difference in configuration between the eastern and western portions of the mountain. On the eastern side (roughly the first two ridges) the strata are severely folded or bent. Here karst topography is everywhere evident in protruding rock masses (some standing like weathered towers), scattered boulders, and numerous caves and sinks. Little surface drainage occurs except in the wet season, then only temporarily. Even permanent springs form rivulets that soon vanish underground. Two major springs handle discharge from the subterranean channels: the *nacimiento* of the Río Sabinas, not far upstream from Pano Ayuctle, and the *nacimiento* of the Río Frío, just south of Gómez Farías.

We could not have foreseen that we would have many occasions during subsequent years to experience the diversity of mountain life, thanks to the main logging roads. On this day, exploration was not on our minds; our concern was reaching Rancho del Cielo. Frank's gate was only about fifteen minutes behind us, but already my resolve to enjoy the remainder of the ride had eroded in the face of reality. The bouncing and jostling had not decreased appreciably, and even in the shade of the forest it was insufferably hot; the only breeze was that created by the overloaded Jeep.

The novelty of our surroundings gradually diminished. The forest slipped slowly past with little change of character except where rock formations altered the landscape. As far as we could see there was more forest, and a trail (generously called a road) that weaved its way under a canopy that permitted little sunlight to relieve a surface of brown leaf litter and gray rock.

Civilization, a.k.a. Gómez Farías, was only miles away, but it could as well have been in another galaxy. Here in the forest we had encountered no human presence other than ourselves, nor were there signs of human habitation along the route. The forest belonged to bird and beast, and the latter rested by day in myriad hideaways. We had entered a land where we must tread softly, for we were intruders and knew not the rules of the realm.

For a fleeting moment I felt a curious release, a freedom from the ordinariness of existence, a surge of exhilaration—but quickly tempered by uneasiness. I sensed a need to belong, to relate to the wilderness. How to achieve that intimacy, except through experience?

My current passion, birds, came to mind. We had looked for birds through the windows of the Jeep, only to glimpse shadows darting, vanishing against the greenery. To experience and relate we must identify, but visual contact had failed us. Occasionally a song reached us over the clamor of the vehicle; no familiarity here. We were in an enchanted woodland, where phantom wings beckoned, inviting us to share their secrets, mocking with unseen voices when we tried. It would take time and patience to win over the forest and its denizens.

We came to a fork in the road. Ahead, a hundred yards or so, the main road would skirt the cleared area known as Paul's Field at the locality called San Pablo, from where it would continue northward to the lumber camp at

Julilo, but that itinerary was not for us today. A right turn here would take us to Rancho del Cielo.

From this point it only seemed a long distance, perhaps because we were anxious, and the going was slow and rough. Then a steep climb, a coast downhill to level ground, and we were at John's gate. John detailed Leon to pull aside the barbed-wire barrier and reattach it to the gate post when we cleared the opening.

We were at forest edge. Beyond, we could see John's cabin perched at the crest of a small rise. A castle on a mountaintop would have been no more welcome. Moments later, the Jeep groaned to a halt alongside the cabin. We disentangled ourselves and stumbled to the ground.

I took a panoramic impression of our surroundings: the small clearing bordered by forest giants, another cabin across the way, a haze-shrouded ridge beyond a hillside to the west.

Then I noticed the small man standing beside the Jeep. Frank Harrison? Small and wiry—was this a man who would challenge the Mexican wilderness? I tried not to stare, but he was looking at the group, not at me. Curious, I noted the unpressed blue cotton pants and shirt, faded but clean, and the scuffed and moisture-stained shoes. It all seemed to fit—the rustic gentleman tidied up to welcome friends.

"It's paradise!" Marie exclaimed.

"I'm glad you could come."

The weathered face was fixed in a slight smile. I had an instant impression of cordiality, and when Frank Harrison spoke you knew that he would never be a stranger.

3

ORE than two years later we had occasion to examine some of
Frank's personal papers, which enable us to describe the man
with more accuracy than reliance on fallible memory. His Canadian passport, dated November 2, 1955, supplied basic data: John William
Francis Harrison, Canadian by birth, rancher; born in Ridout Township,
Ontario, Canada, June 20, 1901; Mexican resident; height 5' 6½"; blue eyes,
brown hair; no "visible peculiarities."

A personal description in his "Documento Migratorio Unico del In-
migrante," dated August 17, 1955, was more detailed (as translated): white
race, thin constitution, average countenance, thick brows, straight nose,
oval chin, small mouth. Religion: Protestant. Occupation: farmer. *Domi-
cilio actual* was listed as Rancho "El Cielo," Municipio de Gómez Farías,
Tamaulipas.

We never gathered much information regarding Frank Harrison's pre-
Mexico years, or those years prior to his coming to Rancho del Cielo. Remi-
niscing with Frank seemed to reach a barrier at April 1935, beyond which
point we were not to proceed. Perhaps it was our reluctance to exhume
events long ago laid to rest, for although Frank Harrison was outgoing and
hospitable to friend and stranger alike, I always felt that he was a private
man, that he would share bits of his life story at his own pace and on his
own terms. Or perhaps—and I believe this was most likely—we were so
enthralled by events at Rancho del Cielo during more recent years that we
relegated probing of the remote past to some future opportunity. We could
not have known then that our opportunity was, as is often the case, for a
limited time only.

The fragment of a letter (presumably from his sister in Canada) and
scraps of information gleaned from other sources enabled us to sketch Frank
Harrison's earlier years.

The family moved to Chatham, in southern Ontario, in 1912, where
Frank graduated from Chatham Collegiate Institute in June 1918 or 1919.
Because of a manpower shortage during World War I, the government requested that college seniors work on farms. Frank found employment with
a nurseryman and florist; this was fortunate, as he had acquired an intense

Rufous-capped Brush-Finch

interest in nature in general and in plants in particular during his elementary school days.

Frank's access to an abundance of books reputedly spawned a wander-lust, and he decided that the Inca ruins in Peru would be his destiny. Instead of which—or perhaps in preparation for such an expedition—he went to California (about 1923), where he worked for about eighteen months on an aqueduct under construction to bring water from the mountains to the city of Los Angeles. (Other sources state that Frank's brother was with him in California. Frank told Marie that he discovered the Gómez Farías region while traveling with his brother on holiday.) After a visit with the family in Canada, Frank went to Mexico where he started a fruit farm—"I think in El Limón"—only to have the project terminated by a hurricane. (El Limón is in the lowlands south of Gómez Farías.) These events occurred some-time between 1925 and 1933. The sister's letter concludes: "From this he contracted malaria, and went into the mountains."

According to other sources, Frank Harrison came to Mexico in 1925 or 1926, settling in the Chamal colony, municipality of Ocampo, at the southern terminus of the Sierra de Guatemala, where he taught school and farmed in a nearby valley. The farm was destroyed in a hurricane in September 1933.

Two yellowed photographs that came into our possession shed some light on the early years. One, labeled simply "Chamal 1930," shows a wagon, drawn by two mules, in front of a house. We assume that the man on the wagon, holding the reins, is Frank Harrison. The house is small (probably one room), squarish, with dirt floor and heavily thatched roof and sides. The thatch is provided by palm leaves; several palm trees, possibly 50 feet tall, dominate the jungle just beyond the dooryard.

A second photograph shows a man in front of the same house. These words are inscribed on the back of the picture: "Frank Harrison and Mexican palm leaf house built by us at Chamal." It is signed "Pancho Klingensmith."

It is said that after a siege of malaria, Frank was advised by doctors to move to a higher elevation. While on an earlier hunting expedition into the mountains, he had come across a weathered, long-abandoned cabin in an overgrown clearing in the cloud forest, the present Rancho del Cielo. Frank moved up to the site in April 1935.

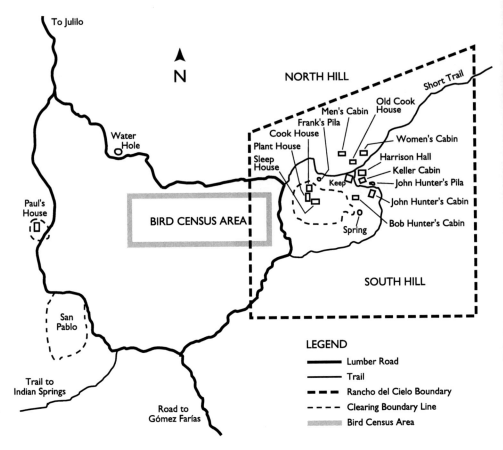

To Julilo

N

NORTH HILL

Short Trail

Water Hole

Old Cook House

Men's Cabin

Frank's Pila

Cook House

Women's Cabin

Plant House

Harrison Hall

Sleep House

Keller Cabin

Keep

John Hunter's Pila

Paul's House

John Hunter's Cabin

BIRD CENSUS AREA

Bob Hunter's Cabin

Spring

SOUTH HILL

San Pablo

Trail to Indian Springs

Road to Gómez Farías

LEGEND

Lumber Road

Trail

Rancho del Cielo Boundary

Clearing Boundary Line

Bird Census Area

Rancho del Cielo.

We assume that Frank chose an uncertain future in a mountain wilderness over a possibly miserable existence in the lowlands, and that escape from malaria was the primary motivation. There were rumors, in later years, that Frank had placed second in a romantic triangle involving a business partner and a woman whose name was not revealed to us; hence, his retreat to the mountain. According to John Hunter, who knew Frank as well as anyone did, the story of love spurned was merely a fabrication.

"Frank never indicated anything like that to me," John said in a taped conversation, "but these women cooked up that story. He told me he had malaria, and he thought he'd come up here and stay three or four years and get rid of that. It was the only way they knew to get rid of malaria in those days."

And now 29 years had passed.

Quite some time later, I overheard a conversation between two women, one a Chamal woman, the other an old-timer in the region. In essence, it was said that Frank Harrison came to Mexico with a gentleman named Klingensmith, and they became partners in an orchard ranch. Later, Mr. Klingensmith married an Effia Nichols and left, and Frank came to the mountain.

Frank had preceded us to John's cabin, removed the padlock from the back door (the primary entrance), and waited to render assistance in unloading the Jeep.

The cabin itself now became my concern. It was small and unpretentious, built of tough oak timber harvested somewhere in the forest, obviously never painted, and graying as it weathered. Widely spaced windows, screenless, were flanked by solid board shutters. A wooden platform by the back door supported barrels that collected rainwater from the ridged tin roof. The building was rectangular, oriented more or less north-south. A roofed porch graced two-thirds of the front (east) side but was terminated by a solid wall, beyond which a room branched off the south end of the building to complete the rectangle.

The cabin interior was basically one long room, perhaps 40 by 50 feet. The smaller room served as a bedroom. The main room actually provided more sleep capacity than the former, with a king-sized metal bed and three cots headed up against the north wall. Two or three old trunks held bed linens and blankets. For privacy, dark green curtains could be pulled across the sleeping area.

The cabin looked and smelled its role, a beloved retreat. Years of use and care showed in the faded wood of floor and wall and rafters, and in the arrangement of scant furnishings in limited space. A dining table and wooden benches occupied the center of the big room. The south third was kitchen space. A wood-burning stove squatted by the back door, poking its very authentic stovepipe into the roof.

A sink and counter lined the south wall, under a generous expanse of window, which, affording an unobstructed view of nearby forest, could relieve the drudgery of dish washing. Shelves for dishes and glasses flanked the window, with shelves for large utensils below the counter. A floor-to-rafter cabinet dominated the east side of the kitchen area, with a butane-fueled hot plate to the right and the bedroom door to the left. There was even room for a small cabinet between the bedroom door and the door to the back porch.

A small, short-legged worktable, equipped with cigar boxes to hold silverware, occupied the center of the kitchen area. It was in the vicinity of the worktable that a perceptive visitor might notice a small rug, too worn and insignificant-looking to elicit comment; however, the rug concealed a trapdoor. A small, narrow pit under the floor, accessible by ladder, served as storage area for cans and jars of food items needing a cool environment during periods when the cabin was unoccupied. Also, it was a safe haven for hard liquor (a commodity worth the risk of a break-in) and John's shotgun.

Among the more obvious features of the cabin, other than those already mentioned, a few are especially memorable. One was the arrangement of flowers, which Frank Harrison had cut from his garden or plant house and placed on a shelf or on the dining table in anticipation of John's arrival. Another was John's kerosene lamp, which, when not being coaxed into functioning, hung over the same table. The lighting of the lamp was a ritual that John reserved for his own amusement, we decided. Another sacred chore was the lighting of the old butane-equipped refrigerator, which sat on the porch next to the door. Getting the refrigerator started was not an end to the matter; I recall John, like an anxious parent, sitting with it at all hours of the night.

We had not picked the best time to visit the mountain, although for John there was no bad time. In later years we would choose the wet months,

June through September, when the forest was most lushly verdant, the rocks coated softly with mosses, and overnight rains cleansed earth and air. Not so on our first visit. It was the hottest day that he had experienced at the ranch, Frank Harrison declared — 95 degrees. We were accustomed to high summer temperatures in Texas, but the ride from Ciudad Victoria had been debilitating. As soon as we had unloaded what was immediately necessary from the Jeep, I pulled a chair outside the cabin and sat.

I suppose I was at least partially motivated by a birder's obsessive desire to see birds regardless of circumstances, but birds, it would seem, were taking an extended siesta, and those few songs that rang through the clearing continued to frustrate me. Thus thwarted, I had ample time to make a more detailed assessment of our surroundings.

I was now convinced that we would find little level ground on the ranch. John's cabin sat on the crest of a slope. I avoid the word "hill," which implies a mound with a top and slanting sides. East of the cabin and beyond the entry road, the hillside was lost in heavy forest, which formed a canopy receding downslope, yet effectively blocking any view of the valley of the Río Sabinas.

To the south, John had about 20 yards of open space before the forest plunged into a depression culminating in a large sinkhole cave (Harrison Cave, the cavers called it, 186 feet deep), but only a thicket of trees and shrubs could be seen from the clearing. To the west, a shallow sink, planted to fruit trees, separated John's from Bob Hunter's cabin. What lay beyond Bob's rock wall and adjoining hillside was for the moment a mystery; I could distinguish only what we came to know as West Ridge, looming in the hazy distance.

On the north side of John's cabin the surface slanted upward to Sam Hill. Along the base of Sam Hill (a whimsical designation) was John's pila, a rectangular concrete reservoir for collecting rainwater, a process supplemented by a sheet of tin laid along the upside. Water was piped a short distance downhill to the cabin.

We had not been led to expect a third cabin. It sat below Sam Hill, about 50 yards north of John's. At the time of our first visit to the mountain, it was known as the Keller cabin; other parties would share ownership at a later date.

From John's cabin, the road (better, trail) headed toward Bob's before curving right; it then passed the Keller cabin and disappeared into the forest. We would soon discover that the road skirted the north side of the ranch and meandered in a northwesterly direction until it joined the primary logging road, which we had left in order to reach Rancho del Cielo.

Our surroundings begged for exploration, but there were chores to attend to. I was assigned to bring water from the spring. Spring water was for drinking, rainwater from the roof for kitchen use, and pila water for any other purpose. Frank's spring was nearby, at the base of a steep slope planted to fruit trees. A large loquat tree shaded the spring. The dry winter season had lowered the water level significantly, and it was necessary for me to bend double in order to draw a bucketful from the rock-lined pit. This I did with some trepidation, imagining being set upon by some creature, animal or insect, lurking in the moss-lined crevices. The tall grasses and forbs growing about the site caused further concern, and I felt vindicated at a later date when the excited scolding of Green Jays alerted me to the presence of a fer-de-lance, a tropical pit viper.

After a long day on the road and the completion of various duties, refreshing of the body was imperative. We were not surprised that John's cabin did not offer all the amenities of home. For a shower, we went to Bob Hunter's improvised facility. Bob had placed two large drums on a platform, from which roof runoff was piped to a shed large enough to accommodate one person. Had we insisted on a warm shower, we could have built a fire under the drums; however, we did not want to bother, and cold water seemed fitting on a hot evening.

John's indoor plumbing was limited to the kitchen sink, supplied by a line from the rain barrels. Water from the pila emerged from a hydrant by the back door; a garden hose could furnish a shower without privacy, the reason John sent us away from the cabin for a short while. Thankfully, a full measure of privacy was afforded by an outhouse (a weathered, tottering structure affectionately called the "hurry house"), a short walk from the cabin.

On the mountain, the approach of nightfall brings a sense of expectation, a tension that seems to fill the lightless vacuum. More often than not, during the summer months, evening thunderstorms roll up from the lowlands and drench the forest for several hours. By midnight the cloud curtain may have parted, and if no moon rises to expose the nightscape, a star sea unfolds above, clear and crisp and silent.

Rain did not come on our first trip to Rancho del Cielo. We watched the sun drop over West Ridge with no clouds to give form to the evening pastels. Dusk settled quickly, with no fanfare, only a few chickenlike clucks of a Clay-colored Robin from the forest depths. Shortly, the real world had no shape. Perhaps later, moonlight would transform the forest with a mystical sheen.

On many future occasions, the coming of night would draw our little party, like moths, to the kerosene lamp hanging over the dining table. Evenings of conversation and games around the table were a tradition of the mountain, but on our first evening we were too tired for games or idle talk. As soon as the supper dishes were put away, and John made a final adjustment (hopefully) on the refrigerator, we took to bed.

Marie and Elizabeth had the bedroom. The men had the main room, John the big bed in the northwest corner. With the lamp extinguished, the cabin could have been the bowels of the earth. John left the doors and windows wide open in warm weather; even so, there was no air circulation on this occasion. Consequently, I resigned myself to a miserable night of perspiring and swatting at mosquitoes. I could not believe John when he said that the mosquitoes would become inactive as soon as the lights were out, but I was pleased to discover that he had spoken the truth. The pesky insects buzzed about in total darkness for a few minutes, then seemed to lose interest.

I was able now to focus on other concerns, one of which was the presence of vampire bats. In Gómez Farías we had seen a burro with a telltale mark on its hindquarters, and John assured us that the creatures did occur at the ranch—but no cause to worry! For my part, I reasoned, no cause to worry if I kept my fingers and toes covered, since, I had read somewhere, vampire bats relish exposed digits. The bat threat thus somewhat alleviated, I could ponder the chances of a jaguar's exploring the cabin. Of course, jaguars usually avoid humans, and anyway, most of the big cats had been eliminated from the mountain.

I may have been ready to revise my opinion of jaguar behavior when, some time later, we were all awakened by a tremendous din from the kitchen area. Flashlights quickly revealed the source. Something had knocked the silverware box off the kitchen table. We dismissed all possibility of a poltergeist, theorizing that some small mammal had hopped onto the table and clumsily nudged the box off the edge. Of course, most mammals are not that clumsy, unless the culprit was sniffing a utensil not thoroughly cleaned from supper. Whatever our visitor, it had departed without sound or trace.

Now a persistence of strange sounds was drumming on my subconscious. Still not fully alert, but driven by impulse, I stumbled to the back door. For moments my eyes adjusted to a scene in soft half-light, wilderness night transformed to a magical realm, every feature of the clearing delineated and identifiable.

As though I could doubt the source, I squinted at a full moon, directly overhead. A more deliberate look about the clearing brought an uneasy thought: darkness held us hostage, for the forest caught moonlight only on its margins, beyond which night secrets were inviolate.

The puzzling sounds drew my attention again; they were coming from the direction of the pila. Frogs, of course—I should have suspected. But the voices were unfamiliar. One was a guttural, raspy drone rising and falling almost imperceptibly over a three-second span and repeated with hypnotic regularity about every three seconds. Another I likened to short toots from an old-time automobile horn, a series with some variation in pitch and motif, sounding hollow against the walls of the pila. Like ghostly echoes, answering calls drifted from some distant colony.

Translation of creature sounds into syllables of human speech may vary widely from person to person, and my interpretation of frog voices likely would be rejected by frog specialists; therefore, it was fortunate that on a later occasion we were able to inspect the pila population by flashlight and identified two species: Mexican treefrog (*Smilisca baudinii*) and a leopard frog (*Rana berlandieri*).

Aside from the frog population, the forest seemed to sleep. It was a silent calm that belied the activity of countless nocturnal creatures. Bats and moths fly, unseen, on silent wings, and land-bound mammals tread softly on the leafy forest floor. Myriad life-forms, I was certain, swarmed through the darkened woodland and across the moonlit clearing.

When we became more familiar with the forest, we would marvel at the numerous rock crevices and tree hollows where night prowlers could spend the daylight hours. One twilight, sitting on a honeycombed boulder in the depths of the forest, I was aware that a tiny animal had emerged from a hole in the rock, within arm's reach, and was looking about curiously. As suddenly as it had appeared, this white-footed mouse scampered off on its nightly hunt, perhaps to one of the cabins. We knew that coatimundi visited the garbage dump under cover of darkness, and there was the chance that a bear or big cat might enter the clearing; sometimes jaguar tracks were found on the roadbed following an overnight rain.

The dark hours belonged to the wild creatures, and I was content to leave it that way. Even the local people (and there were a few small settlements scattered across the mountain) would not be wandering about after night-fall. Superstition was a compelling force in rural areas, John had reminded us, and paranormal encounters, personally experienced or passed by word of mouth, were an effective deterrent to night excursions.

Aside from superstition, the uneven terrain was enough to discourage movement through the forest after dark. Foot travel on the roadways was reasonably safe with a good light, but walking the forest trails called for agile footwork and constant vigilance in avoiding pitfalls. On a future occasion I would experience the unwelcome thrills of a nocturnal hike, but for the moment a visit to the hurry house was quite sufficient.

We had no trouble sleeping that night, although the cabin remained open to bats and jaguars and the unexplained. John's calm demeanor must have assured us that all was well in his special place.

Brown-backed Solitaire

4

F OR the truly dedicated birder, sleeping late at Rancho del Cielo is out of the question. The dawn chorus is hypnotic; it compels attention. One may stubbornly refuse to leave the comfort of bed, but slumber will not return, for the birder's ear has been conditioned to receive and process any bird-produced sound.

The dawn chorus starts modestly. At the first incursion of daylight, the Greater Pewee breaks the predawn stillness with his plaintive, whistled "José, José, José, Ma-ree-ah" from the forest margin. For about two minutes this small flycatcher rules the dawn with his persistent recitation, until the tentative whistled notes, without discernible song pattern, of an Audubon's Oriole sound from the orchard. A Mottled Owl, returning to its diurnal retreat in a nearby sinkhole, barks its typical five bass notes, as though reluctant to relinquish the night. Blue-crowned Motmots hoot back and forth from sequestered haunts.

Light intensifies. The thin, trilled song of a Rufous-capped Brush-Finch erupts from the garden. Green Jays invade the orchard, chattering shrilly. The pewee's song fades into background as Black-headed Nightingale-Thrushes deliver their frenzied, jumbled warbling from the forest understory. Now White-throated and Clay-colored Robins, Blue Mockingbirds, and Flame-colored Tanagers add their more structured melodies.

The chorus has become an insistent blend of sound with no dominant voice until a Brown-backed Solitaire, stationed in lofty treetop, fashions an incredible cascade of notes. Only momentarily, the solitaire's song fills the clearing, then confusion returns.

We did not need birdsong to arouse us on our first morning at the ranch. John was an early riser, and it was impossible to ignore his lumbering tread on the cabin floor, followed shortly by a variety of intrusive sounds attendant to starting a fire in the wood-burning stove. Breakfast, as with other meals in John's cabin, was not taken lightly. We would soon learn that a day's activities climaxed on three occasions: breakfast, lunch, and supper. We found ourselves, not unwillingly, trapped in the routine of anticipation.

At home in Brownsville, John never helped Caroline with the cooking, but on the mountain he cheerfully shared cooking chores. Even more, he loved to putter around the kitchen area (perhaps it was some compensation for limited physical activity), preparing his particular version of familiar recipes and concocting some totally unique. On one occasion, driven by boredom or, most likely, by a well-known mischievous bent, he set out to create a synthetic piecrust, having no idea how authentic piecrust is made. A sheet of butcher paper was laid out, smeared with butter, and sprinkled liberally with sugar and cinnamon, then heated sufficiently for the ingredients to meld properly. John met me at the back door as I returned from a morning's walk and offered to share this delicacy. I should have known from the devilish twinkle in his eyes that all was not as perceived, but I was not long in discovering the deception. In retrospect, I questioned the wisdom of having reminisced with John, the night before, about our grandmothers' leftover piecrust.

Memory of our first breakfast in the cabin has long escaped recall, but I am certain that it was ample to sustain us on a morning of exploration. Frank Harrison's clearing was our primary objective that morning, and as we climbed the hillside that concealed the view of his house and grounds, curiosity overcame any urge to pause and identify the birds we heard along the way.

Frank's quarters topped a gentle rise from his orchard and garden on the south and backed up to a wooded lot on the north. The clearing was relatively small, bordered by forest on the south and west, and adjoined the Hunters' smaller clearing on the east. Considering that Frank's property extended not a great distance beyond the clearings, it may seem odd that the designation "rancho" would be used.

The lower (in elevation) or southernmost of two cabins provided sleeping and living quarters for Frank, although the single room often was occupied by visiting scientists or wayfarers, for which reason we always referred to it as the guest house. Accommodations inside would be basic, as suggested by the unpainted vertical board walls. A covered porch fronted the cabin, and a covered walkway (which Frank called a "patio") bordered the rear. The latter had once sheltered Frank's "cooking corner" but now provided shelving for potted plants, apparently overflow from the adjacent "plant house," a tottering open framework with benches and a corrugated tin roof. The plant house rested on a shelf of rock, at the edge of which a species of night-blooming cactus towered like a sentinel.

The newer of the two cabins sat a short distance to the rear of the first.

This was Frank's "new house," according to a photograph dated July 1954, but we always knew it as his cook house. It was small, simple, and rustic, a cabin of board and sheet metal, put together rather haphazardly, I thought. Even in the early photograph it gave the appearance of long occupancy.

Frank deferred his morning chores long enough to give us a short tour of the premises. His first stop was the plant house, as though he had sensed Marie's interest. Here he had done the research and labor that eventually brought him a measure of fame and introduced the cloud forest to the North American consciousness. In this modest and uncluttered laboratory exotica prevailed: fuchsia, gloxinia, orchid, everything that we would not dare try to cultivate in our central Texas environment. Curiously, many of the specimens displayed their elegance from rusted tins.

Marie was enchanted. "I love this begonia." She indicated clusters of strikingly beautiful pink blossoms in a crowded basket.

"It's a hybrid. I named it after my sister."

I may have been rude to change the subject so quickly, but Frank's gloxinias were on my mind. "We heard about the gloxinias. Where are they?"

Frank pointed to the patio. They would bloom later in the month. I was disappointed. He told us something we had not known about the gloxinias; they had been sent to him by someone who had tried to grow them in the lower Rio Grande Valley of Texas. Frank's initial efforts with the plants had been discouraging, and he set them aside to fend for themselves, which they did with surprising results.

I was puzzled that the plant house was completely open-sided.

"The roof protects them from hard rain," Frank explained. "If it frosts, I can take some indoors."

After some time spent admiring the plants and listening to Frank's commentary, we ventured into the orchard and garden area, which stretched from the house to the tree line south and west. The two crowded amaryllis patches had recently finished peak bloom, but the gladioli sent spikes of pastel colors skyward. We noticed a hummingbird feeding on the glads and determined that it was a Red-billed Azurecrown. We wavered over the identification, inasmuch as only the lower mandible of the bird was a pink-red. Some years later the "red-billed" would be deleted from the species' common name—not soon enough to prevent frequent discussion by fellow birders.

Frank had maintained a diverse orchard in his earlier years at the ranch, with considerable grafting and experimenting. The trees were old now but still bearing exceptional fruit. Near the south edge of the amaryllis bed he pointed out a gnarled, aged walnut tree. Unlike forest giants, this cultivated version had never attained great height, but it was distinguished in its own right: it marked the home site of the first settlers at Rancho del Cielo.

We had heard the story of the McPhersons, but we wanted to hear it from Frank. Later, as though driven by premonition, we would urge him to recall various events and facts from the early years, and his comments were duly recorded (written) in his own words. Now we stood on hallowed ground, reaching back to happenings shrouded in the mists of time past, where memories swirled through the gloom like tormented wraiths, difficult to grasp and hold.

According to Frank's recollections, as later dictated, Murdock Cameron's daughter, Virginia, married a man by the name of Mac McPherson and in 1912 moved to the area now known as Rancho del Cielo. Here they cleared three acres and built a log cabin with roof of oak shakes, all hand hewn, with an ax as the primary tool. The floor was laid with stone. Like other dwellings of that era, the roof was low and extended well out from the structure, enabling a person to work under the eaves in wet weather, a relief from the dark, smoky interior of the cabin.

The McPhersons and Camerons left Mexico "lock, stock, and barrel" at the time of the Mexican revolution. Thereafter, the McPherson homestead lay unoccupied, allowing the forest to reclaim the clearing until, on a hunting expedition across the mountain, Frank Harrison fell under its spell. The McPherson place lay on the regular trail from Gómez Farías to La Joya de Salas on the back side of the range. In Frank's words, "When I lived in Chamal, several friends and I made the trip to La Joya de Salas. At that time there was considerable deer there, and during one of the trips we stayed at the McPherson place on the Cameron property. I liked it so well I decided to move up there and get out of the intense heat and insects of the lower valley." Subsequently, he and a friend, Paul Gellrich, moved onto the McPherson property. "I have never regretted it."

Frank elaborated. "When I came onto the mountain in April 1935, this part of the mountain was just as God made it. . . . The sweetgums had gotten to be twenty to thirty feet tall [referring to second-growth trees]. Only communication into the area was via mule trail to Gómez Farías. . . . At that time several Mexicans from Gómez Farías had a few head of cattle up here, and once a week they would come and give them salt. The jaguars would get the cattle quite often."

Frank and Paul "lived in the McPherson cabin for one year and then built their first cabin, twenty feet by thirty feet, oak shingle roof, and surrounded by a porch on all sides."

Years later we came into possession of a weathered notebook in Frank's handwriting, a journal that he called "Garden Notes," spanning the period March 10, 1937, to June 3, 1939. Several entries refer to a house constructed prior to the "present sleeping quarters." Although the journal starts on March 10, the first mention of the house is on April 3: "shingled house." On April 6, "Felix [Burgos] started to work on timber to make boards for floor." Shingling was completed on April 12. On May 16, "painted on roof of house." On May 20, "worked on roof to try and stop leaks. Took out poles in floor and put in boards."

The fate of the McPherson cabin is given little attention in Frank's journal. We learn that on September 8, 1937, he "fixed old house to keep animals from getting pig." On February 10, 1938, the pig was slaughtered and dressed, ending the final function of the cabin. The entry on March 2 reads, "tore down part of old house and burned poles and shingles."

We are told that Frank's new house was built adjacent to the McPherson cabin, in the vicinity of the old walnut tree and the big amaryllis patch and convenient to the spring. We do not know when that house was demolished or when the guest house was built, except that the latter preceded the cook house. We assume that this was the house that George M. Sutton described in his book *At a Bend in a Mexican River:* "So filled with ferns and begonias was the little house and so open to the breeze that it seemed to have grown there, along with the forest. The roof reached down to within five or six feet of the ground." The year was 1949.

Now it had been almost 30 years since Frank Harrison had come to an overgrown clearing. Only an old, gnarled walnut tree stood guard over the ghosts of memory.

Frank excused himself after showing us the vegetable garden, to one side of the orchard. With the dissipation of the early morning clouds, we were ready to retreat to shade; the porch of the guest house offered an immediate haven and a vantage point from which we could scan most of the orchard and gardens.

Birdlife had settled from frenzied activity to midday lull. A Greater Pewee called plaintively from a lofty perch, and a Black-headed Nightingale-Thrush (seldom ever quiet) sang halfheartedly from the forest floor, while occasionally a Mountain Trogon's "cowh" series or an abbreviated robin song ventured from the woodland. A hummingbird feeding at the far end of the gladiolus bed, a company of rather subdued Green Jays raiding the orchard, and a tethered burro chomping grass claimed our attention for a while.

My eyes wandered beyond the orchard to South Hill, which rose above the shallow canyon at the edge of the clearing, blocking the view of the mountain range to the south. West Ridge dominated to our far right, rising to the pine-oak zone; the outline of pines delineated its crest.

Beyond the ranch clearing, the terrain presented uninterrupted greenery under a sky clear except for wisps of cloud drifting up from the lowlands, tracing ribbons of shadow over the forest canopy, only to vanish before reaching West Ridge. I wondered at the air currents that swirled over the cloud forest in summer, bringing plural inches of rain in evening thunderstorms to sustain the lush environment.

The view from Frank's was mesmerizing on a hot midday. I may have been sinking into a trance when Marie pulled me back from the edge.

"Is that a chain saw?" I sensed annoyance in her tone.

I try to deny unpleasantness. "This is an old house, and all this moisture—they have very large termites."

"The termites are in your head," Marie suggested.

"All right, it's Frank cutting firewood."

"Not with a chain saw. Someone is cutting a tree."

"Or a log, for firewood."

"A tree that will become a log."

I let Marie have the last word rather than try to sustain a leaky argument. I stared at the forest in a new light. Its green expanse hid not only beauty but also an ugliness that might be eating away at its heart. The forest had been logged some years before; it was reported that trees were cut up to—and even on—ranch property. My inexperienced forester's eye had not noticed any cutover areas as we drove to the ranch, but, I reasoned, second growth may have concealed traces of harvesting from earlier times.

Now the chain saw was silent. The birds and the insects and the burro, still grazing, seemed unaffected. I was aware of various domestic sounds from the direction of John's cabin.

"Maybe we can help John with lunch," Marie said.

I agreed.

Flame-colored Tanager

5

WE have a photograph taken in 1964 of ourselves, John, Frank, and Elizabeth; we are sitting on a rock wall near John's cabin. According to an inscription, we were discussing a likely site for a building for Texas Southmost College, a two-year school in Brownsville.

This after-lunch conference came as a surprise to us. We had been so immersed in our own agenda that we had not sensed the degree of John's enthusiasm for developing a working relationship between the college and Rancho del Cielo, or Frank's eagerness to promote an appreciation of the forest's resources for educational and research purposes. Neither did we realize that momentum had been building toward this goal for several years. It was obvious that we had some catching up to do.

We had been assured that Frank's interest in the cloud forest was greatly stimulated by a number of scientists who visited the ranch years before. Guests at Rancho del Cielo found Frank Harrison a gracious host and an invaluable trail guide. He, on the other hand, gleaned and retained a wealth of knowledge from the visitors.

As mentioned previously, completion of the Pan-American Highway in the early 1930s opened the Gómez Farías region to the world. Some commercial exploitation followed, but most significant to the future integrity of the environment was the coming of students of various natural science disciplines to study on a new frontier.

One of the earlier forays into the region was that of the John B. Semple expedition in the spring of 1938, as related in *The Auk* of January 1942. The senior author of the paper, George M. Sutton (later to become a close friend of Frank Harrison's), wrote of himself that

> he participated in a cursory survey of the bird life on the Rancho Rinconada, a partly cultivated stretch of floodplain on the east bank of the Río Sabinas, not far from the hill village of Gómez Farías. So impressed was he with the tropical aspect of the region, so puzzled by the dissimilarities between it and that of Victoria, only fifty miles to the north, and so convinced that what he had seen was but a faint indication of what might be discovered that he resolved to return, as

soon as possible, to undertake a thoroughgoing study of the breeding birds.

Sutton's opportunity came in the spring of 1941. He and Olin Sewall Pettingill, Jr., coleaders of the Cornell University–Carleton College Ornithological Expedition, set up headquarters at the Rancho Rinconada to study birds of the lowlands. But it was not until March 1949 that Sutton first made the climb to the cloud forest—somewhat belatedly, as he had been preceded by several scientists and students.

Even as the world was becoming aware of the singular biodiversity of the Gómez Farías region, lumbering interests were showing appreciation of the mountain's timber resources. It is likely that a lumber company was already operating when Frank Harrison started his garden journal. An entry on July 1, 1937, states, "went with engineers and people from Company looking at timber." (The party included a man from Monterrey.) On August 28 Frank wrote, "E.W.S. [Everts Storms] came up with men who have taken over lumber company."

We have derived the following account from other sources: Some time later, we assume in 1938, a company from Monterrey (possibly Lumber Company Fernández) bought lumber rights from the Cameron estate. From a location on the east slope of the mountain, north of Rancho del Cielo, called the Malacate ("hoist"), the company installed a tramway and cable system to send oak, sweetgum, maple, and other hardwood logs to a mill on the Río Sabinas. A steam locomotive carried lumber from the Sabinas to El Encino. Later, a road was built from the foot of the mountain to El Encino.

Frank's memoirs relate the following: "Lumbering started with taking out the oaks and sweetgum. This was unsatisfactory as the wood [was improperly cured and] split and warped as it dried and [was] of little value. . . . Old-fashioned methods of lumbering were used with cross-cut saw and rolling it [a log] to the road by hand."

It is said that an insufficient volume of lumber was produced, and with prices very low, the company went broke in 1941. Apparently it did not exploit the pine at higher elevations, although Frank recorded on July 2, 1937, that the lumbermen had made "a trip to the pines on West Mountain."

Surprisingly, the cloud forest was in "nearly natural condition" when Byron Eugene Harrell did fieldwork for his thesis for a master of arts degree with the University of Minnesota, *The Birds of Rancho del Cielo: An Ecological Investigation in the Oak–Sweet Gum Forest of Tamaulipas, Mexico.* Harrell first packed in by mule with Frank Harrison on April 2, 1949, and had completed his field investigations by late May or early June of 1950.

Harrell wrote, "There are six small clearings from about one-quarter to three and one-half hectares in size; in total undoubtedly less than one percent (about 20 hectares) of the forest area. . . . Two of the now abandoned clearings were used by lumber companies in unsuccessful attempts to exploit the timber. The Malacate, a compensation hoist, is also a relic of these attempts. Three other clearings which are now abandoned were made by the late Paul Gellrich." The only clearing then in use was the one at Rancho del Cielo.

During the interlude that followed the failed efforts at lumbering, Frank was delighted to host a team of botanists, comprising Aaron J. Sharp, Efraim Hernández X., Howard A. Crum, and William B. Fox. Between August 22 and 29, 1950, they collected and observed. Descriptions of the vegetation were published by Dr. Sharp et al., of the University of Tennessee, in 1950 and by Sr. Hernández et al. in 1951. They were responsible for the oak-sweetgum forest's designation as cloud forest.

Lumbering resumed in 1951, with several business interests involved. Change was rapid and dramatic. The situation was explained graphically by Joyce Heckenlaible LeFebvre in her thesis for a master of science degree at the University of Minnesota, *A Comparative Study of Four Thrushes in a Mexican Cloud Forest* (January 1959). She had looked forward to conducting investigations in a "primeval forest." Instead she found that lumbering operations already had "advanced to the Rancho del Cielo proper, but the topography of this area prevented complete destruction of the timber so that I was able to study both undisturbed and disturbed sections of the forest."

Further, "On my arrival in 1953 I found new lumber roads dissecting the forest and large slash piles scattered throughout the cut areas. Wasteful cutting was evident everywhere. Large trees were felled but never utilized and stacked logs had been forgotten. Wherever lumber roads led, destruction of the forest was evident."

Apparently the resurgence of lumbering had started with the purchase of land by the Ancira family of Monterrey from a José Garza. They worked the land south and west of the Cameron estate (Alta Cima area). The Anciras built the road from Gómez Farías to Alta Cima and then up to San José, the site of a large sawmill.

At about the same time, Luis Ubando Flores of Mexico City bought lumbering rights from the Cameron estate. He built the road from the Aguacates junction northward at least as far as San Pablo, where he established a sawmill, probably in 1952. (San Pablo was the property of Paul Gellrich and the site of his homestead.) Byron Harrell was the first of Frank's friends to use the new road up from the Aguacates. He made the trip from Gómez Farías in a jeep in 1951, bringing a cooking stove to Frank. How he got the stove all the way to Rancho del Cielo is not clear, as the spur road was not built by Fred Blesse until 1953.

Luis Ubando Flores found it expedient to leave the region after a man was killed in an incident in a cantina in El Limón, a highway town north of San Gerardo. In 1953 he sold his lumber rights to a Dr. Meyers, a German immigrant, and Miguel Alcocer. In 1955 Dr. Meyers extended the road from San Pablo north and moved the San Pablo camp to Company Clearing.

The scientific community (at least those individuals who had worked in the region) responded to the actions of the lumbering interests with a scheme to purchase and preserve as much of the area as possible. An informal committee was formed to solicit funds for the project. The plan is explained in a letter from A. J. Sharp, chairman, dated March 6, 1953. Sharp begins with a description of the subject:

> The forest community is unique in composition; the unusual mixture of genera is indicated by the presence of beech, sugar maple, redbud, shagbark hickory, polycarpous yew, fir, oaks, *Heliosoma, Lysiloma,* the palms *Brahea* and *Chamaedorea, Trichilia,* etc. . . . Further, the forest is the northernmost representation of Middle American cloud forest formation.
>
> Unfortunately, this forest is now being destroyed by lumbering. Even slender trees are being cut out for railroad ties. Unless some conservation measure is effected soon, the forest will be almost completely destroyed. Over half the forest is already gone; the entire area around Harrison's rancho is cut and piled with slash.

The committee was to solicit funds from scientists who had worked in the Gómez Farías region, as well as other interested parties, to purchase a "small representative area which, added to the pockets that the lumbermen cannot reach, would be sufficient to serve in the future for field laboratory and museum purposes."

The purchase of land was to be arranged in the name of the Instituto Mexicano de Recursos Naturales Renovables, headed by Dr. Enrique Beltrán, with Frank Harrison as warden. Contributions were to be sent to L. Irby Davis, who served as treasurer of the project, apparently because of his familiarity with and nearness to Mexico (he resided in Harlingen, Texas, at the time).

Years later Irby Davis told us that between $500 and $1,000 had been raised and a seller found. At only a few dollars an acre, a tract of several hundred acres was visualized. It would be adjacent to Rancho del Cielo.

The dream never materialized. In a 1969 conversation, Irby Davis recalled being instructed to send the money to "the man in Mexico City" who was handling negotiations and who asserted that he was ready to buy the tract. The sum was then converted from U.S. dollars into Mexican pesos and deposited in a Mexican bank. Shortly thereafter, the peso was drastically devalued. What little remained of the account was turned over to "the conservancy."

While attempts to save the forest were aborting, timber cutting progressed unchecked. Still, enough must have remained of the forest to impress John Hunter on his first trip in 1954 with Fred Blesse. Four years later, developments forged another link between the Hunter family and the mountain.

In the meantime, Meyers had extended the main road farther north (now four miles from San Pablo), abandoned camp at Company Clearing, and set up a sawmill settlement that he named Julilo ("little Julio"), after his son. In 1958, following Meyers's death, his widow sold lumbering rights and the equipment at Julilo to Ernest McCollum, Sr., Elizabeth's husband. The McCollums had lived in Ciudad Victoria for many years, farming and ranching. The elder McCollum was considered a speculator; one of his acquisitions was a box factory, for which lumber had been procured from Meyers, who had been logging pine above Julilo.

By 1960, Julilo was a bustling community with more than 200 men employed in logging operations. Still, McCollum was not one to turn his back on opportunity; soon he was engaged in mining barite ore at a site on the ridge west of the Malacate.

McCollum's activities on the mountain were short-lived; he died in 1962.

His lumbering interests were sold to Carlos Diez Gutiérrez, who had been associated with both McCollum and Meyers. By this time, cutting had spread far into the humid pine-oak and dry oak-pine forests above and to the west of the cloud forest. Gutiérrez had sawmills at Las Canoas and other localities in the higher country, establishments we would visit before they vanished from the mountain, leaving only mounds of sawdust to mark the sites where people had worked and lived.

But now it was May 1964, and we were sitting on a rock wall listening as John and Frank spoke of their expectations for Rancho del Cielo and the surrounding forest.

Involvement by Texas Southmost College personnel at Rancho del Cielo began with a field trip in April 1962. John Hunter, a trustee of the college, had been promoting the mountain for some time. John announced his success in a letter to Frank Harrison: "Next Thursday, April 5th, the Junior College has a field trip of about seven or eight girls and five or six boys accompanied by three or four teachers, and they asked me if we would let them use the cabin for at least one night and maybe four. . . . They expect to leave here by bus and then transfer to jeep at Victoria to the mountain." John anticipated that Barbara T. Warburton and Tom and Mary Keller would be with the group; however, Warburton, a professor of biology, was not able to make the trip, nor was John, who had experienced "a little flare-up with my heart."

Tom Keller, a chemistry instructor at the college, and his wife, Mary, did accompany the group, with the result that negotiations were under way immediately for space on which to construct another private cabin. The plan met with John's wholehearted approval. "Keller is as thoroughly sold on the place as I was after my first trip. I will be very happy to have him and Mrs. Keller on the mountain. They are fine people," John wrote us later. "They are young enough and free enough to where they can come down more often than an old one like me." Work on the cabin was under way that summer, just uphill and north of John's. It would follow the floor plan of the two Hunter cabins: a large and a small bedroom and a porch.

The April 1962 trip was declared a success, to the extent that one student was ready to gather a group to go to the mountain the very next weekend.

As Mary Keller wrote to Frank, "We suggested that they might better wait awhile. I'm sure that all you need with those Ph.D.s [Paul Martin and party were expected at the ranch] is a group of giddy girls."

"Awhile" turned out to be a full year of waiting for another student trip. Finally, in April 1963, Barbara Warburton led a second expedition to the ranch. It, too, was a success, and definitely an adventure for the 35 participants. The story of the trip is a classic, chosen from a reservoir of countless expeditions, which Barbara delighted in recounting to visiting groups in later years. We give the facts here, deprived of her flair for storytelling.

Tom Keller was in charge of transportation for the trip and managed to have a chartered bus cross over to Texas (not the usual procedure) and meet the group of 25 students and 10 sponsors at Texas Southmost College, only a stone's throw from the International Bridge. Loading was under way at midnight on the appointed date. One unusual item of freight was a refrigerator hull, which was used as an ice chest. It and the working parts (to be shipped later) were destined for Bob Hunter's cabin.

By 6 A.M. the bus was in the vicinity of Ciudad Victoria. Some time later it arrived at El Encino. At that point, the driver was persuaded, after appropriate protest, to take the bus through and beyond the village on a narrow and unimproved road; it was an exercise not in the original trip plan. Tom Keller had arranged with Carlos Gutiérrez to provide two lumber trucks; they would be at the patio where the milled lumber was stored.

After much encouragement from Tom Keller, a relieved driver pulled up to the patio and 35 passengers alighted, only to sit around on stacks of lumber while one of the lumber trucks was outfitted for the trip up the mountain. To accommodate passengers, rather than logs, the truckbeds were fitted with "something like benches," in Barbara's words, "old-fashioned benches in the church."

Eventually, two trucks with 35 persons, assorted luggage, and a dismantled refrigerator set off through the cane fields. For a while the riders were enthralled by the strange vegetation, particularly the palo de rosa tree (*Tabebuia rosea*), covered with pinkish blossoms preceding emergence of its leaves, and a plethora of bromeliads.

Crossing the Río Sabinas on the low-water bridge proved no problem, as spring rains had not pushed the river to flood stage. Giant Montezuma bald cypress (*Taxodium mucronatum*) lining the streamside and contributing largely to the gallery forest were renewing needles lost in winter. Social Fly-catchers were screaming and twittering as they worked their riverine habitat for flying insects.

Sometime beyond the river, 35 riders realized that their necks, understandably strained from gazing up and about, were not the only painful parts of their anatomy. Consequently, the trucks were halted and all dismounted to collect rocks, which were then used to pound nails back into the loose bench boards. This procedure was repeated three times before the expedition reached Rancho del Cielo.

The northern route (El Encino to Julilo to Rancho del Cielo) is about sixteen miles. The first leg (twelve miles to Julilo) provides a relatively comfortable trip in a four-wheel-drive vehicle, but the road from Julilo to Rancho del Cielo is more challenging. Traversing this route on the bed of a lumber truck is a memorable experience.

The trucks arrived at Rancho del Cielo about dusk, in a light rain. The boys rolled out their sleeping bags in the Kellers' new cabin, which at this time consisted of one room and a porch. The girls and the sponsors went down to the Hunter cabins.

Barbara Warburton claimed that her introduction to the ranch was standing over a wood-burning stove and cooking meals for 35 people. Without refrigeration her options were limited. So, as she recalled, she would cook a dishpan full of rice, open tins of chicken, and "make a big old mess of something." On one occasion Tom Keller led most of the group up the mountain to check out the barite mine. The hikers failed to return for lunch, and instead came straggling in late in the evening, too tired to eat. "I tell you, we had the best fed local dog," Barbara remarked.

Despite various inconveniences encountered on her first trip to Rancho del Cielo, Barbara fell under the mystical spell that draws one back to the cloud forest. Also, there was a practical consideration. She was intrigued by Frank Harrison's interest in the forest as a laboratory for scientific study and his willingness to offer Rancho del Cielo as a base.

At the same time that Barbara was discovering Rancho del Cielo, there was a growing emphasis on fieldwork in the natural sciences on the part of colleges nationwide, and a "fascinating article" came to her attention encouraging junior colleges to participate, contending that they could do many things as well as senior colleges. "Sometimes there were derogatory remarks made about our little regional college," she recalled, "and I thought about this place up here in the mountains." To establish "a permanent bio-logical station for general ecological studies" would give the college a boost.

It was in October 1963 that Barbara Warburton approached C. J. Garland, president of Texas Southmost College, with her proposal. Garland wanted to consult John Hunter on the matter. John, as Barbara explained to us later, took it up and carried it forward. "We wouldn't have this if John hadn't lent emphasis to us."

Meanwhile, Garland was doing his part. In a letter to Dr. Efraim Hernández X. of Mexico City, dated December 13, 1963, he wrote,

> Our botanical and biological students have been going down to El Rancho del Cielo, Mr. Harrison's ranch in the Municipality of Gómez Farías, for the field trips, the last two Aprils, and all of us have enjoyed it very much. We would like to figure on making these trips every year, and if possible another trip in the summer or fall.
>
> Mr. John Hunter, one of the college trustees has a cabin there, and the owners of the other two cabins have been kind enough to let us use their cabins. There were thirty-five students and professors this last April. We do not wish to impose on our friends too much so we have asked Mr. Harrison to rent to us two hectares to construct our own cabins and he has agreed.

Garland inquired as to the possibility of a guarantee from the Mexican government that the cabins would be respected as the college property. Frank Harrison would be able to legally rent out the land for fifteen years, for which he would receive 50 pesos a year "to allow for the increase in his taxes."

Further, Garland pleaded for a cessation of timber cutting in the cloud forest, expressing the desire to see a national park established. "The agaristas are still trying to get a foot hold here, and if something is not done soon it will be as it is north and west of the Rancho del Cielo. We would appreciate it very much if this forest could be protected as there is very little natural forest left."

According to minutes of the college board in spring 1964, permission was granted for construction of buildings on the order of the existing private cabins. Funding for the project presented a problem, but not for long. Although the board refused to allow the use of tax money in Mexico, they agreed on April 29 to allocate $2,500 from the Carlo Zeimet Science Fund.

Zeimet, a Belgian immigrant, had served as an entomologist with the U.S. Department of Agriculture before his retirement. He had given his home in Riverside Addition to the college. The college board voted to sell the home and establish the fund. Zeimet had stipulated that funds from his gift be used for science.

It was a time for celebration for students and faculty of the science department. As Barbara wrote in a letter to Frank Harrison, dated May 1, 1964, "The students and I have been rejoicing and find it hard to settle down to the routine coming up for the end of school."

So it was on May 4, 1964, that Marie and I found ourselves privy to the latest development in the establishment of a biological research station, as it would come to be designated. The school campus, it was decided, would be located just north of the Keller cabin, an area of towering trees shading a cluster of ancient Indian house mounds. Construction would begin before the end of the year.

6

THE matter of a building site received little attention during the remainder of our trip. John wished to show us other parts of the range; hence, sometime during the following morning, with Frank Harrison added to the entourage, John herded us into the Jeep. John was not only a gracious host but also an exemplary tour guide, always eager to share his knowledge of places and people in both current and historical context.

We headed north, past the Keller cabin, around Frank's cow lot, and entered the forest on a road that Tom Keller and the college had built to connect with the San Pablo–Julilo segment of the north-south route, the portion that Dr. Meyers had built.

Scarcely had we left the ranch when Frank pointed out the area that Byron Harrell had studied in his survey of cloud forest birds. At Frank's suggestion, Harrell had chosen a least-disturbed portion of the forest, and one convenient to the ranch. We passed the census area without comment, and certainly with no inkling of the role that patch of forest would play in our near future.

The trip to Julilo was much like our introductory cruise through the cloud forest: we recall trees adorned with bromeliads and countless other biota, rock outcroppings crisp with mosses and ferns awaiting the onslaught of the rainy season, and birdsongs without physical accompaniment.

Points of interest along the route included the roadside water hole (or mud hole), a depression with a red clay base that holds rainwater over an extended period, where birds bathe when a noisy vehicle is not approaching and beasts of the forest come to drink after nightfall. Shortly we were on the main road. The next landmark was Company Clearing, the lumber camp site now returning to woodland, which was a great place to find Bumblebee Hummingbirds until second-growth trees supplanted brush patches.

We were basically following a trough between the first and second mountain ridges, although the forest largely obscured that terrain. A road opening appeared to our left.

"That's the Mine Road," John said. "They had a barite mine up there, about five thousand feet up the ridge. It didn't work out." John did not mention the mine cave, a favorite cavern of Texas Southmost students before it became too dangerous to enter.

Gray Silky-Flycatcher

Farther along we passed a road on our right that led to the Malacate, site of the initial lumbering operation on the mountain, where logs were sent below by hoist. Now only a tiny settlement remained, a cluster of frame houses on the eastern slope, remote from the main road, ringed by heavy forest. We would chance upon it on a future occasion when Frank led us on a hike from the ranch. I recall fog hanging thick over the Malacate, house and fence vanishing and reappearing at the whim of the cloud mass, mere ghostly forms materializing from cool, creeping vapor. And there was the overlook; quite abruptly, forest gave way to rock and agave and a cliff bathed in mist. The hoist had been there.

We had been climbing to nearly 5,000 feet elevation. Pine mixed now with oak and sweetgum, and we heard our first Gray-breasted Jay, a bird indicative of the pine-oak zone, just as the Jeep nosed into a sizable clearing.

Julilo was two rows of unpainted frame houses facing a dirt road that sloped downhill to the lumber mill. Potted plants lined porch rails; bushes bloomed in profusion behind weathered wooden fences that failed to restrain poultry, pigs, and dogs. John turned the Jeep toward the mill.

"That's Juan Moreno's house down there"—at the far end of the village, just before the road plunged into forest and headed toward the Río Sabinas. The Moreno house was almost hidden behind yard foliage.

"Will they be there?" Elizabeth wondered. "This is Cinco de Mayo."

I had forgotten. May 5, a cultural holiday in Mexico, commemorates a victory over the French at Puebla in 1862. Many local people made the trek down the mountain for the occasion. Perhaps that was the reason there was no discernible activity at the mill.

The Morenos were at home. Juan and Ladislada had become close friends of Frank's. Juan, brother of Virginia (wife of the late Dr. Meyers), was time-keeper and paymaster of the camp, the head man. Juan was stout and soft-spoken. We were interested to learn that he had attended St. Edward's University in our hometown, Austin. Ladislada was ostensibly the dutiful wife and charming hostess, but also a woman of strong character. Her cultivated plants, particularly her hybridized begonias, won Marie over immediately. But our visit with the Morenos was brief; it was nearing noon, and breakfast was a distant memory.

We turned back up the road, past the mill (open sheds with lumber scraps piled outside), past the frame houses, where a few faces peered at us from the shadow of doorways. A small brick building seemed out of character with the village. We were curious.

"The *forestal* uses it," John said. "They're like forest rangers—check on lumbering. That big frame building up on the hill is the *tienda de comestibles.*"

Elizabeth sensed our puzzlement: "Grocery store."

Frank admitted to being a *cliente*. It was a convenience he welcomed when the lumber people came. "You'll need pesos," he added. "American dollars won't do."

We had not planned to shop. Besides, as we talked, we had slipped back into forest; Julilo was lost to view.

Our next destination, John had promised, was Charco de la Perra ("puddle of the bitch"). The puddle or pond reference, we later learned, derived from a nearby depression that retained water in the wet season, becoming a virtual marsh. The locality appears on some maps as El Porvenir ("the future"). The settlement was properly referred to as El Porvenir, but we knew the place as simply Charco or La Perra.

We climbed to about 6,500 feet elevation through humid pine-oak forest. I remember particularly the strangely shaped rock outcroppings, some of them rugged spires, loaded with terrestrial bromeliads, agaves, and an assortment of unfamiliar plant types.

Unlike Marie, who was enthralled by all aspects of the terrain and its biota, I was mainly interested in the bird population. Although some cloud forest birds spill over into the pine-oak areas, many inhabitants of this zone were new to us. Of the Mexican endemics, the Golden-browed Warbler was most in evidence. We were surprised to find that some species common to the western United States bred in these mountains, a matter of altitudinal rather than latitudinal preference; prominent on the list are Acorn Woodpecker, Cordilleran Flycatcher, Hutton's Vireo, Painted Redstart, Hepatic Tanager, Black-headed Grosbeak, and Rufous-sided Towhee.

The reluctance of most of the birds to be observed diminished our pleasure somewhat, but by this time we had become accustomed to such rude treatment and focused on the vocalizations of the unidentified species.

Refreshed by a lunch break in the shade of a rock overhang, we rode into La Perra. This lumber camp had the unpainted, frame, tin-roofed houses such as in Julilo, potted plants in rusting tins, and clean-swept dooryards without a blade of grass. The configuration of street and buildings was somewhat haphazard, however, in deference to scattered outcroppings of gray limestone. The village's time-worn appearance belied its recent origin, and it was difficult to imagine that the entire settlement might disappear totally overnight.

The setting was idyllic, a mountaintop meadow, dominated only by a higher ridge hard to the west. The most prominent landmark was a balanced rock, a huge anvil-shaped mass perched on the eastern perimeter of the village, commanding a view of the lower ridge to the east and the valley of the Río Sabinas beyond. A decorated cross adorned the rock's rather flat top. On closer inspection we realized that each house had a cross displayed prominently. The decorations on each cross were wooden flowers, cleverly crafted by local workers.

We were accustomed to seeing crosses along the highways in Mexico, commemorating tragic accidents. I made an offhand remark about the house crosses.

"Those are festive crosses," Marie explained. "They are celebrating Cinco de Mayo."

If not a religious occasion, it was at least a time of thanksgiving, I conceded, and let the matter drop.

A small lumber truck with an overload of pine logs was parked by the sawmill. Six logs were entirely too many, and we expected the imminent collapse of the vehicle. How these World War II leftovers could be coaxed along primitive mountain roads defied our understanding.

The mill itself was something special, not for what could be observed but for what was concealed from the casual observer. We would never have suspected its secrets had it not been for Barbara Warburton's insatiable curiosity, the scientific mind at work. Also, there was her acuity in matters diplomatic, rightly valuing communication with the lumber people as an information channel. Further, good rapport meant that a visit to a lumber camp could produce several months' supply of kindling wood for the stoves at the ranch.

The secrets of the sawmill were revealed in the following fashion.

Several years after our first visit to La Perra, Marie joined the college group on one of Barbara's exploratory jaunts into the highlands. Charco de la Perra was one of the designated stops on the trip.

The stage had been set, as it were, some time before, on August 26, 1967. On this occasion the college trucks had started up the Aguacates grade, bound for the ranch, when they encountered a broken-down lumber truck blocking their path. The truck was on its way to La Perra with the head man of the camp. As was their custom, the college crew went to the aid of the loggers.

Marie recalls that while repairs were being made, the matter of caves was broached between Barbara and the lumberman. Sr. Humberto Manjares assured Barbara that the mine cave so popular with the students was nothing compared to La Cueva de la Perra.

The bait was too much to refuse, and on September 2, Barbara, her charges, and an eager Marie headed for the highlands. Manjares joined them at La Perra and guided them to the cave nearby, which, Marie assured me, was in essence a cavern.

Back at La Perra, Manjares invited Barbara into his office to look at maps of the area. In Marie's words, "The inside walls were beautifully paneled and nicely furnished." Manjares pointed out the position of his wall safe behind the paneling.

The foreman at La Perra was not at all like Juan Moreno at Julilo. He was a tall, trim man who left no doubt as to who was in charge. Marie was interested to learn that Sra. Manjares taught botany and that of four children, two were in college and two in high school. Manjares had come north from the state of Michoacán, as did most if not all of his workers.

Before leaving, Barbara was given a set of deer antlers, a board to mount them on, a deer skull and skin, plus samples of lollipop sticks made at the mill. As the average sawmill on the mountain certainly did not produce lollipop sticks, Barbara must have wondered about the extent of Manjares's operation. That, she would learn, was his secret.

As Barbara explained it: "They had a light-generating plant for up here. The light plant came from Czechoslovakia. He told me that the engineer was sent in with the light plant to help them install it. . . . I'd been up there several times, and here were these old ramshackle fences, and I thought there were just more places back of them where people live. He took me back in there, and I have never seen so much sophisticated machinery. They could make tongue-and-groove oak flooring down to making lollipop sticks."

On a work trip to another part of the mountain on August 15, 1970,

Barbara's crew stopped by La Perra. Marie recorded the incident. "There were very few people in La Perra. The sawdust pile was twice as large as last year, the machinery was uncovered, and Manjares was in the process of leaving." Apparently, the pine had been lumbered out.

We last saw La Perra in June 1997. The day remains etched in my memory. The cool morning air of the highlands had succumbed to midday sun. Scattered cumulus hung idle, diminishing to grotesque forms before dissipating altogether. The feathery branches of the pines scarcely trembled. We approached La Perra from the west, through a canyon and then a short climb to the ridgetop. We paid no heed when racing shadows vanished from the roadway and mist drifted on silent wings through the tree canopy; we were conditioned to such mood changes on the mountain. But La Perra was somewhat of a shock.

La Perra had become a grassy meadow broken only by rock outcroppings and a scattering of shrubs. Gray of sky matched gray of limestone and, like a hungry sea, lowered to devour stone behind an opaque curtain. Occasionally the cloud relented, and for moments the adjacent ridge displayed its ghostly tree shapes only to fade back into some netherworld.

There was no village, no sawmill. We found the sawdust mound, toward the canyon side, and the balanced rock eastward. The cross we remembered had long abandoned the rock; an adjacent tree had grown to overshadow the balanced mass.

Yet La Perra lingered in the high grass—bits of rusted truck parts scattered about, lengths of cable like huge snakes concealed by grass. La Perra was in a cluster of alien gladioli flowering above the grass heads.

The future had come to El Porvenir, and it was the past. But that was the way on the mountain.

On Cinco de Mayo we did not linger in La Perra. The sun was merciless, and John wanted to show us a scenic overlook. We returned to Julilo and took another road out of town, to the highlands again but away from La Perra.

We did not reach the overlook on this occasion. The road was fairly good for a logging road, and we were enjoying the pine-oak woodland when the Jeep balked at a rough spot.

"Everybody hold on," John said cheerily. "I'm going to give it a jerk."

Marie, sitting on the right rear side, felt something give, but John was not through. Another jerk, and the Jeep spring was finished.

We always recommend that two vehicles travel together on the mountain, one to aid the other or carry out stranded riders. John usually traveled alone out of necessity and could handle minor breakdowns, but not a broken spring—and it was Cinco de Mayo. We doubted that any company trucks would be operating on that special day.

Fortunately we had not progressed far beyond Julilo. Frank and I walked back to seek help from Juan Moreno, returning shortly with two lumbermen and a truck. We had heard that the local people could fix anything with a little baling wire; it was a matter of survival. In our case the men simply cut a strip of wood from a sapling and placed it in the position of the spring. This simple repair enabled us to drive the Jeep to Julilo, where we left it overnight. The lumber truck carried us back to the ranch.

The day's adventure had enlightened us and given us a measure of respect for the people who, from our perspective, were spoiling the forest.

7

W E were to leave the ranch the following day, but we had the morning to devote to serious birdwatching. We had been told by Frank that Jacinto Osorio, a friend and part-time helper, could take us to places frequented by the ajol. "Ajol" is the Mexican name for the Crested Guan, a black, almost turkey-sized bird species that characteristically moves about high in the larger trees. The bird was a favorite target for hunters and hence was increasingly difficult to find.

Our quest led us down through John's gate, around South Hill, and eventually to that section of San Pablo known as Paul's Field. Once the site of a lumbering operation, San Pablo was merely a deserted clearing when first we viewed it. Lacking the gift of prescience, we could not know the role this location was to play in the drama of Rancho del Cielo. The principal object of interest on this day was a house Jacinto was building, a small one-room structure standing on a bank that overlooked the flat depression that was Paul's Field.

The story of San Pablo past, as had been told us by John and Frank, became the substance of reality as we stood by Jacinto's house, looking across the still, deserted clearing, absorbing morning sun rays. Beyond was the ever-present forest and, farther, West Ridge, with the pines standing sentinel on its crest. West Ridge seemed so near that one could reach forth and touch it, but that nearness was deceptive; a tangle of vegetation and a chaos of rock barred the way. We had learned that on the mountain, distance is often measured in time rather than in miles.

Paul Gellrich must have loved the view as he worked his field. This clearing was only one of several he owned, we were told. His home was to the west, on a slope above the clearing, beyond sight of any passerby. We searched for the site on a later trip and found what appeared to be the rock foundation for a cabin. If there was other evidence of a homestead, memory fails us. There should have been no relics, for on the mountain no material or article remains unused; an abandoned house is hauled away, board by board, and utilized elsewhere.

Paul Gellrich moved up to Rancho del Cielo with Frank Harrison in 1935. He had died long before we even heard of Rancho del Cielo, but papers

Crested Guan

that came into our hands after Frank Harrison's death provide a profile of the man as well as a patchwork narrative of his life.

Paul Gellrich was born July 28, 1892, in Silesia, Germany, son of Albert Gellrich and Franziska Volkner. Paul was described as five feet ten inches tall, white skin with ruddy complexion, chestnut hair, blue eyes, hawk nose, round chin, smooth-shaven face, medium mouth, and little finger of the right hand "cut" (presumably meaning "cut off"). He was a Protestant and spoke English as well as German, but he was not fluent in Spanish. He entered the United States in 1913 and engaged in "agriculture and lumber" for seventeen years (apparently he went from lumberjack to farmer). He entered Mexico at Ciudad Juárez on November 5, 1930, and again engaged in agriculture.

We do not know the circumstances of his friendship with Frank Harrison. They shared quarters until late summer of 1938, when Paul began construction of his own house. Frank's "Garden Notes" first recall his helping Paul on the house on September 7, working all day on at least two occasions. September 13 was spent shingling, but the job was not completed until September 26. On September 23, however, "Paul started to cook his supper and dinner at his house." The two men continued to cooperate closely, often sharing chores.

Paul called his place (formerly part of the Cameron estate) Rancho de Las Piedras. A land registration document dated January 8, 1940, shows he had two hectares in cultivation and planned to cultivate four more.

World War II proved a serious disruption in Paul's plans. Bits extracted from papers no longer in existence tell a fragmented and confusing story. Paul, "a lumberjack and farmer on the Cameron estate," was detained on July 7, 1942, and taken to Mexico City. The reason for his detention is not clear. He had served in the German army during the period of October 12, 1911, to September 18, 1913, driving field artillery. One paper indicates that he belonged to an anti-Nazi guerrilla organization, presumably in Mexico. Marie, who was privileged to see Paul's papers before they were destroyed inadvertently, thinks that his receiving money from Germany (a family pension or inheritance) caused the Mexican authorities to suspect him of subversive intent. According to Marie's recollections of the story, Paul's use of the Spanish language was so limited that he was unable to exonerate himself, and he was sent to a labor camp in southern Mexico. In his absence, Frank kept Paul's tax payments up to date.

A letter dated May 14, 1945, from Paul Gellrich and Paul Strobelt, Estación Migratoria, Perote, Veracruz, to the Secretaría de Gobernación, México, D.F., stated that they had been there for two years, were not sympathetic to the Nazis, feared that a junta might develop, and asked for help in preventing the government from imprisoning them. The significance of the preceding is not clear to us; however, they were released by order of the president of the Republic of Mexico in the latter part of May 1945.

Gellrich returned to the mountain, but we know little of his activities after that. A note written on the back of a 1949 calendar (September-October), apparently in Paul's handwriting, may be enlightening. It is written to a Mr. Verlager.

Having decided to sell my place up here on the mountain I thought I write you first. It is a good opportunity for a family with children. The road from Gomez Farias very likely will be finished this coming year. There is enough timber on the place to pay for [illegible]. With a small sawmill of his own he could make good money out of it. All kinds of fruit can be grown here as my neighbor, Mr. Frank Harrison, can tell you. Personally I want to go to a logging camp to work. I got a recorded deed of 49 Hectar and buying another 12 hectar which is sure. If your interested please let me know. More people coming around now as the climate is very good and the road is coming. It would be better for you to come and see the land yourself and after we can make a deal. Will sell reasonable.

The sale never happened. A letter from Everts Storms to Paul Martin, dated February 1, 1950, tells the story.

Frank was down a few days ago. He is well, but had quite a shock. He found Paul hanged in his house. Frank had moved Paul over to his place and came to the ranch [Pano Ayuctle] on the 3rd of January. He did not go home until the 5th. When he got there Paul was gone, but Frank thought that he had gone to work for the lumber company. He had been working there before and had left his clothes there. When Frank took Paul's mule and turned him in Paul's field, he went by the yard fence, but saw nothing amiss. In a few days he got worried, and when a Mexican went up there they went to Paul's house and found that he had hanged himself. He jumped off a table. He had been dead about a week. He told Frank a few days before he came down here on January 3rd that if he could get some strychnine he would kill himself. Frank hid his strychnine. He had been in bad health, and I think that he went to see a doctor at Mante about a week or ten days before, and the doctor probably told him there was no hope for him.

For several years after his death, Paul Gellrich's name continued to appear on certain documents. His taxes were receipted through 1959, as Marie discovered before the receipts were destroyed. Another document, "Manifesto de Propiedad Rústica," filed in Gómez Farías on September 27, 1958, is a *revisado* (revision or review) of Paul's property. "Rancho de Piedra" consisted of 49 hectares valued at $10 each, with surrounding property on all sides belonging to Arturo Arguello. Curiously, this document is signed by Paul Gellrich and Evaristo W. Storms, but we detect some similarity in the handwriting.

After removal of the sawmill in 1955, Paul Gellrich's land lay idle. John Hunter looked at it before buying the Welch cabin, and Aaron J. Sharp, the botanist from the University of Tennessee, considered purchasing land there, although nothing came of the plan.

Jacinto Osorio did finish his house at San Pablo but never lived there; his wife refused to make the move. Nor was Jacinto able to show us an ajol.

Later that day the lumber truck came and took us to Julilo, where we boarded John's Jeep, sans repairs, and headed down the mountain. John drove with unusual caution, but before we reached Rudolph's Corner, about four miles below Julilo, it was necessary to stop and adjust the wooden spring.

"You'll have to get under it," John told me, referring to the Jeep. "Use this duct tape."

I know that John would have done the job gladly had it not been for his size. I pretended not to mind, and Marie gleefully photographed the event, my first time ever under a vehicle of any sort. John was sitting beside the road, directing. I don't know whether he was more amused or more concerned about my being able to do the job.

John lightened the trip down the mountain with his commentary on aspects of the route. Rudolph's Corner was a most fitting subject. Here, at an unusually wide turn in the road, we noticed a small shrine perched on a boulder at road's edge. The rock itself presents the carved outline of an equine-type beast. (Marie insisted the figure was that of a mule rather than a burro, and indeed, the mule was a favored beast of burden at the time the carving was done.) The shrine, a boxlike structure with a pitched roof, sat atop a platform on the rock. The side facing the road was open and nicely arched at the top. Candles and perhaps other items were placed inside.

The story of Rudolph's Corner differs somewhat, depending on who tells the story and how often. According to Frank, a man named Rudolph was coming down from the Malacate with his two burros (or mules) when they encountered a swarm of huahichiles. These vicious little hornets nest in the bottom of old oak and sweetgum trees and, when leaving to feed, travel en masse in long columns, undulating between three and six feet above ground level. They will attack any living creature in their path, usually concentrating on one target if there are more than one available. The hornets set upon one of the burros and began stinging. The animal was so tormented that it bounded off the mountainside. The other burro and the man, we understand, were not attacked, but the loss of a single burro and whatever burden it may have carried was a serious matter.

Beyond Rudolph's Corner we were on a section of road built by Elizabeth's husband, completing the road that Meyers had started from Julilo. McCollum put a bridge across the Río Sabinas in 1959–1960, which made it possible to reach Rancho del Cielo from the highway town of El Encino via Julilo. This route was considerably longer (at about sixteen miles) but generally easier to drive than the road from Gómez Farías. Thinking he could make others pay to use the new road, McCollum installed a gate with a lock, but the authorities ruled it illegal.

We do not recall Elizabeth mentioning her husband or his activities as we descended toward the Río Sabinas, but memories must have moved gently through her mind, much like the morpho butterfly bouncing airily before the Jeep, only to melt into forest obscurity.

We reached Ciudad Victoria before sunset. The spring problem was corrected overnight, testimony to what can be accomplished in Mexico with the right connections, in this case, Ernest "Sonny" McCollum.

8

OUR next trip to Rancho del Cielo was in September 1964. In the interim, plans for a college presence at the ranch were going forward, albeit at a slower pace than some had hoped.

An article in the Brownsville newspaper of May 1, 1964, disclosed the plan. "The college will build two dormitories, one each for boys and girls, and a mess hall. This will keep out the elements and that's about all, Texas Southmost College president C. J. Garland said."

John Hunter, trying to keep things moving, wrote to Frank Harrison on June 6, 1964. "Sonny [McCollum] has instructions to get Carlos [Gutiérrez] on the job as soon as possible and get it [the lumber] hauled down to you at the cabin. . . . If there is any way you can put pressure on Carlos and the lumber people to get moving, I sure will appreciate it, because the project is dragging." Bud Crain, maintenance man at Texas Southmost College, planned to go to the ranch on July 15. "If you can hire some extra men to make the foundations of the building . . . they could start the carpenter work just as soon as they come. The two small buildings will be 16'×20', the large building will be 16'×30' with an eight-foot porch. . . . If you can get Jacinto or someone to cut and hew the rafter poles which will have to be 16 feet long . . ."

The first measurements for building foundations were said to have been done on the July trip.

Our September trip was notable in two respects: it was our first trip with Barbara Warburton, and it was Mabel Deshayes's introduction to the cloud forest. We were John's guests, and he graciously welcomed our friend Mabel. Mabel and her husband, Bob, of Houston, would play significant roles in the future of Rancho del Cielo.

The party traveled in John's Jeep and one of two army-surplus (Korean war vintage) weapons carriers that the college had acquired for mountain climbing. The carriers were junkyard material, but with extensive repair and refitting, and discounting frequent breakdowns, they served the college well for a number of years.

On September 5 we turned off the Pan-American Highway at El Encino, picked up Juan Moreno at the lumber patio, and headed for the Río Sabinas. Here, at the river, we had our most exciting experience of the trip. The

Hooded Grosbeak

rainy season was not yet over, and the river ran two feet over the low-water bridge that Ernest McCollum had built. It was not impassable, we decided, as we watched a man practically pull two reluctant burros across the current. We volunteered Jimmy James, one of Barbara's students, to wade ahead and test the depths, as well as to point out the edge of the concrete. We followed Jimmy, the Jeep in the lead, John driving with unaccustomed caution and at least one passenger admitting to some trepidation. We arrived safely on the opposite bank.

Crossing the river at flood stage was not to be taken lightly. Sr. Manjares had lost a truck to the current. Dr. Sharp and his party, on a much earlier date, had been forced to make the passage in a dugout canoe.

We dropped Juan Moreno off at Julilo, presented Ladislada with a colorful hat that Marie had brought from Texas, and bounced on to Rancho del Cielo for several days of typical rancho activity—birding, hiking, and exploring.

We found that an area north of the Keller cabin, along the road that passed behind Frank's clearing, had been cleared for future college buildings. It was the site of several Indian house mounds, which were discernible only by the configuration of the terrain. No artifacts lay on the surface now, but after a heavy rain shards were sometimes found on the roadway, reminders of a culture of which we knew little.

Indian house mounds were said to have been common on the mountain. A trained eye might spot traces of the ancient habitations, but most evidence lay under centuries of sediment. Frank Harrison, in the late 1930s, came across telltale signs while digging a drainage ditch by his garden. He noticed two "lines of rocks" about a foot apart that looked as though they had been placed there. It reminded him of the "round Indian mounds like in the north part of Chamal." Between the two lines the soil was rich and black, unlike the clay of the garden. Two feet below the surface he began to find pieces of red pottery and charcoal; nothing of the sort could be found beyond the rock barriers.

Area caves were more productive in yielding artifacts, but they have been raided for profit by local people as well as outsiders. Around the turn of the century, Murdock Cameron had shown wisdom in dealing with cave exploration. According to Barbara Warburton's interview with Cameron's descendants, his boys were instructed to look but not touch or take, on threat of a whipping. Sometime, he was reported to have said, somebody with understanding and great knowledge "will come up here and need to see those caves with the contents untouched."

The Indian caves of the area are pre-Huastecan, dating back to 5000 B.C. The Huastecan is a pre-Columbian culture, linguistically related to the Mayan, which is found farther south in Mexico. Studies made in extensive settlements in adjacent lowlands show similarity of artifacts with those found in the mountains. These people were not studied by the Europeans, having vanished long before colonial days.

Barbara was interested in exploring the entire mountain range and lost no opportunity in accomplishing this, bit by bit. On our September trip we motored into the pine-oak zone to visit Indian Cave. The cave was, in reality, an extensive overhang with a high ceiling that receded gradually to ground level at the rear. A man was tilling a patch of land in front of the cave for a corn field and in the meantime working the cave. He was happy to show us the site, and bones and pottery that he had extracted from the thick dust of the floor.

On forthcoming trips the college students would work in another Indian cave on the flank of South Hill, just off ranch property, a shallow, low-ceilinged horizontal cave consisting of several small chambers with limestone deposits caused by water seeping through rock. Artifacts and bones were (and possibly some still are) covered with centuries of powdered soil. This cave is now off-limits to outsiders and concealed by encroaching vegetation.

As though determined to follow the Indian motif, we hiked to Indian Spring, up on West Ridge. The trail up the slope was reached by a logging road that branched from the north-south road near San Pablo. At the time, we could drive as far as the base of Canyon Diablo, a spot marked by sheer rock walls (aptly called the Rock Pile) and a maple tree that we were convinced must be the world's largest. From there a steady climb through deep woods, on a path beset by boulders and fissures and rattlesnakes, took us to a rivulet and the spring.

The lumber people had piped water from the spring down to San Pablo. (Paul Gellrich, earlier, had been obliged to haul water from Frank's spring or the mud hole.) Some time later the spring would be enclosed by a concrete structure and a water line run down to Gómez Farías, but on our first visit we enjoyed the clear, cold stream, the moss-covered waterfall, and the spring.

The college building program had not been advanced on this trip, but we had learned more of the mountain and, like Barbara Warburton, had whetted our appetites for exploration. The time had passed too quickly.

For our party, the trip down the mountain was uneventful. John left the ranch before the weapons carriers, and we had reached the vicinity of Llera, just south of the Río Guayalejo, before John decided to stop and let the college party catch up. We sat in a little roadside café and waited. An hour passed. By this time John was concerned, so we backtracked to San Gerardo. Still the carrier was not to be seen. We proceeded toward Gómez Farías for four miles, at which point a road branches to the left.

"Maybe they went to the Frío," John suggested, more hopeful than convinced. I was instructed to remain at the junction "in case they come by." John drove off toward the river.

The Río Frío originates in a spring a short distance from the road. It would have been a fun place for the students to visit, and I fully expected to see them follow John back. Instead, the carrier appeared shortly from the direction of Gómez Farías in a cloud of dust, headed for the highway at full speed (carrier version).

Somebody shouted, "We can't stop!" Nor did they. We found them at San Gerardo, by the highway.

Not far from the ranch the carrier had run over a six-foot-long board lying parallel to the ruts, with a nail protruding from each end. Both front and back tires on one side were punctured, and they carried but one spare. Lucas Romero, Frank's helper, who was riding down with the group, led one of the boys back through a forest shortcut to the ranch to fetch the tire pump. Six pumping sessions later the carrier passed me at the Río Frío junction.

Now the Jeep demanded attention; the radiator was leaking. Someone suggested an application of raw eggs. We purchased two eggs from the people at San Gerardo and dropped the contents into the radiator. Then it was off to Llera again where tire repair was available, with only one pumping stop en route. The eggs got the Jeep to Ciudad Victoria.

John was a faithful letter writer and kept us abreast of developments at Rancho del Cielo. A letter dated October 14 revealed that two or three workers were spending the week "up there, so they will pretty well get the foundations laid out. Most of the lumber has been delivered."

John took us to the mountain again in mid-November. The foundations had been completed, but no work toward construction was going on during our week at the ranch, perhaps because some amount of time was required for fresh-cut lumber to cure.

Fall is a delightful time in the cloud forest. The weather is mild. Oaks, sweetgum, maple, and other deciduous species still hold most of their leaves, and the rocks are still green with mosses and ferns, souvenirs of summer rains. Migratory birds from boreal breeding grounds have passed through to southerly latitudes, winter visitors are still appearing on northerly winds, and summer residents of the higher forests have made their vertical migration, some to the cloud forest, some as far down as the Río Sabinas. It is a season of surprises and excitement for the birder. It was a particular treat to see warbler flocks of eastern and western United States species intermingled with Mexican endemics of different altitudinal affinities.

We did not return to the ranch while the college buildings were going up, but John kept us informed. A letter from John dated December 16 reported that "by the first of last week the college work crew had all the floors laid and all the materials on hand—thought they could get the roof and side walls up before they came down this weekend." On January 7, 1965, John wrote, "The college crowd went down before Christmas and got their buildings—all three—up and weathertight. I don't think the plumbing and some of the interior work is complete." Then, in a letter dated January 26 John announced, "I just got back from a trip to the mountain. . . . the college buildings are now complete."

While the administration and board of trustees at Texas Southmost College applauded the accomplishments at Rancho del Cielo, at least one segment of the Brownsville population took a dim view of the project. A piece titled "Mickey Invades Mexico" appeared in the *Brownsville Herald*, the city's daily newspaper.

> We see our friends architect Wilhite and Heister have gone down to the rain forest area of Mexico to do something or other at the camp of Texas Southmost College in Rancho del Cielo, Mexico.
>
> Along with the architects were some of the trustees of the college. There has been no official word of the significance of this jour-

ney, but we woke up last night in a cold sweat, dreaming that Texas Southmost College had just announced the opening of their new Rain Forest Branch campus—a complex of eleven 12-sided buildings, connected by malls—and named it the Miguel Maus University of Rancho del Cielo, Republica de Mexico.

Whew!

John Hunter was not about to let the matter rest. He wrote to D. R. Segal, editor:

In reply to your editorial, "Mickey Invades Mexico," I wish to state that architects Wilhite and Heister were taken to the Rancho del Cielo campus, along with an eminent architect from Houston, primarily to show them that there were educational facilities still being built on the square; that is rectangularly shaped in more or less 90 degree corners. The Rancho del Cielo campus was built without benefit of the architectural profession; Mrs. Barbara Warburton drew the plans; the material specifications were set up by Frank Harrison; Bud Crain consulted both design experts and executed the work, and the Board, after due inspection, approved the resulting project.

I do not believe that you need have any fear of the Texas Southmost College Board, as now constituted, ever building a 12-sided, round, or concaved-walled building on any of their campuses. . . .

Sometime when you are feeling tough enough and want to take a delightful weekend in Mexico, I will be glad to take you down and show you the Rancho del Cielo campus. I think that even you, with your warped ideas on education, would at least appreciate the architecture, and the utility of the project. Incidentally, it might help your conscience out to know that it was entirely paid for by privately donated funds of a man interested primarily in wildlife. . . . Not one cent of local tax funds or Federal money has been invested in the Rancho del Cielo campus.

John then wrote to Frank, "We have a newspaper in Brownsville that is poison on all public education. This is one time that if I get up there with him, I would like to have a breakdown or even get him close to a sink hole and push him in."

We first saw the completed college buildings in late February 1965. The pine wood was fresh and yellowish, a shade that would soon turn to a weathered gray. (No exterior or interior paint was used on the buildings.) The tin roofs, yet clear of forest debris, glistened with newness. Overall, the effect was one of attractive simplicity.

The windows (showing their early origin in the uneven glass surfaces) and all plumbing accessories had been used in old Fort Brown in Brownsville. The Texas Southmost College campus occupies the former grounds of the defunct military base and has access to material from the demolished buildings. The science club at the college occupied the very building wherein William Crawford Gorgas, renowned U.S. Army surgeon, operated during his tour of duty in Brownsville.

Members of the Gorgas Science Society were the students who, under Barbara Warburton's direction, played a major role in the Rancho del Cielo project. In 1965 there were only 600 or more students registered at Texas Southmost College, then a two-year school. As is the case today, the vast majority of them were of Latin American origin. Some were residents of Mexico who crossed over from Matamoros to attend class; others had family members in Mexico. Most spoke fluent Spanish.

The campus on the mountain does not have access to public utilities, nor are generators used. Lights, water heaters, and refrigerators run on butane fuel. Rainfall supplies all water used in the cabins. In the beginning, rainwater was collected by roof runoff into metal tanks (U.S. Navy surplus); later, pilas supplemented the roof water. Before indoor water heaters were installed, shower water was heated outside by a fire set under a metal drum and piped into the shower area.

Although building lumber came from the mountain, and an abundance of rock for the foundations was at hand, all else was brought up the mountain from Brownsville or Ciudad Mante in the college vehicles, a challenge and a daunting task.

9

OUR February trip came at a time of transition, when winter holds hands with spring in a brief mingling of the seasons. Winter is of short duration in the cloud forest, and already, in February, some sweetgum, oak, hickory, and other species were budding or pushing out tender leaves, and redbuds were in full spring glory. Meanwhile, some forest giants yet clung to foliage of spring past, as though reluctant to bare themselves completely; brown, worn leaves still drifted downward when nudged by an impatient breeze and added to the crispness of the forest floor.

Podocarpus reichei, a tropical species, is the most prominent evergreen tree; magnolias are in lesser number. At this time of year we are more aware of the affinity of this forest with temperate woodlands of the United States. The sweetgum, maple, hickory, walnut, western soapberry, and others give a sense of familiarity to the visitor from the north, as do the oaks, except that these oaks have tropical origins and are difficult to identify.

Winter is the dry season, as reflected in shriveled ferns and dormant mosses awaiting the fulfillment of summer rains. Rain does fall in occasional winter and spring showers, and protracted rainy spells are not unknown, but these are not dependable. In the interim, fog is a frequent visitor; clouds engulf the forest, moisture gathering on remnant leaves and dripping off the tips. This is cloud forest, not rain forest.

In February Frank Harrison's orchard was bright with peach blossoms, and loquat trees were forming fruit. Amaryllis had started opening, displaying the huge variegated hybrids that Frank had developed. Along the drive from John's gate to his cabin, the azalea bushes were aflame.

We were John's guests again, along with Mabel Deshayes. This time no college personnel were present. With the buildings ready, students and staff would work trips in as the school schedule permitted.

We spent most of our time birding. We did take one trip worthy of note, a Jeep ride to an area we had only read about, the back side of the mountain range. This is the dry oak-pine forest, the land of the rain shadow. We must confess that we have seen this area quite wet on occasion, but usually summer rains coming against the mountains on easterly trade winds play out before reaching the west side.

It was a long ride, through Julilo and then into the highlands and down

White-collared Swift

McGOWAN

the western slope, about fourteen road miles from the ranch to La Joya de Salas, our destination. The road was fairly good out of Julilo, but there were no settlements, not a single farmhouse, between Julilo and La Joya de Salas, and without a second vehicle we would have been in trouble in the event of a breakdown. Apparently John, always confident in his ability to overcome adversity, did not consider the possibility of trouble sufficient cause to remain at the cabin.

The lengthy trip only enhanced our awareness of the biological diversity of the sierra. This was evident in the vegetative associations. We were deep into the wet pine-oak zone after we left Julilo. Then the transition to dry oak-pine was gradual, complicated by the succession of canyons and peaks that provided pockets of diverse environments, where amount of sunlight and moisture retention contrasted with that of contiguous habitats. (Mentions of peaks and canyons should not evoke visions of the Andes. The highest point in the Sierra de Guatemala is thought not to exceed 8,000 feet above sea level. We probably topped 6,000 feet on the road to La Joya de Salas.)

By the time we had crossed what I assumed to be the second north-south ridge of the range (moving westward) the tall oaks gave way to gnarly trunked, round topped specimens seldom reaching 65 feet in height. Mosses and liverworts were no longer in evidence, and lianas, which strung their cables throughout the cloud forest, had long disappeared. However, present were epiphytic orchids, ferns, and Spanish moss (particularly in the oaks), and a strange mixture of ground-cover plants.

Had we been mindful, we might have noticed that compound-leaved trees are rare in this woodland. The most common trees in the dry oak-pine zone are oaks of several species, Montezuma and jelecote pines, and drooping juniper (*Juniperus flaccida*). We thought the jelecote pine (*Pinus patula*) most curious for its fine green needles, which drooped like a long patch of human hair. It prefers higher, more humid sites than the Montezuma pine, which we soon found to be common in La Joya's basin. A familiar small tree confined to the dry side of the mountain is the madrone (*Arbutus* species). Like the madrone in our Texas hill country and the unrelated chaca (*Bursera*) tree of the tropical deciduous forest, this variety has smooth, reddish brown bark that peels off in thin sheets.

As we left the more humid region for drier country the forest seemed to thin somewhat, possibly because rock outcroppings provided less support, and obviously because much pine had been cut out. Logging trails, most abandoned and overgrown now, branched from the main road like collapsed veins that had drained the lifeblood of the forest. We saw no indication of recent cutting, but the view from the road is necessarily myopic.

We had reached Tierra Colorada. Far behind now were any reminders of humid pine-oak woodland. Tierra Colorada had been a lumber camp at one time. It was merely a clearing now, red clay under a thin glaze of pine needles, but a convenient place to stop and relax before a downhill drive to La Joya de Salas. Nearby we had our first panoramic view to the west, an undulating horizon clothed in blue haze, wooded mountains in disorderly configuration. Farther beyond, visualized only in our imaginations, would be the vast, arid central plateau of Mexico.

Nowhere was there a hint of recent human activity. We had eluded civilization, and the loneliness was almost tangible. We could look above to scattered cumulus clouds floating in an incredibly blue sea, a background for pines that waved branchlets to vagrant air currents. With the Jeep's wheezing stilled for the moment, we heard unfamiliar bird calls against the sibilant orchestration of wind in tree.

It was all downhill from Tierra Colorada. We navigated a stretch of solid rock surface and, dipping into a narrow canyon, were at once engulfed in sun-peppered shadow. The road hugged one side of the dry water course and, after a long downhill glide, became less clearly defined as we came into a wide valley. The valley, walled in by long wooded ridges, reminded me somewhat of the Texas hill country. Here, too, was a dwarf forest, but the vegetation was noticeably different; the oaks and junipers were different species from those in Texas, the limestone more fragmented, not confined to traceable strata.

A little birding produced some truly western U.S. species: Bridled Titmouse, Hutton's Vireo, Painted Redstart. The Gray-breasted Jays were raucous, and to our surprise we heard the unmistakable "coaah" of the Elegant Trogon, a species we had left in the tropical deciduous forest on the eastern flank of the sierra.

We picked our way across a valley floor deeply gouged by forgotten rain torrents, now grass-covered except where wheel ruts rambled aimlessly. In wet weather the whitish clay was as slick as ice, and we would have floundered in it and had to turn back. Today we wove our way forward with the ruts, past a rock-walled enclosure that protected a house, fruit trees, domestic animals, and whatever, and came into a much greater valley. The vegetation that had covered the valley floor in ancient times was but a memory, in its place bare earth reaching to the flank of surrounding peaks. Overgrazing had robbed the land even of grass cover; only scattered thickets of acacia species remained. Cows, horses, and pigs took what forage they could find.

The valley had two natural attractions, a small lake that seldom went dry and an enormous sinkhole. The Sótano de la Joya de Salas is a wide slit-trench opening with a depth of 896 feet and a free fall of about 600 feet. The hole acts as a gigantic drain in the event of torrential rains, sucking in any object not anchored.

The village of La Joya de Salas lay beyond the lake, a small cluster of picturesque houses and gardens. Frank Harrison was familiar with the area and had known the people there. Hunting game must have been particularly good on the west side of the range; the people of Gómez Farías and the lowlands often crossed the mountain in search of deer and turkey. It was on such an expedition that Frank stayed overnight at the abandoned McPherson homestead (now Rancho del Cielo). The trip to "Jolla" (Frank's term for the area) was made on foot with mule or horse, as there were only primitive trails until the lumber people came. Rancho del Cielo was on the main trail to the back side, with countless travelers taking shelter in the old cabin. Later, Frank put them up overnight in his new house. From the ranch, it is likely that the trail cut directly over West Ridge, north of the mine but south of Julilo and La Perra. With John, we had taken a longer, less direct route farther north.

Frank stayed with friends at La Joya de Salas or at a nearby ranch and hunted day or night with infrequent success. In his earlier days at Rancho del Cielo, he made several trips across the mountain each year, in late summer or fall. In September 1937 he wrote of killing a seven-point buck, taking it first to La Joya and then to the ranch, minus one front shoulder (the buck's); no doubt he had the services of his mule or horse.

We did what all visitors do at the Sótano, we looked over the edge. Then we dropped a pebble or two to test the sound of rock hitting the first ledge, and in the process flushed out the resident Canyon Wren. John walked to the rocky rim with the help of his cane, and Marie, with no support and a total lack of fear, leaned as far as she could over the abyss.

I was relieved when we had satisfied our curiosity and could spare a moment to observe the birdlife on the grass-deprived, acacia-dotted meadow.

Violet-green Swallows swooped tirelessly around the sinkhole. A male Vermilion Flycatcher was a Christmas ornament misplaced in a scraggly acacia. Some familiar duck species were on the pond, with Killdeer and Least Sandpiper foraging along the waterline. Waterbirds spot the lake as they migrate overhead, this tiny jewel ringed by mountains. In summertime, on future trips, we could count on seeing Lesser Goldfinch, Blue Grosbeak, Black Phoebe, and other Texas species that breed in the valley of La Joya.

We drove through the village and beyond, down to another wide valley, one with ample pasture and a scattering of pines. It could have been a park and, in fact, would come to be known, at least to Warburton's students, as TSC park. For the most part, however, it was home to horses. For us, it was the farthest point of the day's journey, time to petition for an uneventful trip back to the ranch.

On this trip in February, we had more on our mind than just birding. John had lured us to the mountain initially by dangling before us not a carrot but Byron Harrell's thesis. Had we not perused that scholarly work, I doubt that we would have exposed ourselves to the mountain's addictive charm. Nor would Harrell have done his study in the cloud forest had it not been for our friend, Irby Davis. According to Irby, George M. Sutton (later renowned as a bird artist and writer) had sent Harrell to see Everts Storms to arrange additional ornithological investigation in the Sabinas lowlands. On the way to Mexico, Harrell stayed overnight with Irby, at which time Irby suggested that the young scientist could "avoid the tick-infested lowlands," where studies had already been done, and go up to the cloud forest. There he could make a unique contribution.

Harrell did his work at the ranch in 1949 and 1950, mainly during the months of April, May, and June. Now fifteen years had passed.

I don't recall just when the inspiration came or exactly what I said to Marie. I do know that we were in Austin, between Mexico trips, probably looking for an excuse to return to the mountain. I can imagine the conversation.

"I've been thinking about Harrell's thesis."

"Oh?" Marie was perusing the morning paper, over breakfast.

"How do you think the bird populations would compare, then to now?"

Marie looked up. I had gotten through; given the circumstances, that was an accomplishment. A moment passed. "I don't know," she responded thoughtfully. She expected more.

"It's been some time now. I think it would be interesting to find out."

Marie had placed the paper on the table. "And how would you go about this?"

The ball was definitely in my court now; actually, I thought I would have to defend my suggestion. Picking the right words would be crucial.

"I was thinking a census, like Harrell's. Checking every day or so. Over a period of weeks."

Marie had an intent look. I hoped for the best. "We would have to do it, I suppose," I said tentatively.

"We?"

"Well, you." I was employed, Marie was not, at the time. "Not by yourself," I added quickly. "Maybe you could interest Mabel."

Mabel was interested indeed, as was John Hunter. Frank Harrison was delighted. Not surprisingly, Marie was excited at the chance for a prolonged visit to Rancho del Cielo.

Black-headed Nightingale-Thrush

10

I F we were to study the nesting birds of the cloud forest, we would need
to establish a census area. This was one objective of our February trip.
Breeding activity would start soon for some bird species, and we must
decide on a location. Despite the perceived urgency, we delayed acting until
the day before we were to leave the ranch.

Our options seemed limitless, although we preferred a site within easy
walking distance of the cabins. We were aiming for 30 acres of heavy forest and would not settle for less than 15. My specifications called for laying
out north-south and east-west lines that were 148, 209, 256, 295, or 330 feet
apart, creating a grid subdividing the area into units of ½, 1, 1½, 2, or 2½
acres.

We chose to investigate an area just north of North Hill, the steep incline directly north of Frank's clearing. A trail leading to the north side of
the hill intersected an abandoned, overgrown logging road. Frank had taken
us to the area on an earlier occasion to see Cathedral Cave, which was a
short distance off the road.

Cathedral Cave is really a sink (about 40 feet deep when we first saw it),
with vertical walls. A person descending could count on permanent residence in the hole were his rope to slip from its mooring. Some sinks we
had encountered were bowllike with gently sloping sides, others were sheer
drops, but none we had seen was as wide as Cathedral Cave.

Sinkholes were unpredictable. Barbara Warburton cautioned her students to walk only on the forest trails, but to tread softly if it was necessary
to move on untested ground, for a thin layer of surface soil could collapse
under the pressure of a boot. It is doubtful that hikers give much thought
to being swallowed partially or totally.

Cathedral Cave notwithstanding, we liked the forest thereabout and
started measuring along the road. It was when we ventured from the road
that our resolve wavered.

I summed up our reactions. "That terrain is rougher than I expected."

"We would need to do a lot of clearing for trails," Marie added. Hacking
through the forest was out of the question; we did not have the tools, the
workers, or the time. The project was deferred but not abandoned.

We returned to the mountain with John on April 11. Mabel Deshayes and her husband accompanied us. This time Marie and Mabel were equipped for an extended visit, as John would not be expected back for about a month. Preparations had included assembling clothing and other personal items, binoculars, cameras, and various materials to be used in conducting a field study. We had planned carefully and thoroughly.

One matter had not been resolved, however: where to do the work. Harrell's thesis included a map of his study area. It all but adjoined the ranch clearing on the west side and paralleled the road connecting the ranch with the main road, creating a rectangular tract consisting of three squares aligned east-west. It seemed logical that a time-comparison study be made in the same area; why we had not considered this previously, I do not know. When Frank declared that he could locate Harrell's corner marker, we were elated. True to his word, Frank led us to Harrell's marker stake at the northeast corner of the tract.

Harrell's forest plot remained relatively undisturbed, a prerequisite for a reasonable comparison of bird populations. Logging had occurred in adjacent areas since Harrell's sojourn, and it would have been difficult to find another convenient location that had not been affected.

We characterized the study area as a mature oak-sweetgum forest. Some sweetgums exceeded 100 feet in height and 3 feet in diameter. Oak species composed over half the number of trees, sweetgum about a quarter, hickory a substantial number, and maple a minor factor. Smaller trees and shrubs included redbud, wild cherry, *Clethra macrophylla*, buckthorn species, magnolia, *Eugenia capuli*, *Podocarpus reichei*, and persimmon. The trees and shrubs present a confusing mixture of temperate (particularly eastern deciduous forest) and tropical species, which raises speculation as to the origin of the forest components. Tropical elements are found especially in the smaller trees and shrubs. The *Clethra*, *Eugenia*, and *Podocarpus* species, for which we lack English names, are tropical. Of these, *Podocarpus* is considered to be a tropical cloud forest indicator. (Other *Podocarpus* species are Australasian.) The oaks have both temperate and tropical affinities and may hybridize.

Like most of the forest, the census area has a very uneven floor, sprinkled liberally with boulders, rocky hillocks, and sinks. Harrell noted four sinkhole caves in his 20-acre study plot. Epiphytes (lichens, mosses, ferns, bromeliads, orchids) abound on trees and rocks, adding to the tropical aspect.

For our project, we took all or part of Harrell's original tract (depending on the accuracy of our measurements) and enlarged it to a 30-acre rectangle, 700 × 1,000 feet. The tract, when trails were cut, would present a grid of eleven north-south lines and eight east-west lines, including the borders of the tract. North-south lines would each receive a number, one through eleven; east-west lines would be lettered A through H. Within the grid, each intersection of lines would receive a tag bearing the number and letter of that intersection. We printed a supply of maps with that format, one sheet to be used for one day's work. The numbered/lettered intersections would be reference points to locate birds seen or heard singing. After a series of daily maps were accumulated, a cluster of daily entries would mark the general location (territory) of a breeding pair in the event the nest was not located.

We thought we had a wonderful plan; only implementation stood in our way. That business was quickly addressed, as on April 13 we began laying out our trails.

The forest floor is relatively open in this area, but to make reasonably straight paths, we cut a few saplings, bypassed tree trunks, and detoured around boulders. A few hillocks, piled high with jagged rock and crowned with sharp-leaved agave plants, were insurmountable; here the trail was fragmented. With Marie using the compass, Bob, Mabel, and I measured the trails with a retracting 50-foot tape, hanging a strip of orange engineer's tape at each 50-foot spot. Every 100 feet we left an orange strip with an aluminum tag bearing the number and letter of the intersection, such as 3-G.

We had finished laying out the census area by April 16, and on April 17 Bob and I hiked down to Gómez Farías, where he had left his car, our destination Texas. John had left on a previous day with the college group. Now Marie and Mabel were on their own.

If we have left the impression that Frank lived the life of a recluse, we must set the record straight. Even in the early years Frank and Paul hosted travelers crossing the mountain between Gómez Farías and La Joya de Salas. Some people came up to hunt stray cows or to buy amaryllis bulbs or flowers from Frank. Some came up just to see Frank (people from Gómez Farías, especially good friend Félix Burgos, old friends from the Chamal colony, and Everts Storms from Pano Ayuctle), and there were part-time helpers from below. Later, the scientists came for protracted visits. After Paul moved to his own place, and on occasion when no visitors were present, Frank was quite alone, however, and when he ventured into unfamiliar places, looking for errant cattle, he must have felt the isolation. It is true that Rancho del Cielo was in a wilderness, reached only by mule trail, and even today a person may walk through the forest for hours without encountering a fellow human and, once straying from the trail, could be lost for days.

During the spring of 1965, Frank's visitors generally remained beyond view of John's cabin, and once Marie and Mabel reached the census area solitude was a reality. The road passed nearby, but thanks to the forest and the uneven terrain, visibility at ground level seldom exceeded 100 feet, and sound projection was limited.

One of Frank's visitors aroused Marie's curiosity. The brief encounter occurred on the road bordering the census tract. Marie was walking to an entry point when she passed a local man headed for the ranch. He was not the average wayfarer one encounters on forest trails; this man was dressed more appropriately for a business meeting than for a stroll in the woods — not that he wore suit and tie. He came from the direction of Julilo, but it seemed unlikely that he sought to buy produce or a pail of milk, as would be expected of the Julilo people. Frank did not mention the man's visit, and the matter was not broached by Marie.

Although Marie attached no significance to the man in the road at the time, two other encounters were definitely of a disquieting nature. On one occasion Marie and Mabel had walked to the water hole, not far north of the census tract (a good birding spot, particularly in dry weather), only to find three women doing their laundry. Like other rural women of the area, they were dressed conservatively in long skirts; Indian ancestry was apparent in their skin color and facial characteristics. They were said to be living at San Pablo, but they were not local people; they had come from southern Mexico with the workers at Julilo.

The women moved across the road from the pond to rocks on which they scrubbed their garments. The pond water had a high silt content, but it was their only recourse. The pipeline from Indian Spring that had served the sawmill at San Pablo had long since been abandoned, which left Frank's spring the nearest source of good water, and its level dropped over the winter.

"Did they drink that stuff?" I asked Marie later, referring to the water hole.

"It's all they had. They asked Frank for water, and he let them have some from the pila, but not from the spring." Frank's pila held collected rainwater, well seasoned with tree droppings and occupied by frogs and a goldfish someone had donated. "The livestock need water too," Marie reminded me. "Water can be quite scarce in the dry season, even in the cloud forest."

I knew that. My thoughts returned to the women at the pond. "Did you speak to them?"

"We didn't speak. They wouldn't look at us."

Marie recalls one other encounter of a similar nature during the census period. She and Mabel were taking Frank to a sinkhole where the Mottled Owl was nesting. It was past the southwestern corner of the census area, and to reach it one crossed a natural basin or hollow. On that particular day a man was working in the basin to clear a patch for a corn field.

The man had no title to the land. It may have belonged to Paul Gellrich at one time. It may have been part of the land sold to Jacinto Osorio and later to lumbering interests. As with other small plots of land scattered throughout the forest, often tucked away from prying eyes, possession meant only hope of future ownership, and squatters were seldom challenged. Marie did not know the man with the machete, nor did they inquire. He paid no attention to them, never pausing in his slashing. Frank, who was among the friendliest of men, made no attempt to speak.

John graciously turned his cabin over to the women, and they were sole occupants for most of their sojourn on the mountain. John made one trip up with the college trustees and the fixings for spaghetti and meatballs. "I am to cook it for this mob (16) for supper," Marie wrote. "Plus apple pie." They always "ate good" when John came up.

Barbara Warburton and the students made one trip to the mountain in late May, bringing needed food staples. Fresh meat had been packed for the trip, but the carrier with the meat broke down at San Fernando, 100 miles out of Matamoros, and limped back to Brownsville in low gear. Altogether, it was a fairly typical college trip.

Marie and Mabel settled into a daily routine of sorts. The day began whenever one awoke, the clocks and watches having ceased to function.

One can imagine that the dawn bird chorus hindered sleeping late. After a few days of culinary confusion, a plan was devised for breakfast chores. "Today we are starting a new policy," Marie wrote. "One will start the fire and cook and the other will do the dishes. This way one of us can be birding most of the time."

Frank kept John's cabin stocked with firewood, piled to one side of the porch. The art of starting and maintaining a fire in the wood-burning stove was one cultivated and fine-tuned through practice. The fire could not be rushed, so the dishwasher was able to enjoy quality birding minutes in John's clearing, or sit in John's rocking chair on the porch while the sun sent shafts of golden light through the forest, finally to nudge its way over the canopy. There were always birds in John's garden, which sloped sharply to the road as far as the gate. Shortly beyond, the forest eased into Canyon Tableta, concealing the surface contours. From the porch, there was a forest wall; all else was left to the imagination.

For the dishwasher, birding could resume as soon as the breakfast dishes were collected. A wide window was set over the sink, framing a portion of the clearing and nearby forest. The datura bush outside the window was a favorite perch for the little Rufous-capped Brush-Finch that sometimes lit on the windowsill or even explored the cabin. Hummingbirds checked out the large trumpet-shaped flowers of the datura before they wilted in mid-morning.

Without John's influence, breakfast was reduced to a minor inconvenience, and on mornings when Marie and Mabel were to go into the census area, the formality was quickly satisfied. An early start meant more bird activity to observe.

"So you were out there at the crack of dawn," I guessed, as we were reviewing the trip summary.

"It was after breakfast, some time after breakfast, depending on what time we got up. We probably slept late if we were up late the night before."

"For what? You walked down to the cantina at Gómez?"

Marie regarded me with a degree of tolerance. "Canasta. You know Frank came down for supper and to play canasta, and he stayed till he won."

That being the case, at whatever time they could, the two women set out with binoculars, camera, canteen, clipboard and maps, a plastic bag to sit on (because moss-covered rocks and fallen tree trunks were often wet), and a sandwich, for a day in the woods.

Photographs by Marie Webster unless otherwise noted.

Frank Harrison (LEFT) **and Everts Storms, Pano Ayuctle, circa 1940**
(photographer unknown).

Frank Harrison at old house, Rancho del Cielo, 1930s *(photographer unknown*

LEFT TO RIGHT: *George M. Sutton, Frank Harrison, Paul S. Martin, emetrio Osario, Roger Hurd, Everts Storms, Bill Heed at Rancho del Cie. March 21, 1949* (photograph courtesy Paul S. Martin).

Frank Harrison (LEFT) *and Demetrio Osario at new house, Rancho del Cielo, July 1954* (photographer unknown).

Texas Southmost College party at market, Ciudad Victoria, April 1969.

Gunsight Pass, south of Tropic of Cancer, July 1964
(photograph courtesy Alfred Richardson).

Río Sabinas crossing near El Encino, August 1964.

San Gerardo junction, old road to Gómez Farías, July 1967.

Plaza at Gómez Farías, February 1965.

*Marie Webster at memorial shrine, Blesse's Corner, November 1964
(photograph courtesy Fred Webster).*

The road to El Cielo, November 1964.

John Hunter's Jeep at the red gate in the cloud forest, April 1965.

John Hunter's cabin, Rancho del Cielo, May 1965.

John Hunter trimming his favorite lantern, December 1965
(photograph courtesy Ruth Black).

Looking toward West Ridge, Bob Hunter's cabin in foreground, October 1965.

Rancho del Cielo clearing, North Hill in background, February 1964
(photograph courtesy Alfred Richardson).

Frank Harrison in the cloud forest, September 1964.

LEFT TO RIGHT: *Nancy McGowan, Suzanne Winckler, Fred Webster, Edgar Kincaid, atop North Hill, July 1970.*

Looking south from North Hill, storm clouds moving up east slope, October 1973 (photograph courtesy James Pruitt).

Amaryllis bed, Rancho del Cielo, April 1965.

Frank Harrison (LEFT), Ladislada and Juan Moreno, Christmas cactus a
lant house, Rancho del Cielo, December 1965 (photograph courtesy Ruth Blac

LEFT TO RIGHT: *Juan, Pablo, Blanca, and Celestine Cordova at Rancho del Cielo, 1972.*

Cook house (first college building), Rancho del Cielo, October 1965.

Preparing dinner in cook house, Rancho del Cielo, 1975.

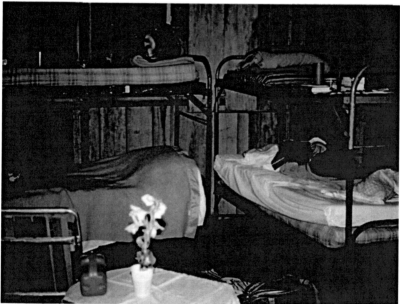

Men's cabin, Rancho del Cielo, June 1985.

Interior, men's cabin, Rancho del Cielo, June 1985
(photograph courtesy Alfred Richardson).

Harrison Hall, Rancho del Cielo, June 1971.

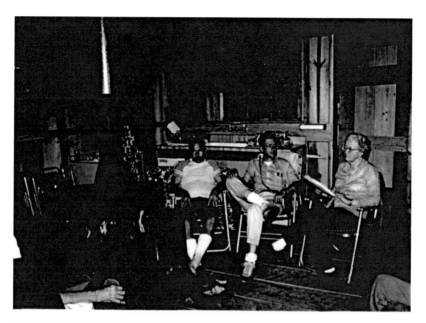

Barbara Warburton lecturing to tour group, Harrison Hall, June 1981
(photograph courtesy Constance Tatum).

The Keep, Rancho del Cielo, August 1975.

*Larry Lof cranking ice cream freezer, Rancho del Cielo, June 1981
(photograph courtesy Constance Tatum).*

'reparing dinner in the Keep, June 1981 (photograph courtesy Constance Tatum

Mabel Deshayes entering bird census area, Rancho del Cielo, May 1965.

Bird census tract, May 1965.

San Pablo clearing, Frank Harrison's cattle, August 1966.

Julilo, sawmill on right, September 1964.

Sawmill at El Porvenir, May 1964.

Ejido Alta Cima, June 1971.

San José, April 1968.

Elephant Rock at El Elefante, August 1974.

Bridge at Casa Piedras, August 1970.

Waterfall and pool at Casa Piedras, August 1970.

Barbara Warburton leading students up waterfall above Indian Springs
August 1967.

Looking east from West Ridge, November 1964.

Rock formation, humid pine-oak forest, road to La Joya de Salas, August 1983.

Tierra Colorada, dry pine-oak forest, road to La Joya de Salas, June 1988

Sinkhole at La Joya de Salas, February 1965.

Lake at La Joya de Salas, August 1987.

Larry Lof overlooking canyon of the macaws, June 1992.

aura Alcalá Vargas (LEFT) *and Barbara T. Warburton (photographer unknow*

Thoughts of supper came when the sun had retired over West Ridge, pulling after it the curtain of night, and the birds (Blue Mockingbird, nightingale-thrush, and robin), no longer to be observed, greeted encroaching darkness with parting calls. The datura blossoms would be opening outside the kitchen window to entice their nocturnal pollinators. The Mottled Owl, aroused from daytime rest, would send an eerie scream through the forest, as though to challenge other creatures of the night.

Then Frank Harrison, having finished watering and tending his cattle, would walk down from his cook house, flashlight in hand, to have supper with Marie and Mabel. If rain was imminent, Marie remembered, Frank was prepared. "He usually wore his rubber boots and carried his raincoat, hoping that it would rain. He had a pretty good idea when it would rain. He would sit on his doorstep evenings and watch the clouds build up in the east. And we really did need rain then. John had drained his pila, expecting it to rain, so the hot water tank was empty. Since water from the rain barrel was used in the kitchen sink, and we drank the spring water, we were limited in bathing. You can be sure, when it did rain, we showered and washed our hair in roof runoff on the east side of the cabin, hoping no one would come up the road."

(Some water remained in the pila, below the outlet pipe. Frank used this less desirable remnant for his cattle, hauling it to three steel drums he kept by the Keller cabin. He customarily carried three full buckets at a time, one by hand and two suspended from a yoke over his shoulders.)

Marie and Mabel prepared supper, but Frank assisted on such occasions as the night they made kumquat jelly and preserves. One night Frank brought walnuts "and made the best walnut fudge imaginable."

"If Frank really likes you," John had told them, "he'll bring you some of his walnuts."

Frank's walnuts were special. He had grafted English walnut to two native black walnut trees years before. They were an excellent source of protein, Marie reminded me in Frank's defense, and he did not dispense them frivolously. John Hunter had expressed regret that Frank had never given him walnuts, but that was no reflection on their friendship.

After supper a game of canasta was inevitable. The dining table was cleared, and under the light of John's lamp the three played for blood, until weariness or Frank won, or the lamp gave up the ghost.

Sleep comes quickly on the mountain for the initiated. Night sounds are embraced: frogs and insects, owl calls, white-footed mice scurrying over cabin rafters, wind in trees, thunder of an approaching storm. Too, there are sounds that delay sleep, of source undetermined: nocturnal groaning of old cabin planks, window shutters nudging a cabin wall, clatter on the tin roof, a rustling of leaves beyond the window.

"Were you ever frightened at night?" I asked Marie later.

"Why?"

The question had been ill-conceived. "Well, I thought . . ."

"What was there to be afraid of? Frank was up at his cabin. No one else was around."

At least not in the immediate vicinity. Of course the local people avoid moving about at night, so no point in bringing that up.

"Did you go out at night, except to the hurry house?"

"We have the palacio," Marie reminded me.

True. An indoor facility had been installed in March, adjacent to the small bedroom. John proudly called it the palacio.

"We went outside to see the owls," Marie added.

"Well, you did lock yourself in at night."

"Me? We shut the door, only because of the time the silverware was pushed off the table. Some night animal might come in to explore."

Or to have supper. I turned my attention to windows.

"We left the windows open!" She thought my questions were ridiculous.

"I was thinking about vampire bats."

Marie admitted with her mischievous grin that she slept in John's big bed under the open window. Mabel slept on a cot in the corner.

I could not share what I perceived to be Marie's lack of concern for her safety. As for myself, I am always sniffing for danger in the most tranquil surroundings. Oddly, I was not particularly worried about Marie in the forest. The forest was to be enjoyed, not feared, and preferably in solitude. Although Marie and Mabel usually went into the census area together, they worked separate sections in order to cover half of the total acreage during a day's outing. If all they had to worry about were wild creatures, I was content.

The census did not monopolize the women's attention. Some days were given over to other activities, particularly exploration. One such hike took them to Paul's Field (San Pablo), where Jacinto Osorio had built his house. The field was weed-grown and occupied only by some of Frank's cattle, which liked particularly to go there in late afternoon. On that day it was a tranquil scene, the main activity being furnished by a feeding calf.

Jacinto's house was intact but unoccupied. There was an additional structure toward the eastern edge of the clearing, a tiny stick and mud building with a hipped roof and an open-roofed area at the front. An oven in the patio claimed Marie's attention. It rested on a wooden platform. The oven had a metal sheet at the bottom and top and rock walls plastered with red clay.

"They couldn't build a fire under the contraption," I said when I saw Marie's photograph of the oven.

"Of course not. I suppose they baked bread or whatever with charcoal."

Some distance behind the new building, where the forest edge appeared to have been pushed back, was the pole framework for another structure.

No one was seen or heard at Paul's Field on that occasion. It seemed reasonable to assume that the women washing at the water hole and the man clearing land were living in the area, but we had failed to record the exact dates of those encounters.

We were not informed regarding the agrarian situation. No mention of the subject appears in our letters and notes of that period, or in letters from John or Frank. In retrospect, we are certain that Frank considered it his problem to solve; he never spoke of it to Marie and Mabel.

Agrarian demands certainly were nothing new. In an entry in his journal dated July 17, 1938, Frank wrote, "Felix says that the [lumber company] engineer told him that the agrarians are going to take all of Cameron mountain lands."

According to one dictionary, the noun "agrarian" is defined as "a person who favors the equal division of landed property and the promotion of agricultural interests." That seems to fit land reform, or "the agrarian movement," in Mexico. Since 1910, large landholdings have been broken up and a pre-Columbian communal system of land ownership applied. A number of families may get together and petition for the division of a tract of land. The community so derived is called an *ejido*. Each family concerned is given a small plot of land to utilize; these serve as subsistence plots but are not as economically productive as large tracts. (To retain large holdings, a land-rich family may divide ownership between family members, each being responsible for a legal-sized tract while working in conjunction with other members.)

The agrarians currently active on the mountain were persons employed by the lumber companies. The people of Julilo had been brought in from the southwestern state of Michoacán to log and work at the mill. When timber cutting ceased and the mill closed, they would be left without a major source of subsistence. According to local gossip, a "leftish activist" was fomenting trouble on the mountain, encouraging some residents of Julilo to move in and squat on forest land. Generally, these were poorly educated people, ignorant of their rights and prohibitions, persuaded that they could move onto unoccupied land or even take over the ranch with impunity; however, they had not been granted ejido status.

II

ISSENSION with the squatters seemed remote in 1965. I was back in Austin, trying to keep the house in order and two Irish setters happy, and missing Marie more by the day. The women had at first planned to spend six weeks on the mountain (it stretched to nine), but after three weeks I gave in and started looking for a companion to travel with me. Luckily, Nancy, who had been with us on an earlier trip, was free, had an understanding and trusting husband, and had a station wagon available.

We left Matamoros at 8:45 A.M. on May 15 and arrived in Ciudad Victoria around 2 P.M. After a visit with Sonny McCollum, we were on our way again at 3:45 P.M.

Marie had urged me, and whoever would accompany me, to catch a ride on a lumber truck at El Encino to Julilo, then walk on to the ranch from there. It would be easier than walking up from Gómez Farías, Marie said. If the roads were dry enough, the lumber truck would visit the *tendero de comestibles* (retailer of groceries) on the highway, pick up supplies, and leave from the patio for Julilo. We were to inquire of Don Arturo, the *tendero*, as to the chances of catching ride.

Despite repeated pleas in letters from Marie, I characteristically rejected her suggestions, and we did not pause until Nancy's station wagon overheated on the road up to Gómez Farías, wherewith we birded along the road while the wagon boiled over and cooled off. An hour and a quarter later, at 5 P.M., we had parked the vehicle at the home of Félix Burgos in Gómez Farías and were ready for the hike up to Rancho del Cielo. We had backpacks. In addition, I carried binoculars, a canteen, and a raincoat. Nancy, unknown to me, left her canteen behind, an oversight we would both regret.

Clouds hung over the mountain but seemed too thin to promise much-needed rain. Throughout the lowlands the air was heavy with haze, and it was hot. Shade, when available, made the heat bearable, and birders, when immersed in the chase, seem impervious to both searing heat and bone-chilling cold.

Once beyond the village proper and descending into the valley that edged the first mountain ridge, we slowed to a leisurely walk and tallied all the

Wedge-tailed Sabrewing

birds we could see. Many of the lowland birds would not be found in the cloud forest, so we made the most of Elegant Trogon, Brown Jay, Scrub Euphonia, Altamira Oriole, Black-headed Saltator, and others.

By 6 P.M. we had passed Lucas's Bottom, headed for Fred Blesse's corner, then climbed the first steep grade to Breakdown Bend (the college truck had stalled here on the April trip), when two Crested Guans appeared on rocks above the road, looking quite as surprised as we were, if less thrilled.

It was after seven now. The sun was long lost beyond the canyon, and shadows were blending into featureless gloom. A Singing Quail called from deep within the brush, in single loud hesitant whistles, followed by a frantic chorus of "gin-ger ale, gin-ger ale, gin-ger ale" (or perhaps it was "sing-ing quail"—even authorities disagree on the translation). By now we would have been hard put to see a quail were we about to trod on it. To convince us that diurnal birding was truly at an end, a pair of screech owls called, one from the canyon below, one from the steep slope on our right, back and forth across the road. Bats, mere darting specks, crisscrossed a patch of fading sky above the canyon walls.

Twin probing lights appeared ahead, materializing in a jeep with official-looking occupants. We were greeted politely as the vehicle rattled past us toward civilization. We would see no other vehicle nor other human being between that spot and the ranch.

I must have been confident as we trudged through the canyon. I had walked the entire route before in daylight, had even hiked partway up the Aguacates grade at night with only moonlight to show the way; that had been a lark, while John waited below for the college's weapons carrier to undergo repairs. But this time we would have no vehicle to pick us up some-where along the way. We did have a full moon, if it would emerge from a cloud-smeared sky, and flashlights. And two canteens—until I learned that mine was the only one.

We had been hearing the sound of music, faint or fainter as the breeze sent fitful puffs of cooling air from down-canyon. In daylight we could look back to the outskirts of Gómez Farías. Tonight we could discern no topo-graphical features, but where we knew Gómez Farías to be there was a sprin-kling of lights. "They're dancing in the plaza," I suggested.

"My throat's dry," Nancy said. "May I have a drink, please?"

The plaza, sunbaked by day, came alive at night. Even on no-event nights, people walked about or sat on benches watching other people walk about. "We could have stayed for the dance and slept in the station wagon," I said.

"We could have. We didn't," Nancy replied a little testily. She took a gulp from my canteen.

We reached the Aguacates and started the long, steep climb, flashlights alert for loose rocks and fallen branches. The breeze deserted us entirely as impenetrable walls of vegetation closed in; heat and humidity intensified. Fireflies danced ahead of us, as though luring us farther into their enchanted shadow realm. The little beetles reminded me of home. At least for a moment the darting, twinkling spots of yellow light eased a feeling of apprehension that had been assailing me in waves since we could no longer bird. "They're looking for mates," I said.

"Who is?" Nancy was panting.

"The fireflies."

"I'm looking for a water fountain," she said suggestively.

The romantic fantasy of the fireflies was extinguished. Nancy desired my canteen. Thunder rolled across the ridges. Once distant, it seemed to be closing in on us as the storm built. "The mountain is having indigestion," I remarked.

"Water," Nancy pleaded, "water."

"Make it a sip. We've got to conserve." I surrendered the canteen reluctantly. We felt the first raindrops.

"Here." Nancy handed me the canteen. "Hold it open if it rains hard."

It didn't, not enough to dilute the sweat, not until we reached Frank's red gate, our portal into the cloud forest. Rain met us there, with thunder and lightning, but like many promising mountain tempests, it dissipated faster than it had formed.

We had made the long, hard climb, but it was still about four miles from the red gate to the ranch, and miles tended to stretch on mountain roads. "It's clear sailing from here," I lied.

Nancy was either too tired to respond or was formulating a statement.

We were several hundred yards past the gate when I stopped to shake the canteen. I replaced it on my belt without drinking, hoping Nancy had not noticed.

"If I recall," she said belatedly and sternly, "it's clear sailing up and down, up and down, and then that killer hill just before Mister Hunter's cabin. How about another sip. Water."

"It's real low, Nancy. Let's wait. We may need it more later."

Nancy's silence was ominous. I was tempted to suggest that she absorb moisture through the skin, for clouds had settled earthward and submerged us in a sea of billowing vapor where fireflies flashed by like plankton in a ship's wake, but at the moment I had no stomach for the picturesque. We were exhausted from the climb up the Aguacates grade, yet it was agreed that we would limit rest stops to a few minutes at a time. I walked ahead, Nancy following closely. We were using only one flashlight at a time now, and wondering when both would succumb to the inevitable. Despite Nancy's descriptive protestations, I was very strict in doling out the remaining water.

I recall little about the hike after we left Frank's gate. I do remember, with painful clarity, placing one boot ahead of the other for millions of repetitions. I do remember Nancy's chronic thirst, and how I worried when she finally stopped asking for water. When some unseen creature rustled the leaf clutter at roadside, the thought of a charging jaguar did cross my mind, but it really didn't seem important. I was absorbed in my own little world, a meager patch of road that kept moving ahead, swaying from side to side, dimly, interminably.

We arrived at John's cabin at midnight, like witches out of the abyss, and we probably looked the role. Marie had expected me (or us) earlier, but after nightfall she and Mabel had given up and eventually retired for the night.

Our greeting lacked the traditional amenities. Marie distinctly remembers a pitiful, quavering voice outside her window. "Water. Water. Water for the famished!"

Marie shone the flashlight across the windowsill to assure herself that she wasn't dreaming, then met me at the back door.

"What did we do then?" I asked Marie years later, trying to recall details. She usually is better at that than I am.

"What could we do! I guess I gave you a glass of water."

"Funny I should remember, but I've always thought you gave me a glass of milk and a piece of cake. That's what I always tell people."

"Pie, maybe?"

More likely, on the mountain, or I may have been hallucinating. "What did Nancy have to say?"

"You don't want to know."

I still think it was cake.

Traveling through the forest by motor, the visitor passes a never-ending repetition of tree and rock until monotony diminishes fascination. Such would not be the case if one could walk into the forest, unfettered by time constraints, and experience the life pulse of the wilderness. One discovers that while trees and rocks surely abound, there is diversity unexpected in the interrelationship of plant life and geology. Where the rocks have gathered into hillocks too soil-poor to support or sustain a mature tree, a unique plant community may flourish under open skies. Rock piles typically support agave and terrestrial bromeliads and orchids that would not be found on the forest floor; likewise, ground cover under the tree canopy is limited to a scattering of bushes among fern-and-moss-covered boulders. Openings caused, for example, by large trees felled by lightning create temporary niches for light-loving plants and encourage invasion by the opportunistic mala mujer.

The census tract offered all the above features in a variety that we had failed to appreciate when we were marking trails through the area. As Marie guided me through the tract, I felt a bit of the excitement—and tranquillity—of lingering in a wild place long enough to meld with the environment, to absorb the sounds and sights of ever-busy inhabitants.

Marie showed me her favorite places: the rock formation where she would sit as one enthroned, quiet and motionless, unnoticed or ignored by resident birds and, on rare occasions, mammals (tayra, red weasel, brocket deer); the rocky hillock encircled by a garden of begonias and purple achimenes and topped by a *Bouvardia* species whose red tubular flowers lured the Amethyst-throated Hummingbird from its deep forest haunts; the cave where Canyon Wren and Vaux's Swift nested in harmony beyond the glare of sunlight; the tree whose base hosted a colony of butterworts, invitingly pretty violetlike blossoms with a rosette of leaves that trapped and consumed small insects. We stood under the tree that supported the copa de oro (*Solandra nitida*), a vine whose large chalice-shaped golden flowers reach for the sun and, having served their destiny, carpet the forest floor with limp, browning blossoms. These were the special places, offered only to those who would wander beyond the logging roads, foot paths, and cattle trails to accept the forest's invitation.

Time spent on the census tract was a continuing revelation. A quiet vigil on a rock or moss-covered log worked as a shield of invisibility about the observer; forest creatures were soon at ease and resumed their normal routine. The behavior of birds was best studied by this stratagem, and nests most readily discovered.

The Black-headed Nightingale-Thrush was by far the most common breeding bird on the tract, with 34 territorial males located by song. This small thrush with black head, yellow bill, and red-rimmed eyes lives in the heavier shade of the forest and nests on or near the surface. Marie showed me a nest in a small depression and one set in a crevice on the sheer side of a sinkhole; the former was later trampled by a cow. By contrast, a nest of the Gray-collared Becard was located high under the canopy, a "clump of green moss about one foot across to not quite as high," with an entry on the downside, more than adequate for a six-inch-long bird.

The Blue-crowned Motmot was strictly a ground nester, in a rock crevice or more likely a burrow in the dirt side of a sinkhole. This strange bird with the racket-tipped tail often perched upright on a horizontal liana and moved its tail slowly from side to side like a pendulum.

The large, beautiful Mountain Trogon preferred nesting in holes already prepared by large woodpeckers. The sexes took turns sitting in the nest, at which time the male's bright red breast was totally hidden, with only the yellow bill and the top of the head (and the tail elevated behind it) visible. The woodcreepers looked for slits that gave access to hollow places in tree trunks, a safe haven from most predators.

Other than the nightingale-thrush, the most numerous species on the tract were White-throated Robin (eight territories), Amethyst-throated Hummingbird (six), Mountain Trogon (five), and Brown-backed Solitaire (five); next were Green Jay, Blue Mockingbird, Singing Quail, Blue-crowned Motmot, Chestnut-sided Warbler, and Hooded Grosbeak, each with four territories.

Other presumed nesting birds, in descending order of number, were Audubon's Oriole, Flame-colored Tanager, Ivory-billed Woodcreeper, Spot-crowned Woodcreeper, Olivaceous Flycatcher, Rufescent Tinamou, Bumblebee Hummingbird, Gray-collared Becard, Rufous-capped Brush-Finch,

Bronze-winged Woodpecker, Olivaceous Woodcreeper, Spot-breasted Wren, White-tipped Dove, Canyon Wren, Vaux's Swift, Brown-capped Vireo, Ornate Hawk-Eagle, Crested Guan, Vermiculated Screech-Owl, Least Pygmy-Owl, Mottled Owl, Wedge-tailed Sabrewing, Azure-crowned Hummingbird, Magnificent Hummingbird, Smoky-brown Woodpecker, Pale-billed Woodpecker, Greater Pewee, Clay-colored Robin, Rufous-browed Peppershrike, Tropical Parula, and Olive Sparrow. (Some species common names have been changed since the census was published; we have used the currently preferred names.)

Visitors to the census tract included Gray Hawk, Common Black-Hawk, Crane Hawk, Military Macaw, White-crowned Parrot, White-collared Swift, Streaked Flycatcher, Boat-billed Flycatcher, Long-billed Thrasher, Gray-crowned Yellowthroat, Bronzed Cowbird, White-winged Tanager, and Blue Bunting. (These species all nest in the region; the list does not include migrating species.)

Among the more interesting observations were Mottled Owls residing in a cave at the bottom of a 75-foot sinkhole and a Wedge-tailed Sabrewing (hummingbird) nesting in a small cave on the side of a steep hill.

A summary of the 1965 census results, compared with findings by Byron Harrell, indicated only a few changes in bird populations in that part of the forest; notably, the Mountain Trogon had declined about 50 percent, while Audubon's Oriole had increased about 50 percent.

Marie and Mabel made a final foray onto the census tract on June 9 and returned to Texas soon thereafter.

12

WHILE we were preoccupied with birds, a move was afoot that would dramatically change the status quo at Rancho del Cielo. First in order of business was the future of the ranch. This was being discussed even as the college campus took shape.

Frank Harrison felt that he was approaching an age when he should think of a final disposition of his property. His family had no interest in Mexico. On the other hand, the enthusiasm and appreciation shown by Texas Southmost students and staff made the decision easy. The problem was how to effect a transfer. John Hunter initiated and pushed negotiations over a tiring span of months and can be credited in bringing the plan to fruition.

Besides John, the principal players were two lawyers, Juan Zorilla, in Ciudad Victoria, and an old friend of John's, Burnell Goodrich, in Mexico City.

A letter from Goodrich to John, dated November 23, 1964, reads in part,

The Victoria lawyer was correct about Southmost acquiring title. Actually, the law does not prohibit this, but the Department of Foreign Relations which issues permits would turn this down almost certainly. . . .

Probably the most viable method of handling this is through the organization of a small company by Mr. Harrison. He could do this in conjunction with one or two other friends, either Mexican or with immigrant papers in Mexico. Probably young McCollum or Elizabeth would qualify. After the land is in the company name, there should be no trouble in transferring the interest in the company to whomsoever Mr. Harrison wishes. As the land is owned by an alien and as it would be transferred to a company owned in truth by aliens, there should be no problems if the aliens transfer their interest to another alien so long as the transferee is not a foreign government or a foreign government entity.

It would be preferable if Mr. Harrison would make the transfer of his interest in the company during his lifetime with appropriate arrangements for life tenancy and complete control of the property as far as its operation, management, construction, etc., is concerned.

Singing Quail

In a December 2 letter to John, Goodrich suggested that the business would best be handled in Ciudad Victoria or Gómez Farías. He, Goodrich, would prepare a draft of articles for the company and another for the transfer of land to the company. Frank Harrison would sign both applications, "return them to us and we will process them through the Ministry of Foreign Relations. We would then send Mr. Harrison the permit, together with the drafts of articles and a local notary can proceed with the company's organization. . . . we will need a copy of the deed by which Mr. Harrison acquired the property and his Mexico immigration papers. . . . The company must have a name which you should supply to us."

Another letter from Goodrich to John, dated February 16, 1965, reads, "We have run into a slight snag in connection with preparing for the organization of the company and transfer of Mr. Harrison's land to it. After discussing the matter with my partner, Lic. Eduardo Vazquez who will attend to this matter and with whom you and Mr. Harrison may communicate, we have concluded that the best thing is to make an application to the Foreign Office embodying request for permission to organize a 'sociedad civil' and at the same time to transfer to it at the time of organization the real estate."

The land transfer was culminated in July. The trip to accomplish it was rather typical (that is, unpredictable) and is described in a letter from John Hunter to "Dear Bird-Watchers."

> Frank and I had an appointment with the lawyer at Victoria at ten o'clock Tuesday morning, and we fooled around until six o'clock in the afternoon and couldn't get our work finished, so I headed out for the mountain just about six o'clock. We had a good trip until we got to Rudolph's corner, and there we met a truck with the front spring broken, and we worked with him until about nine-thirty that night and cobbled him up so he could get out of the road for us. . . . I turned around Wednesday morning and drove back to Brownsville. We had another appointment with the lawyer for Tuesday, the 20th, at ten o'clock in the morning. Frank came down with the Kellers, who had gone up about the same time. We got the papers all signed up and the land legally transferred to the corporation.

It was a nonprofit corporation, to hold property for educational purposes. The expense of organizing the corporation was borne by the college. John commented that Frank seemed "very happy" over the transaction. It had been agreed that he could control any and all parts of the property as long as he lived.

The deal was culminated at the notary's office in Ciudad Victoria, with John representing the college as a trustee and vice president of the board.

While John was preoccupied with legal matters, trouble brewed with the squatters, employees at Julilo and their families, up from Michoacán state. The local people were not involved, and apparently they would have nothing to do with the newcomers. Precisely how the matter stood, we could only wonder, as John and Frank said little.

When we examined Frank's papers much later, we found a letter to Frank from the mayor of Gómez Farías. It stated in effect (as translated from the Spanish) that "in the valley of Gómez Farías, four o'clock (P.M.), Oct. 5, 1965, Mayor Francisco González Martínez" authorized a written agreement that Frank pay damages to Cláudio Hernández, Marcelino Mendieta, and Octáviano Bernal, represented in their suit by their attorney, Federico López Delgado, for damage to corn fields caused by Frank's cattle. Named as guilty of the crime are Frank's cattle. The number of tons of crops (corn) affected is not stated. The agreement is that Frank will pay the cost of the tons of damaged crops or turn the animals over to these men. Frank recognizes the fact that his stock have in the past damaged the men's property and decides to give them the old and young (yellow) bulls under the condition that the bulls be tied up before respectable witnesses. The attorney agrees, and then the agreement is signed by the city secretary, David Morales.

López, who represented the plaintiffs, was listed as a farmer by occupation, not an attorney. Whatever his actual business, he was a major player in the drama. The man was a native of Ciudad Hidalgo, Michoacán. At the time of the negotiations, he was 48 years old, married, and resided in Julilo.

As for the cattle, they were found on Arturo Arguello's land. The damaged property was no more than the plaintiffs' corn crop.

From the beginning, Frank's cattle had roamed at will through the forest, browsing on whatever met their fancy, even leaves of the mala mujer. The area behind Frank's cabin was designated as the cow lot, separated from house, garden, and orchard by a rock fence. Cattle came there for water and salt. A small, rock-walled enclosure near Frank's house was designed to hold calves. Often, calves were born far from the ranch, and Frank might spend days searching the canyons for them, hoping to find them before "el tigre" did. On March 2, 1965, Frank was reported to own sixteen cows, four young bulls, one big bull, and four calves.

John Hunter summed up the situation in a letter to Frank's sister, Nellie McKay of Canada, dated February 7, 1966.

> About two years ago, a group of agrarians began to move into the forest area around Frank's property. He was opposed to this, because he knew that it was impossible for them to farm the land, and they could only destroy parts of the forest, kill off the animal life, and generally disturb the area; and for that reason, he opposed the agrarians' claims and entered protest with the Mexican government. As the situation developed in the next two years' time, there was continued friction. They finally moved into what is known as Paul's Place, about half a mile from Frank's land, and, naturally, his cows broke into their poorly fenced fields; but Frank went before the authorities in Gomez Farias and made a settlement whereby he gave them two yearling calves to liquidate the damage done, which could not have been half the value of the calves. A formal paper was drawn up and the matter was supposedly closed.

As far as we were concerned things were going very well. An October trip provided us a wonderful interlude in the cloud forest. It was a time to harvest the fruits of summer and defer, for a while, the expectations of winter. Rain had come late, but it had come (27-plus inches at the ranch in August), and all the land was lush. Down by the Río Sabinas the sugar cane formed a green, tall jungle; cotton was blooming; corn was ready to pick. In the cloud forest, the sweetgum dangled its many-horned fruit, large and green, while its leaves gave hint of fall colors. The evergreen podocarpus was dropping its berries, soon to turn purple, the size of large peas. Acorns were falling now, several weeks late, delayed by earlier drought. On the census tract, butterworts were still blooming around the big tree, and wild dahlias were opening on a sun-drenched rock pile.

Birds were less vocal than in spring and summer. The ubiquitous nightingale-thrush was quiet and seldom seen, presumably having dispersed to lower elevations, or perhaps southward. The forest no longer resounded to the constant song phrases of White-throated and Clay-colored Robins, whose numbers also decline with the advance of winter. The Brown-backed Solitaire, however, still delivered its cascade of notes from high in the canopy, and Spot-breasted Wren, Blue Mockingbird, and Audubon's Oriole occasionally recalled the excitement of spring.

The Ornate Hawk-Eagle yet soared over the forest, announced by loud whistled notes that, in a typical rendition, we equated with demonic laughter. But the beautiful Plumbeous Kite no longer drew its shadow across Frank's clearing in graceful maneuvers; it was bound for wintering quarters far to the south.

Fall bird migration, which had started as early as July, continued unabated; only the participants were different. Warblers from both eastern and western North America fed in mixed flocks; some would remain until the following spring, others were merely pausing on a long southward journey. Some species that bred in the highlands above the cloud forest were migrating vertically, even to the lowlands of the Río Sabinas. Change flowed on feathered wing.

Over at Frank's, the tuberous begonias were blooming in all their glory, while a plague of pocket gophers undermined garden and orchard. It was time for digging and grubbing, planting and transplanting, budding trees, spreading manure, mending fences.

Day was friendly warm, evening chill, a time to cherish, touching senses with muted impulse of sight and sound, stirring memory. The evening cry of the Crested Guan from deep in the forest was the spirit of wilderness, defiant and free, quickening the pulse of the hearer. Insects took the stage at dusk, buzzing, chirping, comforting in their monotony.

Day surrendered uneasily over the lowlands, white thunderheads threatening, blue sky-field fading. West Ridge retired into obscurity, an evening star pinned above, a sentinel in a gray void. The frogs were awakening in John's pila, joining guttural rumblings with distant thunder. A Mottled Owl screamed from the tree wall, welcoming the moonrise over a cloudbank.

Things were as they should be in the cloud forest — at least, if one could overlook a few blemishes to a perfect world. Logging continued. The lumber yard at El Encino was well stocked. Julilo was active; they were cutting trees in the cloud forest now, between Julilo and Rancho del Cielo. Giant oaks were reduced to cross ties. The area where we had found giant ferns had been violated.

We were loading to leave the mountain when Frank asked me when we would return.

"I don't know. When I find some excuse."

"You don't need any excuse," Frank said. Those were his exact words, and the last words I would hear him utter.

Rancho del Cielo had been converted to a sociedad civil, Rancho Cielo, S.C. The sociedad owned the property. This was a civil partnership, its principal function being for other than commercial purposes.

That having been settled, John Hunter and others were interested in expanding the acreage, not for the sake of ownership but to protect more of the forest from exploitation. This posed a problem, as the lawyer, Mr. Goodrich, explained to John. "I am afraid I can give you little encouragement about owning several thousand acres of land. Acres of this size are particularly subject to expropriation for agrarian purposes."

Goodrich noted that such a large acreage could be protected only by the government designating it as a park site, in which case the entire Rancho del Cielo property would likely be expropriated for park purposes! Appealing to foundations for necessary funds had been considered, but John now advised, "I think we had better go slow on involving the Rancho Cielo property with any of the foundations until we see for sure how the matter could be handled." The question now: How much additional land can be held by the society without danger of expropriation?

In a letter to Frank Harrison, C. J. Garland, Barbara Warburton, and us, John concluded, "I think we had better apply our efforts to raising enough money among ourselves to buy adjoining pieces of land to the extent of what we can hold legally in Mexico, and then let the foundation people work entirely on their own, or at least wait until we could see a little bit more clearly what would happen in case of a large development of public property."

Circumstances forced this matter to go on hold for a while.

Frank Harrison's physical condition was a concern. According to John, Frank had been "considerably breaking in health during the past two years." Marie and I had not been aware of it, but we had little basis for comparison, having known Frank for less than two years. We had been told that he had a hernia, although the work he performed belied any physical discomfort or impairment.

John had urged Frank to come to Brownsville for a thorough physical check and hernia repair. Just before Christmas 1965, John made a trip to the mountain, hoping that Frank would return with him to Brownsville and spend Christmas with the Hunters. However, on December 21, Frank decided that he could not leave the ranch at that time, and John returned home without him. Despite the outcome, John declared that the December trip was one of the best, and the last opportunity for an uninterrupted visit with Frank.

John's next trip to the mountain occurred from January 6 to 9, 1966, when he was accompanied by a group of college officials and three representatives from the Texas Legislature. At that time, he reported, Frank seemed to be in "reasonably good health."

Having transferred his property, Frank desired to have it accurately surveyed. We do not know if a survey had been done when Frank originally acquired the ranch. A document from the local tax collector shows Frank's property registered on April 17, 1942. At that time his land was classified as a "huerta" (orchard of plums, peaches, and apples) and consisted of 25 hectares. Excerpts from later documents are confusing, but one that seems most reasonable lists the ranch as comprising 2 hectares devoted to orchard, 8 hectares of land suitable for agriculture, and 14 hectares of mountains.

To comply with Frank's wishes, a party from the college (students and two professors) picked up an official surveyor in Ciudad Victoria and drove to the ranch in late January. In John's words, they "ran the lines and established the corner markers officially." Later, Barbara Warburton told John that Frank had expressed his satisfaction that the survey had been made, as he felt that "time was running out with him."

One evening in early February we had a telephone call from John Hunter in Brownsville. The tone of his voice was matter-of-fact, as in discussing a business deal; we knew he was serious. Frank Harrison had been killed. Murdered.

13

NOTIFYING all persons who had known Frank Harrison was a monumental task. We do not know how many people were reached. I took it upon myself to write to George M. Sutton at the University of Oklahoma. Now widely respected as an ornithologist, artist, and author, Sutton was best known to many neotropical bird students for his early work on the ornithology of the Río Sabinas lowlands, as eloquently recounted in his book *At a Bend in a Mexican River*. He had visited Rancho del Cielo and become a close friend of Frank's.

"The details of poor dear Frank's death leave me shaking with rage," Sutton wrote. "What under heaven could give anyone, *anyone* I repeat, the feeling that he had a right to bring such a wonderful life as Frank's to an end?"

Events surrounding the tragedy were detailed in a letter from John Hunter to Frank's sister, as well as related in a trip logbook that John kept at the ranch.

The survey party had left Rancho del Cielo between six and seven on the morning of January 29. Frank had eaten an early breakfast with them, leaving milking the cows and other chores until later. When the college people left, he took fresh eggs, bacon, and other perishables up to his cabin and, evidently, started to do his morning chores. He had not changed clothes.

"Two of the agrarians' group way-layed him in the area between his house and the calf-lot close to the house; evidently hit him on the side of his head with a specially shaped club which they left lying in the area. Then they stabbed him three times with a sharp, narrow-bladed knife; the stab wounds all entered the heart."

Sometime that afternoon, a boy from the lumber camp at Julilo went to the ranch to buy milk. There was no response to his calls, and he did not see the body; however, he may have noted that the cows had not been milked. Back at Julilo, the boy told his parents that he could not locate Frank, but the parents waited until the next morning to notify Juan Moreno.

According to John, Juan and Ladislada left Julilo early Sunday morning, January 30, and walked to the ranch. Marie remembers Ladislada saying

Least Pygmy-Owl

that Juan told someone to get a truck to take them to the ranch, and then he and Ladislada started on foot—Juan running. "I feel sure the truck overtook them," Marie added.

At the ranch, the Morenos found Frank's body about 20 feet from his cabin (cook house) door. Juan left Ladislada with Frank and walked (or rode) to Gómez Farías and reported to the police, arranging to have the body brought down. Juan then went to the sawmill near El Encino, where he wrote a letter to the owner of the sawmill requesting that he notify John Hunter.

John Hunter received word of Frank's death around 10 A.M. on Monday. By one o'clock three carloads (two jeeps and a college weapons carrier) of mainly school personnel had left Brownsville. John had phoned ahead to the lawyer, Juan Zorilla, in Ciudad Victoria, to determine the location of the body and to obtain permission for burial at Rancho del Cielo. "We had the usual lot of trouble that is inherent with four-wheel-drive vehicles," John wrote, "and did not reach Victoria until about eight o'clock that night." Bob Hunter had gone ahead to Zorilla's office and secured the burial papers, but it was too late to proceed farther that evening, John decided. Bob Hunter, Gordon McInnis, and Tom Keller drove on to Ciudad Mante, where they spent the night, "in order to go up the mountain as early as possible Tuesday morning by way of Gomez Farias."

John's party left Ciudad Victoria for El Encino about five the following morning. As had been requested the day before, Frank's body had been taken to the patio at El Encino and left at the lumber company office, where employees remained with it all night, awaiting John's arrival.

By good daylight the coffin and a wooden container to house it had been loaded onto the college truck and the trip up the mountain begun. Julilo was reached about nine o'clock. Juan and Ladislada Moreno were picked up there, and the expedition proceeded to Rancho del Cielo, arriving about eleven o'clock.

The party lost no time in deciding where to bury Frank and started digging. The site is on an Indian house mound directly in front of the first college building to be completed, the original cook house. The terrain slopes downward toward the south at this point and levels out short of the remnants of a rock wall. The grave stone, to be installed later, would command a view in all directions.

It is not easy to excavate a hole of any size on the mountain, and John doubted that they would have been able to accomplish the task on that day without the help of Frank's local friends who walked up from Gómez Farías.

"We completed the grave by about four o'clock in the afternoon," John wrote, "and I read the burial services from the Episcopal Common Prayer Book. The Mexican friends present followed the custom of each putting a handful of dirt in the grave. It was all finished in less than an hour's time. The next morning, our boys planted some amaryllis on the mound and outlined the grave with rocks."

John was impressed by the response of the authorities to the crime. "The mountain was swarming with police officers," at least 20 men. Among them were Enrique Lamarque F., head of the state police, "an old friend of ours from Matamoros;" Jesus Chávez Palmares, chief of the Policía Rural from Antigua Morelos; and the "district attorney" (Agency of Public Ministry), Lic. Marco Antonio Mansur A., of Xicoténcatl.

The first police had arrived on Sunday afternoon. They found Frank's cabin "in a shambles; papers, books and other articles scattered about on the floor." Items known to be missing were guns (Frank's and those he kept for other people), a battery-run electric clock that Caroline Hunter had given Frank for Christmas, Frank's radio, and some clothing.

There was no doubt that the men who killed Frank looked for money. Probably he had some on his person, as he had traded a $20 bill for pesos on the morning he was killed, at which time he had remarked that he never kept much money at the cabin. Frank maintained a joint savings account with Mrs. Ethel Williams in the Brownsville Savings and Loan Association and had a peso account in a bank in Ciudad Victoria with Ernest "Sonny" McCollum; the latter, in the event of Frank's death, was to be used to pay off his debts, with any amount left over going to Texas Southmost College.

At some time past Frank had told a Texas Southmost student where he kept money not in pocket or in deposit. That student met the Brownsville caravan at the International Bridge as it was leaving for Mexico and informed a student on the expedition. The latter kept quiet until the police left the ranch, then he directed concerned persons to Frank's plant house. The hidden treasure consisted of 335 pesos in a small jelly jar.

One of the first acts of the police in investigating Frank's murder was to arrest Lucas Romero, Frank's helper for many years. No one aside from the authorities believed that Lucas had any part in the crime. On the day of the murder he had gone down to Gómez Farías with the college group, and his presence there could be confirmed until the time of his arrest. As John re-marked, "The Mexican officers have their way of operating and regardless of our protestation of his innocence, he stayed in jail."

A break came in the case on Monday morning when a man from the settlement at San Pablo appeared at Rancho del Cielo. No explanation has been given for the man's action. He was immediately questioned as to whether he had any guns or ammunition in his house. The man swore that he had none, but he was held while investigators went to San Pablo. John wrote, "They found three loaded rifles and a good supply of ammunition cached in the cabin and behind some large boulders to the side of the cabin."

What happened next is not reported, but the outcome was the arrest of three prime suspects: Enrique Flores, Federico López, and Simon Leal. They were not among the three men who sued Frank's cattle for crop dam-age; however, Federico López Delgado was the "justice of the peace" who had served the papers and acted as attorney in the case. The suspects were all members of what John called "an extreme leftist group in the agrarian movement."

The police left with the three suspects about five o'clock in the after-noon, each man riding in a different car. One man was jailed in Antigua Morelos, about 50 miles south of Gómez Farías, one in Ciudad Mante, and one in Xicoténcatl.

The college party decided to spend the night at the ranch, and Barbara Warburton and Katherine Blesse "managed to feed" the crowd from the college pantry. The following morning they attempted to put Frank's cabin in order. They were now free to remove Frank's personal papers, which amounted to three full boxes of account ledgers, Christmas cards and let-ters from years back, weather reports, and, most interesting, Frank's garden journal from early years.

By eleven o'clock Tuesday the ranch was left in charge of Frank's cows. They had not been milked in three days, "but there was nothing to do but turn the calves loose and leave the place to the mercy of God."

In Gómez Farías, John's party sought out Frank's longtime friend, Félix Burgos, who was serving as presidente municipal, to reimburse him for his expenses in connection with the transportation of the body. It was then that they learned of Lucas's plight. "So," John wrote, "after giving his wife enough pesos to live on for a week or two, we went over to Xicoténcatl to take him some cigarettes and do what we could for him."

Xicoténcatl, east of the main highway, is noted for its sugar mill, railroad station, a huge strangler fig on the plaza, and the regional jail. "The officers allowed us to see him [Lucas] but were very rough with him. They still treated him as if he were involved in the murder." It was an unsettling experience for the visitors.

Only John and his passengers lingered now, the others having started back to Texas. While they were debating their next move, Sr. Lamarque directed them to a food stand on the plaza, paid for their lunch, and requested that they wait a few minutes; he wanted to talk about developments in the case. He, Sr. Chávez, and Lic. Mansur had been up all night questioning the suspects. Lamarque's subject was Enrique Flores.

While they were still eating, an assistant to Mansur drew Lamarque away from the table. A short conversation ensued, after which Lamarque returned and said, "If we could wait for an hour or so he thought they had about broken one man to where he was ready to talk."

That man was Enrique Flores, "who had been with Fred López and Simon Leal when the murder was planned. About an hour later he was talking freely and making a formal statement," taken in writing before witnesses. López and Leal had killed Frank about 10 A.M. on January 29, according to Flores's statement.

John and company left Xicoténcatl about dark for Ciudad Victoria and returned to Brownsville on Thursday, February 3. "It was a hard and sad trip," John summarized, "but we had no car trouble that I recall outside of a couple of flat tires. The Mexican officers were most courteous to us at all times. They worked hard and faithfully on every clue and are certain they will convict the men they are holding." Under Mexican law, the maximum penalty for their crime is 30 years behind bars.

The matter of land ownership settled, there was little left of Frank's estate. While in Ciudad Victoria, on the way home from the trip to bury Frank, John visited with Lic. Zorilla, who agreed to search the records for a will. John was certain that a will existed. In the absence of a will, the estate would go to the government after payment of debts.

Also, Zorilla was requested to appoint Juan Moreno executor for the estate with authorization to sell the cattle quickly. "If they are not sold in the next 30 days," John remarked, "they will disappear without trace. The personal property of a man who dies without someone to take care of his things dissipates quickly in Mexico."

In a letter to Frank's sister, John requested permission to give "what books he had" to the college library. "Outside of these books, a few tools, a few kitchen utensils he had nothing but his flowers."

By "books" we assumed John meant the various papers, letters, ledgers, notebooks, and so forth that they had removed from Frank's cabin. At a much later date the boxes containing that material were placed in the John Hunter room of the Texas Southmost College library. A new librarian, apparently thinking that the boxes had been loaded for disposal, threw them out.

Spot-breasted Wren

14

JOHN HUNTER returned to Brownsville on February 3 after burying Frank and dealing with the authorities. That evening he called to inform us of Frank's death. Aside from the tragedy itself, John was deeply concerned that they had left the ranch without a presence on the grounds to represent the college. Lucas Romero was the logical choice for interim caretaker, but he was still incarcerated, and John's party had been too preoccupied to search for an alternate who might accept temporary status. Until a permanent caretaker could be appointed, it was essential that someone be on the property, as a show of determination that the college was not to be intimidated.

We don't recall if John asked or if we volunteered, but before both parties put down the telephone Marie and I had agreed to go to the ranch if we could find suitable companions for the trip.

I went to work (Statistical Reporting Service, USDA) the following day, but I may as well have stayed at home, except that I was able to enlist Allan Marburger, a young co-worker, for the Mexico trip. Meanwhile, Marie persuaded our friend Ruth Black to join the party. So, after frantic preparations, we left Austin sometime later that day and arrived in Brownsville before midnight.

Most of the morning of February 5 was spent working out the final details of our trip. John's and our good friend Alfred Richardson, whom we had first met on the mountain, was to accompany us to Gómez Farías in his Jeep station wagon, and after we had parked our Dodge, he would carry us up to the ranch. To facilitate matters, John penned a note to Félix Burgos in Gómez Farías, advising him of our intentions. Also, we received an official "To whom it may concern" letter from C. J. Garland, president of Texas Southmost College, certifying that we were authorized to use "John Hunter's cabin at El Rancho del Cielo in order to keep it [the ranch] occupied."

A copy of Garland's letter was sent to Enrique Lamarque F., with a notation by John: "The bearer Mr. Fred Webster is a cousin of my wife and has the key to my cabin and permission to use [it] as long as he wants. If there should be any trouble of any kind he will call on you and please help him all you can."

Thus properly endorsed and certified, our two-vehicle caravan cleared customs at Matamoros around 11 A.M. and was beyond Ciudad Victoria by 4 P.M. South of the Río Guayalejo and the town of Llera we spotted Bob and Mabel Deshayes, who were bound for Brownsville after a trip to southern Mexico. We flagged them down. Of course they had not heard about Frank.

In Gómez Farías we parked the Dodge at Félix Burgos's house and loaded into Alfred's Jeep. We were joined by Pablo Cordova, the one-man police force at Gómez Farías. We left Burgos's house at dusk, passed Lucas's place by 7 P.M., and arrived at the ranch before 9 P.M.

By the time we reached John's gate, the realization that there would be no one to greet us hit home. The thought was depressing and disturbing. The entire area suffocated under a cloak of fine mist. John's cabin was no more than a lurking mass, dark, lifeless, crouched at the edge of the clearing, cowed by forest night. For a moment I felt that we were not welcome, that we should not disturb the brooding stillness.

The padlock at the back door dropped open and I pulled the heavy oak door outward. Hinges squealed in protest, then surrendered with a whisper. Across the threshold was darkness of the pit and silence that intruded on the ear. We entered gingerly, reluctant to violate the still sleep of the cabin. Flashlights sent distorted shadows dancing across the walls, phantom shapes fleeing reality.

John's kerosene lamp restored some semblance of order, but a closer examination of the main room revealed something more disturbing than vanquished shadow. The yellow poncho and high rubber boots that Frank Harrison had worn the morning he was killed had been shoved under John's big bed, but not far enough that they failed to give graphic testimony to the crime. We would not touch them (or whatever else might have been under the bed) during the time that we occupied the cabin.

Marie and Ruth prepared supper after firing up the wood-burning stove. We took to bed soon, the women in the little slant-floored bed chamber off the kitchen corner and the men distributed in some manner in the main room, perhaps overlapping onto the porch.

We slept well, fatigue overriding memories and imagined scenes that had haunted waking hours. There were familiar sounds in the fog-moist clearing that night, where Frank's cows were free to forage and tend to their calves as best they could. Their calls might have been the entreaties of disembodied souls wandering restless through the gloom; I wondered if they felt any sense of loss or disorientation.

Around dawn we heard barking from up toward Frank's clearing. It proved to be Sombra, Frank's four-eyed terrier, a black and tan female with a tan spot over each eye. Frank had tied her up before the college group left the ranch, to keep her from following the trucks. Ladislada had released her when she and Juan found Frank's body. Her presence, while a comfort of sorts, only enhanced the poignancy of Frank's absence.

Alfred Richardson and Willie Bleier, his traveling companion, and Pablo Cordova left us at mid-morning. As the sound of the Jeep faded along the flank of South Hill, we realized with a jolt that we were, for all practical purposes, stranded. Our nearest friendly contact was at Julilo, four miles' walk away; it was not a great distance on a flat, paved road, but a good hike on mountain terrain. The alternative was a walk down to Gómez Farías, about double the distance. As for contacting Lamarque should there be trouble, how were we to accomplish that? Our best plan was to stay close to the ranch; we could think of no reason to do otherwise.

In his letter to Nellie McKay, Frank's sister, John told of our going to the mountain "to stay in my cabin for a week and generally try to tie up any loose ends that they can." In a postscript, John added, "One of the men [presumably Alfred Richardson] who went up the mountain Saturday, February 5, returned this morning. He says the mountain is swarming with soldiers and Mexican law-enforcing men. They have a total of seven men in jail now and are taking away every unemployed or unauthorized man out of the area. It looks like it will be the end of the Agrarian Aggression."

If the mountain was swarming with military and police personnel, they either were swarming at some distance from the ranch or were cleverly camouflaged, as we saw no one during our stay. Nor did we encounter any squatters, although we assumed that some were still living at San Pablo. We further assumed that any San Pablo residents would be women and children left behind when the men were taken away.

The women at San Pablo were not to be taken lightly. They had gone to the ranch while Ladislada was waiting with Frank's body and, we were told, were both insulting and threatening. They had come to steal whatever they could, Marie suggested. "The women told Ladislada that with Frank gone, the ranch and everything was theirs, and no one could stop them from taking possession. Actually, these people had the idea that it was Frank who owned all the uninhabited land on the mountain!"

Marie confessed later that when a dry wind blew from the west, across San Pablo and toward the ranch, she could envision a fire front, deliberately set, advancing toward the clearing through dry forest, trapping us. Marie did not express her fears at the time, and I doubt that Allan or Ruth entertained such a scenario; I did not.

We were alert to the possibility of unwelcome visitors, but when none had appeared after a few days, a degree of complacency set in. Nevertheless, we remained in or near the clearings, venturing only once into the census area and climbing North Hill on another occasion.

How were we to while away the time? There were no chores to attend to, aside from feeding ourselves and keeping our quarters tidy. Had we known how, we could have tended Frank's cattle; it would have been time well spent. His cattle were gentle and a friendly presence, although it was disturbing to hear their calls day and night and not be able to address their needs. At one time we counted 20 of the animals, including a bull and two cows with calves, in Frank's cow lot, at the salt lick and water source.

The area designated for cattle included the cow lot behind Frank's cook house and featured the pila. Frank would dip water from the pila into steel drums just outside the enclosure, where the animals would drink. After Frank was killed, the college people had left the gate to the pila open, assuring access to water.

There was a small calf lot behind the cook house, with a shed where Frank put young calves at night, "to keep the jaguars from getting them," Marie recalled. Also, there was a fenced area east of the calf lot where the cows to be milked were kept; a gate from the calf lot into the milking pen was only wide enough for calves to go through.

Cattle were fenced out of the garden and clearing areas, but we were obliged to chase one cow out of John's orchard, and I suspect that there were other trespassers. Calves were another matter. Without human supervision, the calves tended to wander. On one occasion several calves invaded the college clearing despite a closed gate. Marie and Ruth went after them. Ruth, unaware of the animals' tame nature, "chased after them, shouting, which frightened them," Marie reported. "I had to run around the cook house to head the calves toward the gate. Running down the steep incline on the east side of the cook cabin, I tripped. I landed on my binoculars and my chin." (A genuine birder is never without binoculars, even when chasing livestock.) "I can show you the dent in my binoculars," Marie offered, years later.

I don't know if she was hinting for a new pair.

Our principal activity, given the circumstances, had to be birding. Although this activity served no practical purpose, moving about provided some exercise. The weather was agreeable enough, temperate generally, and no really cold spells. Fog, which came frequently and at any time of day or night, was the only deterrent to good birding conditions.

It was at night that reality became a burden, but we were too weary to do other than retire early. Outside, night fog concealed a half-moon and cloaked the cabin in a protective blanket. We slept better for it.

As long as the weather was favorable we spent little time in John's cabin. For me, there were too many reminders of tragedy, especially after an unfortunate incident—one I completely banished from memory until it surfaced during a conversation years later. There was a metal can in John's cabin (a garbage-can type), which I had not investigated until one day when I was alone in the cabin. Curious, and probably bored, I casually removed the lid from the can. It was stuffed with the clothes Frank had worn when he was killed. They had been cleaned and put away by John's party in a loving gesture. Marie came into the cabin shortly after my discovery.

"What's wrong with you?"

I must have resembled a shell-shocked battle casualty. I couldn't speak. I pointed to the can. Frank's shirt was on top, knife slash painfully evident. My exact feelings at the time are still blocked from recall. I suspect deep sadness and, at least for a moment, homicidal rage.

One day we ventured into Frank's cabins to see if anything needed our attention. The guest house produced only one interesting revelation, when Marie found a few pesos taped under a table top.

The cook house was a different story. John had indicated that they had gone through Frank's possessions, removing certain papers and books, and had cleaned up "the mess" before leaving the ranch. That being the case, someone had been in the cabin later. I made an inventory of items left on Frank's dining table: one-half package of oleo, a small amount of Miracle Whip, two eggs in a carton, an empty marmalade jar, and two Vienna sausages in a dish with a knife. It is surprising that mice had not disposed of the sausage; I made a mental note to avoid that particular brand. Also on the table: sugar in a plastic container, catsup, salt, pepper, and a can of evaporated milk.

We checked the cellar, a feature not to be expected in such rocky terrain. The trap door was inconspicuous and may have been covered, since Frank was discreet in divulging its existence. Steps led to a small chamber with a six-foot-plus high ceiling and lined with shelves. Here Frank stored a treasure of preserved fruits from the orchard and other edibles processed for future use. "If I hadn't known how to preserve," Frank had told Marie, "I wouldn't have made it through the first year."

Like John Hunter's cellar, Frank's was cool in summer and relatively warm in winter. Frank suspected a connection with the subterranean cavities so common on the mountain, but no opening was apparent in the rock, nor did we feel a draft.

Topside, we found a mass of old news magazines and paperback novels. (Fortunately for the purpose of this narrative, Frank seemed reluctant to throw anything away.) Ironically, the paperbacks were mainly murder mysteries that friends had given Frank. Later, we tried to burn them in John's trash pit, but without success.

In addition, there were some letters, cards, and miscellaneous items that the search party had left; either they had been overlooked or were not considered important enough to preserve. We collected them. Little material of use remained in the cabin, aside from cooking utensils that hung in their accustomed places on the wall. After arranging the remaining clutter in a semblance of order, there was nothing further for us to do. Regretfully, we shut the door behind us.

The cook cabin, the sleep cabin, and the plant house, still and deserted by all but plant life, were depressing enough; the orchard and garden spread out below the buildings seemed in denial that their caretaker would not return. A few gladioli were flaunting their beauty to the hummingbirds, and peach trees were testing the season with a scattering of blossoms. There were turnips and carrots in the vegetable garden, now at the mercy of the gophers. Overall, however, the poverty of winter still dominated clearing and forest and weighed heavily on the human spirit.

As we viewed this scene, we began to appreciate more the effort Frank Harrison put into his project, although it would not be until later, after we had gained access to his garden journal, that we realized how much work was involved in running the ranch.

Clay-colored Robin

15

FRANK'S "Garden Notes" covered the period of March 10, 1937, through June 3, 1939. The lined notebook, yellowed and stained and worn about the edges when we acquired it, was appropriately titled; it recounted maintenance chores, orchard and garden conditions, livestock activity, and weather. But comments were not restricted to the garden and cattle, for inserted throughout were invaluable observations concerning life at the ranch, as well as Frank's comings and goings as he engaged in business or pleasurable pursuits, the latter very much the lesser.

Except for occasions when he left the ranch to "go below" or across the mountain to La Joya de Salas, Frank seemed to be constantly at work maintaining or improving garden and orchard, or tending to cultivated plants. The progress of each tree, vegetable, or flowering plant was faithfully recorded, some on an almost daily basis.

During the period encompassed by "Garden Notes," Frank grew the following vegetables: asparagus, beans (various), sugar beets, broccoli, brussels sprouts, cabbage (including Chinese), carrots, cauliflower, celery, chayote (squash), corn (including popcorn), cucumbers, kohlrabi, lettuce, mustard greens, onion, peas, peanuts, peppers, potatoes, pumpkins, radish, rhubarb, squash, sweet potato, tomatillo, tomato (including cherry), and turnip. Berry crops included blackberry, dewberry, huckleberry, strawberry, and youngberry (a dewberry and blackberry cross). Grapes were mentioned; also ginger root and perennial herbs.

The climate at Rancho del Cielo is temperate and the soil good, but we are not told of the success or failure of some of the vegetables listed. Those with which we became familiar had done quite well at the ranch, and we could be persuaded that almost any crop would thrive there with the proper attention.

Frank depended on the sale of some vegetable crops as a source of income. Some potatoes were marketed as early as late May, but the really busy season started in October, a number of trips to market being made by Frank or Paul during each of the last three months of the year. Carrots and lettuce were the cash crops in October, cabbage and carrots in November and December. These vegetables were welcomed in the tropical lowlands, where conditions were unfavorable for production. The volume of other vegetables sold was insignificant.

Most sales were made at Juárez (now Ciudad Mante) and at El Limón, both towns on Highway 85. El Encino is the nearest highway town to Rancho del Cielo, but Frank preferred to stop first at Las Calabasas, Everts Storms' place on the Río Sabinas, to see his old friend. Las Calabasas, the location name that Frank Harrison used in his garden journal, was known as Pano Ayuctle (Pumpkin Ford) by the scientists who worked that area later and by us. From Las Calabasas, on the river, a dirt road connects with the highway, emerging from sugar cane fields less than two miles south of El Encino. The junction is still marked by a sign, "Las Calabasas."

Everts Storms played a major and influential role in events unfolding on the mountain in early days. Lawrence V. Lof, who succeeded Barbara Warburton as director of the Rancho del Cielo project, contributed the following: "His family came to Mexico in the nineteenth century and was prominent in Ciudad Victoria. Everts was friends with many of the people in the Chamal community and around Gómez Farías." Early in the twentieth century he settled at Pano Ayuctle, located at an important crossing of the Río Sabinas and at the foot of the trail to Rancho del Cielo and the Malacate.

Don Evaristo had the skills of a diplomat and was well liked throughout the region. When there were disputes to settle and land titles to straighten out, his friends called on Everts. According to Lof,

> He had helped the Camerons formalize their holdings in the mountain after the revolution. He had also helped Frank Harrison get title to Rancho del Cielo after he bought it from the Cameron family. As scientists began to discover the area, he put them in contact with Frank Harrison and arranged for guides or personally took them up the steep trail to Rancho del Cielo.
>
> Everts loved the mountains that towered above his ranch. With friends, he frequently crossed the mountains on hunting trips to the dry side at La Joya de Salas. And he had a simple cabin high in the mountains at Agua Linda, a retreat from the heat of the spring dry season.

From Rancho del Cielo, Las Calabasas was accessible only by foot. Frank once led us on a hike partway down the mountainside on the east. This was the short trail, as it came to be called; presumably there was a longer trail also. We recall the ancient, rugged walls of the slope and great trees in endless succession, mist swirling a gray film over all, boulders moist-slick, and green leaf tips dripping a melancholy rhythm against fallen comrades on the moldy floor. We were awed and fascinated, but ours was only a sampling, and Frank turned us back before we reached the steeper declines. Not so fortunate were Barbara Warburton and her students, who once elected to take this treacherous route to the base of the mountain, arriving exhausted at the clear, cool waters of the Río Sabinas.

To Frank and Paul the trip was routine, and Frank had little to say about it in his journal except to comment on footing and weather conditions. It was a lonely pilgrimage, with Paul's gray mule or Frank's horse the only companion. There were no way stations, and if other travelers were ever encountered, their passing went without mention in the journal. The time required for the trip down varied according to circumstances at the time: weather, footing, and volume of freight. A time of two hours and ten minutes with an unburdened mule was cited for brevity. One trip back up to the ranch required four hours; Frank was feeling ill on this occasion and admittedly moved at a slow pace.

Once down the mountainside, Frank crossed the Río Sabinas at Pano Ayuctle. If the water was too high, he went upstream to the lumber company bridge. Once, when the river was flooding, he was forced to use the company boat. "An old tree that was cut down" provided passage on another occasion.

Las Calabasas was a home away from home, and Frank was seldom in a hurry to leave the hospitality of Don Evaristo, but time there did not pass idly. There was always some task needing attention and readily addressed. For recreation there was spearing fish in the river or watching "boys" working the cane mill, which was driven by oxen. Visitors were a welcome break in the routine. One never knew whom to expect at Las Calabasas or when, as visitors often appeared unannounced, which in no way diminished their welcome.

When the time came to leave Las Calabasas, a short hike took Frank to the highway. There he could dismiss horse or mule and load onto a bus for points south. Buses ran regularly but often late and sometimes were too crowded to take an additional passenger.

South of El Encino and Las Calabasas the next town of significant size was El Limón. Here Frank picked up his personal mail and merchandise. El Limón is at the junction with a road that runs west to Chamal (the Chamal colony) and to Ocampo, settlements lying at the southern terminus of the Sierra de Guatemala; in early days the road was their only link to the outside world. Also, it is in the vicinity of El Limón that the rivers Frío and Boquilla, having merged to the west, merge again with the south-flowing Sabinas-Guayalejo to form the Río Tamesi, emptying into the Gulf of Mexico at Tampico.

A short distance farther south of El Limón on Highway 85 is the metropolis of the region, Ciudad Mante (old Juárez), nowadays crowded and bustling and usually dusty.

These were the communities that Frank visited most frequently. His trips to the lowlands served multiple purposes: sale of his produce, purchase of supplies, pickup of mail and shipments, and various other errands. Those having been accomplished, he could visit with old friends, particularly in the Chamal colony, where he had farmed and taught school for a number of years. Here, as at Las Calabasas, he shared in a variety of routine tasks.

Gómez Farías was less often a destination than Las Calabasas, but it was a necessary trip at certain times. Frank and Paul, as immigrants, were required to present their cards (*tarjetos*) at the Presidencia (the municipal government headquarters), perhaps fill out forms and make contact with Mexico City. A trip to "Farias" also entailed a visit with friends, particularly Félix Burgos, who in those early days frequently worked for Frank at Rancho del Cielo. By the mid 1960s, when we first met Don Félix, he had become the presidente municipal, an office equivalent to a county judge in Texas. His modest home overlooked the dirt road beyond the plaza; it was here that we left our Dodge when we drove to Gómez Farías, assured that it would not be tampered with.

One of Frank's longer journeys within the time frame of "Garden Notes" was to Ciudad Victoria on "the red bus." A visit to the dentist was the first order of business. Taking in a "show," perhaps a chance encounter with friends, and a night at the Regis Hotel completed the schedule.

Ciudad Victoria offered shopping opportunities, but Frank apparently preferred to buy clothing and shoes at Juárez and other items at El Limón. Whatever he needed at the ranch (items ranging from jar lids to bed springs, a bundle of fruit trees to paint cans) was carried up by Frank and Paul and the mule. Of course, food stocks not grown on the ranch were purchased below. Frank referred to "groceries," but specific items were flour, sugar, salt, coffee, honey, piloncillo (cones of unrefined cane sugar), oranges, bananas, and mangoes.

For an isolated area, Rancho del Cielo had an astonishing array of cultivated plants. It was obvious that much thought went into choice and procurement. Given Frank's background in horticulture and his passion for plants, it is not surprising that he was able to contact the best suppliers. Most seeds, bulbs, and plants that stocked the garden and orchard were shipped to El Limón; little would have been produced locally. As mentioned previously, Frank's success with exotic ornamentals was reported in trade journals.

Frank's journal listed more than 50 species of ornamentals. Many were old garden favorites: chrysanthemum, daisy, delphinium, marigold, pansy, phlox, snapdragon, verbena, and others. Begonia, fuchsia, gloxinia, orchid, and some others were in tins or hanging baskets.

Fruit and nut trees cultivated in the early years included almond, apple, apricot, cherry, crabapple, fig, guava, peach, pear, pecan, plum, prune, and walnut. "Don't forget the kumquat," Marie reminded me when she saw my list. We had admired the kumquat tree with its oblong orange fruit as prominent as Christmas ornaments. Apparently it was the only citrus that did well on the mountain; orange groves were confined to the lowlands.

"Frank didn't mention kumquats."

"Well, the tree looks old enough to have been here back then. Anyway, Frank helped us make kumquat preserves. Delicious! What about papayas?"

"No papayas."

"No? They're doing quite well at the ranch."

I was still on the defensive, it appeared. "Now before you mention mangoes and bananas, Frank had to bring them up from Gómez."

Gómez Farías is renowned for its mangoes nowadays. In season, one can't walk along the road without the threat of being anointed by a ripe fruit. Mango groves thrive in the Sabinas Valley as well, and roadside sales draw touring mango-lovers like juicy yellow magnets. The local mango is the manila, the very best in Marie's expert judgment, a testimonial not to be taken lightly.

"But Frank's walnuts were excellent," Marie pointed out. "Also, walnut grows naturally in the forest. Remember, Frank grafted black walnut with English walnut."

"And he budded peach to almond, and plum to apricot. Imagine what those produce."

"I have no idea."

"Palmonds and apriums?"

We have no clue as to the success or failure of the latter experiments. What we know for certain is that apple, peach, plum, and pear produced very good fruit, which, if spared by the birds and squirrels, found their way into preserves and pies. Marie's reputation as pie-maker was established on the mountain and remains unchallenged.

Frank found that maintenance of a successful orchard demanded constant vigilance. Pruning, cutting suckers, and removing galls were routine tasks. The cloud forest climate encouraged accumulations of mosses and lichens. They could be removed by scraping, if reachable; otherwise spraying was mandatory. A "strong solution of lye" killed the unwanted guests. Lime sulfur was used for insect infestation; Frank boiled a pound of lime and a pound of sulfur to produce the spray.

Lime was obtained by a time-honored but laborious process. An area was prepared for the lime kiln, then a platform of logs was built. "Cut small trees to place on form to burn lime," Frank wrote. "Piled on lime rock to burn." The fire must have burned continuously for several days, as additional wood was cut to feed it. On the third day some lime was removed for boiling, and he "carried some lime and ashes for trees and garden."

After doing what we could in Frank's cook house, we walked below the guest house, at the edge of the orchard. We stood on carpet grass that some outsider had introduced years before; it spread over the knoll we know as the helicopter pad and down toward John's cabin. It was a sickly green and brown patchwork now, in harmony with the skeleton trees, but winter would soon loosen its grip.

"Who will look after things now?" Marie wondered aloud.

"Lucas." It seemed logical that Lucas Romero would be hired. Supposedly he knew more about ranch upkeep than anyone else. "If he gets out of jail."

"It will take more than one Lucas," Marie said.

My gaze took in the orchard and garden to the tree line. It could have been a painting; nothing moved. The forest was in remission; no breeze stirred twig or leaf. For the moment, even birds were atypically silent. A cloud shelf topped South Hill and West Ridge, as immobile as the land-mass.

Actually, I had no concept of the amount of work it had taken to create what was now Rancho del Cielo. In the late 1930s, the clearing had yet to expand to the 1966 boundaries. To expand the clearing, underbrush was macheted and burned, trees felled, logs hauled away, stumps grubbed out and burned. Then rocks were removed. Larger rocks went into a stone wall that ran behind Frank's cook cabin, separating clearing from the semiopen area we called the cow lot. The cow lot, a rocky expanse of cleared forest floor shaded by towering trees, backed up to the base of North Hill. Its major feature was the rock-walled pila, which seemed to replenish itself, perhaps by seepage.

The rock wall, which ran the length of the clearing on the north side, was built up about four feet, not enough to prevent cattle from scaling it on occasion. To build the wall, rock was piled on rock without the advantage of mortar. Even with the material close at hand, the work must have been backbreaking; I was convinced of this after attempting to replace a dislodged member.

When the ground was ready for plowing, Paul's mule or Frank's horse was employed. Then came harrowing to break up dirt clods, and leveling. Frank made a brush harrow of oak branches in one instance, for which his notes offered no explanation. After harrowing came listing.

We noted these maintenance chores from Frank's journal: weeded, hoed, boiled soil to sterilize it and planted seed, covered seed beds with branches of oak leaves, carried manure (often this was bat guano from nearby caves, but Marie remembered Frank placing cow chips around the garden), carried water, cut logs for firewood, cut poles to put across water hole on road, dug drainage ditch, made *calzados* (footwear), fixed fence after cow broke into field.

"What time did he have left to work with his flowers?" Marie wondered when I read the list.

"Or cook, or do the laundry, or slaughter and process his pig, render lard, stuff like that. Not to mention unscheduled activity."

"Like what?"

"Actually, keeping up with the cattle was major."

Frank made no mention of confining his cattle, and his cow lot held little of interest for the beasts other than salt and water. Aside from being restricted from the garden and orchard (by a rock wall and barbed-wire fence), they roamed the forest, grazing on forbs and saplings and whatever grass was available in clearings. The leaves of mala mujer must have been considered a delicacy, as one cow was seen to break off a sizable trunk with its horn to get to the foliage.

The cows' wanderings caused Frank concern when he wanted milk, needed to check for new calves, or treat an animal for vampire bat incisions, which often led to screwworm infection. Many hours were squandered in tracking down the animals. Cattle tracking seems to have been a way of life in the region, as men from Gómez Farías often came up to the cloud forest "hunting cattle."

It appears that at the time the garden journal was written, Frank had only a few head of cattle. He names the blue cow, the yellow cow, and the Jersey, a bull, several heifers, as well as calves that are born during the period. Only once do we hear of an "old black cow" that "got in field."

Frank might devote many hours, sometimes days at a time, looking for a certain cow. His wanderings took him near and far, high and low, deep into canyons toward the Río Sabinas or along the "Jolla trail to the west." When found, he may have attended to the animal on the spot or led it back to the ranch. In the 1930s he would have walked in heavy forest, often on faint trails made by the animals. In the early years, it seems, even Frank had not explored the region to his complete satisfaction, and he spent some time looking for existing trails and cutting new ones.

To the newcomer, the cloud forest and adjacent zones offer a confusing and seemingly endless sequence of ridges and canyons, green-clad except where a cliff face breaks through to expose jagged limestone, gray against green. The forest canopy blends tree with tree until all seem of one kind. Unless the sun is riding a cloudless sky or a landmark such as West Ridge can be discerned, all sense of direction may be lost. Most often, one traveling a forest trail will find that the familiar and recognizable is concealed somewhere beyond flanking curtains of foliage; on the forest trail, one is confined in a realm self-contained and jealous of its secrets, the only way of egress a narrow corridor twisting out of view in either direction, through more forested walls.

We can only marvel at Frank Harrison's familiarity with the terrain and network of footpaths, his sense of direction or perception of location too subtle for the casual hiker to comprehend. Even he was not complete master of the forest. When clouds lower and smother the visible world in a moist cocoon, the most seasoned outdoorsman may be immobilized, or forced to wander aimlessly in search of the familiar. On one such occasion, Frank, who had been looking for the blue cow in the east canyon, reported, "Got lost in fog and spent several hours finding trail."

In searching Frank's journal, we immersed ourselves in a world that time had long passed by, leaving only fragments that we could relate to our own experience. In one area we admit total confusion; we are unable to relate the various canyons of Frank's account to sites with which we had become familiar.

In the cloud forest zone, a canyon can be no more than a ravine or valley separating two ridges. Most often the canyon walls are sloping hillsides, their contours lost in heavy forest. Such are the canyons east of Rancho del Cielo, which for the most part drop gradually and interminably toward the valley of the Río Sabinas. They might more correctly be called irregularities or breaks in the ridge that runs north-south on the eastern face of the mountain. One such canyon starts a short distance beyond John Hunter's cabin; however, just north of Canyon Tableta a gradual slope drops abruptly at a rocky overlook called Cycad Point.

"At least you know Canyon Diablo," Marie said. It started at the Rock Pile and extended up West Ridge toward Indian Spring.

"And well named," I said, visualizing the rocky terrain. "But Canyon Tableta, what does that name tell us?"

"Frank would have known."

Our February sojourn at the ranch was thankfully uneventful, but not without a feeling of inadequacy, a haunting emptiness that burdened the soul. It was not that Frank could no longer communicate with us. Something else was missing; we were out of touch. The wind that blew off West Ridge and rattled skeletal forest giants carried a message so poignant we could not comprehend. The bird chorus, subdued by winter's rule, had a melancholy undertone.

It was only later, when we had immersed ourselves in Frank's garden notes, that we experienced a bonding with a past more distant than our limited experience at the ranch. Names became persons, as familiar to us as the ground they trod. We shared their lives vicariously, and we missed them when they passed from the pages of history. But we had been too quick to dismiss them. In February, we at last realized, we had not been alone. A host of nebulous entities moved restlessly beyond the veil, as surely as mist shrouded the wild creatures when cloud claimed the forest. We were not privileged to see them; perhaps, in a retrospective moment, we had felt their presence. But they were there, restrained by the enemy Time, waiting for memory release. They would always be there, we knew, but ever retreating into obscurity.

Sometime during the day of February 11 we heard gunshots from the direction of South Hill. We were expecting a relief party at any time, but until Pablo Cordova of the Gómez Farías police and Lucas Romero, fresh from jail, appeared on the road below John's cabin, we held our collective breath. The men may have been alerting us to their approach or firing randomly at a squirrel; whatever, we were pleased to see friends.

The realization that our weeklong vigil was nearly over lightened our mood for a time; the ranch seemed a friendlier place. A tiny Black-headed Siskin sang cheerily from a sweetgum tree at the clearing edge, his golden underplumage resplendent in the afternoon sun. But clouds hung over the lowlands, and by nightfall rain was pelting the tin roof of John's cabin and wind was beating at the shutters. Rain on a tin roof is more conducive to sound sleep than to conversation, and we were in bed as soon as supper was over, the dishes washed, and preparations made for the trip down the mountain.

Early February is still winter at Rancho del Cielo. Winter embraces the dry season, which continues through April and sometimes well into May, but winter and spring are not without a dampness. Fog is common. Actually, most of our references to fog describe ground-hugging clouds that may glide through open cabin windows only to vanish like a ghostly presence remembered, or may move through the forest for hours at a time, constantly vacillating in density. Moisture gathers on twig end and remnant leaf and releases droplets to refresh the ground-dwelling plants, the mosses and ferns that cling to rocky outcroppings, to dampen the composting leaf matter that makes it possible for one to tread silently through the forest.

So it was when we aroused ourselves well before dawn on February 12. A heavy fog encased John's cabin; no breeze stirred the mist. But by daybreak a light rain had set in. We were accustomed to hiking in the rain while on the mountain. Marie broke a huge leaf off an elephant-ear plant to hold over her head, knowing that her raincoat would be too oppressive by the time we reached the Aguacates grade. Birdwatching was unproductive, so we slogged along at a steady pace, reaching Frank's red gate by 7:55 A.M. Here we left a rainy cloud forest and started the Aguacates descent in thick fog.

From our first trip with John Hunter, passing through Frank's gate, either coming or going, was an event that never failed to move me. The passage had been symbolic: entry to an enchanted realm, as it were, or exit to the sphere of the familiar and ordinary. In a more prosaic perspective, reaching the gate signaled the relief of victory over the Aguacates or apprehension for the descent to come. On this February occasion, particularly, I felt that we were closing the portals on not just an episode but on an era.

However, I am certain we lost little time pondering the significance of the moment, for it was imperative that we direct our attention to the slippery footing of the descent. There were also birdsongs teasing us from the mist-draped mountainside forest. We attempted to lure the songsters into the open, but only the Golden-crowned Warbler showed enough curiosity to respond to our simulated scold notes. The Spot-breasted Wren mocked us, as usual, from some sequestered place in thick ground cover. The Tropical Parula, foraging among the moss-draped branches of the canopy, was merely an echo from the gloom.

We reached the Aguacates junction and turned toward Gómez Farías. A cool breeze blew up the canyon, sending fog swirling away in tattered ribbons. Soon we could see Sierra Chiquita and the outskirts of Gómez Farías, and the lowlands spread out like a welcome mat.

We passed Fred Blesse's corner and the shrine and reached a corn field just short of Lucas's Bottom about 11 A.M. Two dozen Military Macaws had taken over the site. We studied them, transfixed, for some minutes before we started the walk up to Félix Burgos's house, on feet thoroughly damp and weary, to face the other world.

Crescent-chested Warbler

16

FOLLOWING our sojourn at the ranch, John Hunter lost no time in returning to the mountain. If he had made arrangements with Lucas Romero, he would want to know if they were being carried out. Finding a reliable caretaker was imperative in order to provide a consistent presence on the grounds and to maintain the facility, at least the exterior portion: garden, orchard, fences, cattle, and the rest.

As business manager of the ranch project, John was responsible for both employment and oversight. He would have preferred to hire Juan Moreno as caretaker, but that would have necessitated hiring another person to do the labor, an expense the college budget could not stand. Under the circumstances, Lucas Romero, Frank's longtime helper, seemed the logical choice. He was thought to be honest and reliable. His brief incarceration after Frank's murder was inexplicable except to the Mexican authorities and did not diminish his integrity in the opinion of college personnel.

The owners of the three private cabins were no less concerned than the college. Their presence at the ranch was frequent but sporadic, and they relied heavily on the ranch workers to maintain the grounds. One change had occurred in building ownership. Earl Hunter, John's brother, decided to relinquish his joint ownership in their cabin. Bob and Mabel Deshayes, who visited John and Caroline as they returned from Mexico in February, were quick to assume Earl's half at John's invitation.

Anxious to assure that order and stability be restored at the ranch, John (accompanied by Caroline, Mabel, and Oscar Kieswetter) left Brownsville late on February 16 for the mountain. The trip started smoothly, overnight at the McCollum house in Ciudad Victoria, a morning visit with Enrique Lamarque and Juan Zorilla, lunch, and then to the mountain by the long route, through El Encino. Somewhere along the ascent between the Río Sabinas and Julilo the tenor of the trip changed.

The adventure was duly recorded in John's handwriting in the trip log he kept at the cabin. En route to Julilo the party encountered "four or five" trucks headed downhill. It was the materialization of a driver's nightmare. "In backing up to get out of the way of one truck," John wrote, "I knocked off the tail pipe. It was a cold drizzling day and we kept windows of jeep closed. We were driving the '59 grey jeep.

"When we reached Julilo and were getting out of car I felt dizzy and said to others to be careful. When Caroline got out she fainted and would have fallen if Ladislada, Juan and Oscar had not caught her. She was out several minutes and gave us all a good scare. We lost probably 30 minutes in Julilo.

"It was almost dark when we left. We had no trouble until we almost reached the pila of Frank's when we found a tree across road."

They were merely a good stone's throw from John's cabin, but with the road blocked and neither tools nor manpower to deal with the fallen tree, the only recourse was to double back to the main road and go through San Pablo and thence to the junction with the ranch road.

John continued: "By that time it was raining quite hard and Oscar and I were wringing wet. On going through San Pablo we lost our way and ran into a log road block. Mabel recognized the place and guided us out of San Pablo. We saw no one in the San Pablo area and later found they had been moved out.

"At our cabin we found Lucas and Elías with a good fire going. Mabel and Caroline got in bed and covered up. I made some hot toddies and gave them each one. It seemed to ease their pains. We put on some soup to heat for supper and while it was cooking Oscar, Lucas and Elías polished off the rest of the fifth of whiskey. Caroline and Mabel may have had a second toddy."

John loved to tell a good story, even if it involved some misadventure on his part. One of his favorites evolved on that evening.

"I had bought a sawed-off 16-gauge second hand lever action shotgun and while waiting for the soup to heat we started loading and checking the gun. I fired one shot out of the back door so as to be sure which was 'safety' position. We . . . were sitting around the table and I was reloading the gun when it went off and blew a hole in the hot water tank. It scared me sober in half a minute. Caroline and Mabel didn't turn over. We ate supper and went to bed."

John arranged with Lucas and Elías to stay in the cabin and work during the week and return to Gómez Farías over weekends. Lucas, who was not known to be the bravest of men, would not have remained at the ranch without a companion.

Lucas's hiring became official shortly. John reported that the college board "agreed to back the Rancho Cielo Project to the tune of One Hundred Dollars a month from March through August; and I am going to have to do the very best I can with it during that period. I have written Lucas and offered him a job through the period at a thousand pesos a month, provided he moves onto the place; and I am going to get another family to live there with him."

In addition to his salary, Lucas was to receive one-fifth of the sale of ranch products, with the exception of bulbs sold to Texas Southmost College. Leopoldo "Polo" Garza was to receive 15 pesos per day with five days per week guaranteed, plus 20 pesos per week for food.

The caretaker problem thus was settled for at least several months. Lucas and Polo moved their families to the ranch, and with the addition of Frank's cook stove, all lived in the two rooms of Frank's guest house.

How constant their presence was at the ranch can only be surmised, a walk to Gómez Farías being routine for the locals, but John seemed satisfied. In a letter of April 12 addressed to "Bird-watchers," John reported that "everything at the ranch looked fine; Lucas and his other man are working keeping everything cleaned up really in better shape than they did with Frank, because they are putting in more time; of course, we can't replace Frank's guidance and work in the flowers."

However, the working relationship was destined to deteriorate. In late July John reported that Lucas and Polo had "fallen out with each other, and I told Lucas, if he can't get along with him, to fire him and get somebody else."

A letter from Lucas to John, dated August 3, translates: "In reply to your letter received this week, I will state that I think it won't be hard to get a replacement for Polo; I talked to Pablo Cordova, the policeman at Gómez Farías, and he told me he would be glad to come work with me just as soon as I paid off Polo."

Lucas had a scheme. "I am going to tell Polo that you lent some money to Pablo Cordova and that he is going to pay you back with work and that we are going to have to suspend Polo while Pablo works out his debt and that we will let him know when the loan is repaid and that maybe Polo can come back then; the thing is that I don't want to tell Polo that I simply don't want him because I don't want him to be mad at me."

John did not record his reaction to Lucas's plan, but no action was taken until August 26, when John came in with a college party by way of Julilo and found "no one on duty" at the ranch. John wrote in his trip log, "This caused me to fire Polo when he showed up."

It was apparent that Polo was not without support in Gómez Farías. A letter dated August 29, 1966, to "Uncle John" and signed "E," presumably was from Elizabeth's son, Ernest "Sonny" McCollum of Ciudad Victoria:

> Félix Burgos from Gómez Farías was at Pancho's [Rodríguez] house this evening and his news was as follows: He was wondering when you would be down because he wanted to talk to you, as it has been made public in Gómez Farías that Lucas Romero has in his house guns and a radio that belong to the ranch. They also know that Lucas has a bank account of $3,000 or $4,000 pesos. It is the feeling of the inhabitants of Gómez Farías that this was stolen from Frank Harrison. One of the persons that declared this is a man named Evaristo Garza, who is the father of Leopoldo Garza. Also, there is a person in Gómez Farías who has amaryllis and gladiolus, and they think that Lucas has been selling him these plants. Mr. Burgos has said that the people of Gómez Farías who hear these rumors begin to think that Lucas is a possible accomplice as they think he was involved with the people who murdered Frank. Also, they say Lucas has sold a lot of fruit, plants, and other things that belong to the ranch. And they say the reason the pistol was taken away from Lucas was due to the fact he was drunk and firing the pistol. Pancho is here now and dictated his letter to tell you what he had been told this evening.

Pancho Rodríguez was a good friend to Frank Harrison and Texas Southmost College. He owned a shop in Ciudad Victoria and frequently bought flowers from the ranch.

Whatever credence John gave to the rumors in Gómez Farías, there seems to have been no further reference to the matter, and Lucas and Pablo continued in their respective roles at the ranch. John was pleased with the arrangement, but not everyone shared his enthusiasm, as we soon learned.

We were guests of the college on a late-August trip in 1967. On this occasion the Río Sabinas was flooding, making the low-water crossing out of El Encino too hazardous to attempt. We headed for Gómez Farías. By chance, we met Bob Hunter and his family at the home of Félix Burgos; they had just driven down from the ranch. Bob declared the road badly washed but passable; however, it was his additional remarks that caught my attention. I recorded the gist of the conversation in my trip notes.

"Bob said Lucas's mother-in-law is making trouble again. Pablo and his cousin have been working with Lucas. The cousin said to Bob that Lucas is hard to get along with because of his mother-in-law; thinks she wants to create friction so Lucas will replace Pablo with her son—so she can move up."

Nothing further was heard of the matter, but the woman's reputation as a sorceress was taken seriously by the local people, and her influence was likely to be suspected if ill should befall her antagonists. It may be only coincidence that some years later, Pablo Cordova endured a lingering, debilitating illness that the medical profession was unable to diagnose. It was Pablo's contention that he was a victim of *brujería* (witchcraft).

Lucas's employment lasted for several years, but suspicion was growing that he was engaged in activities not covered in his job description. Inattention to duty at the ranch was a more serious charge. Regarding a trip to the ranch in mid-August 1970, John reported that Lucas was "gone the entire time I was there."

Winter and spring of 1971 was a bad time at the ranch. A fire raged across the mountain for several months. Rain would not fall in appreciable amounts. By April the college pila and Frank's pila, as well as the spring, were dry. According to John, plant life was in "pitiful shape," with flower blooms stunted. Likewise, Lucas's luck had run out.

In a letter dated May 1, John reported,

I had to go down and fire Lucas. He had gotten progressively more slovenly in his ways, and during the last of the month of March and early April he only spent one night out of 15 in the cabin. He would go up on Monday morning and change the [weather] charts and come back down. When he made the March report, he lied to us; and I had warned him that if I caught him lying again when I was at the mountain I would fire him. I also found that he has sold amaryllis bulbs and not reported the sales. He had even gone so far as to dig the choice white amaryllises out of the college bed and also choice amaryllises around Bob and Gordon's house, and I imagine around my cabin, but I am not close enough observer to hold this accusation against him.

The way was clear for Pablo to take over. We had been impressed by the man and his work ethics. Pablo was short in stature, as was Frank, but a bit heavier. A roundish face was quick to break into a wide grin that betrayed dental irregularities, a penalty for drinking local well water. "He was a good-looking man," Marie contributed when I tried to recall Pablo's appearance. I did remember that he was missing two fingers, lost as a sawmill worker in the highlands.

Pablo was well known and well liked in Gómez Farías, where his family had lived for many years. Nor was he without means of support other than his job as a policeman; he owned land and cattle.

"I would like to make a good man out of Pablo, if possible," John said. "If he fails, we will have to hunt for someone else." No further hunt was necessary. Pablo proved to be an efficient and faithful employee for many years and was particularly valuable as a liaison between the college and the local people, old-time residents and newcomers alike.

17

MANAGEMENT of the ranch was of no concern to us in 1966, except that the facility should continue to exist. Title to the land was secure, we assumed, and any nagging problems were being addressed. We had no idea what problems there might be, and John's letters lacked explanation. For example, in his letter of February 26, 1966, John wrote, "I spent yesterday in Ciudad Victoria straightening out the legal matters of the College and had about a two-hour lunch with Mr. Lamarque and the State Treasurer, who turns out to be another friend from Matamoros. I think we did everything we could both legally and politically to work out our troubles. Mr. Garland was with me, and we both think the meetings were satisfactory."

One sentence in John's letter impressed us more than reports of legal maneuvering: "Why don't you folks prepare a trip, say late in April, when Fred and, if possible, Bob could spend a week getting the girls set up and operating on the bird census?"

John's hospitality was widely known, and it came into full flower when he wanted to share his mountain. The bird census was an excellent excuse for a trip or more. Probably we had mentioned to John that we would be interested in a repeat performance.

The work that Marie and Mabel had done the year before had been analyzed, summarized, and submitted to the National Audubon Society. Eventually it appeared in the Breeding Bird Census issue of *Audubon Field Notes* (vol. 19, no. 6). They had compared the results of their study with Byron Harrell's earlier work, thus achieving their original goal. So enamored were they of the forest and the birds (and Frank Harrison) that, I dare say, they had thought to return even before the first census was accomplished. It would be different without Frank to divulge secrets of the forest, to drop in for an evening of canasta, to just be there when they needed him. Nevertheless, the lure overrode the bitterness of loss, and would it not honor Frank's memory to carry on?

John was concerned that the women would be alone except for the caretaker. Someone they could better relate to and converse with would provide meaningful company and, as John phrased it, would "at least show a man with them in the census area." It was John's idea that we invite George M.

Gray-collared Becard

Sutton, who, John was sure, would enjoy painting birds during a stay at the ranch. Sutton had done most of his work along the Río Sabinas many years before, but he had spent some time at the ranch and considered Frank Harrison a special friend. He had not revisited the cloud forest since those earlier days.

John had long wanted to meet Sutton, and we all thought it a great idea to invite the distinguished ornithologist to join the party. So we quickly had a letter in the mail to the Department of Zoology at the University of Oklahoma, where Sutton was research professor. A reply came promptly.

Unfortunately, commitments prevented Sutton from leaving his post at that time. "My book on Oklahoma birds has just gone to press," he wrote in a letter of March 14.

> The Administration here is keen for me to go ahead with painting birds, but they seem to want *Oklahoma* birds just now. . . .
>
> By all means be sure that some able-bodied man is on "the mountain" while the girls are there. I'm not a timid soul, but the fact of Frank's murder stares us in the face. How I miss (and shall miss) that fine man. . . .
>
> I am going to write John Hunter right off asking if there is any way in which I can help with the biological station. That Rancho area has long interested me, and now it has a stronger appeal of sorts than ever.

Despite our failure to enlist an "able-bodied man" to impress the local people, Marie and Mabel had no intention of abandoning the project. By early April John had assured us that the authorities had taken "all of the people" out of Paul's Place (San Pablo) and that the college was having no trouble with any agrarians. "I am sure you can feel perfectly safe at the cabin."

The anticipated expedition got under way on April 30, 1966, with John, Marie, Mabel, and me crowded into the Websters' overloaded Dodge. From the outset, the trip was unusual: we had a leisurely mid-morning start from Brownsville, and we were not in John's Jeep. The Jeep was in Ciudad Victoria undergoing repairs from an April 6 nocturnal encounter with a "big, black cow." The vehicle was projected to be back in running order by April 26.

Predictability set in as soon as we reached Ciudad Victoria, about 2:30

P.M. Two hours were spent waiting to settle the cost of Jeep repairs. Then there was the job of putting the vehicle back together, which effort lasted until about 9 P.M. It was too late to travel, so we had supper at the McCollums and bedded down at El Jardín courts.

The following morning we left the Dodge at Sonny McCollum's box factory and set off in the Jeep. Our first stop was a time-consuming visit to the market in search of kerosene (as well as fresh produce and such staples as sugar, which were cheaper in Mexico), long enough to be delayed by a May Day parade.

By mid-morning we had escaped the crowds and the clamor, finding refuge in the open road. There had been rain; the brushy semiarid country out of Ciudad Victoria was refreshingly green. Down in the valley of the Río Sabinas the jacaranda tree flaunted its lavender-blue blossoms along the roadside, while cassia brightened the woodland with yellow splotches and the petrea vine drooped hyacinth-colored sprays on hillsides. It was a day to celebrate nature's metamorphosis.

As we passed the dirt road to Pano Ayuctle, we complied with tradition by picking out the spot on the western horizon where we thought the ranch was located, a bit difficult today as bands of cloud hovered over the ridge, leveling the horizon.

In high spirits we passed the "Bienvenidos a Gómez Farías" sign at the village edge and proceeded to the plaza, arriving at 12:55 P.M. A few minutes later we were passing Félix Burgos's house, headed for Lucas's Bottom and then the ascent.

It had been a most pleasant and unimpeded trip, the sort that breeds complacency. We did not lose our composure when, just before the Aguacates junction, it began to rain. We were not surprised; the clouds gathering on the mountain front had given promise, and a shower during the dry season was always welcome. As for mechanics, the rejuvenated Jeep was running well and John was in good form. John had made the run many times before in rain.

About one-third of the way up the Aguacates grade the Jeep slithered to the side of the road and came to rest against the right (cliffside) embankment. No amount of coaxing could get traction for the tires on wet clay and rock. Had we been accompanied by a college truck, we would have been winched out. Alone, we were helpless.

One obvious problem was overload. John and I started taking larger items out of the Jeep and piling them on the right-of-way behind the vehicle. Meanwhile, Marie and Mabel, sans rain gear, hiked the several miles to the ranch. Marie loves to walk in the rain, although she prefers some cover. Mud-sloshing, however, is a different matter. Some distance beyond Frank's red gate, in the cloud forest, lies an infamous mud hole (not to be confused with the pond north of the ranch). Here is a low place where, drainage lacking, red clay holds rainwater indefinitely. Now the puddle was at peak volume and extensive, soil having been banked on either side of the road for some inexplicable reason, retaining water while making a bypass out of the question.

"It came up to my knees," Marie reminisced recently. "Mabel is shorter than I am. She wasn't sure she'd get through."

"I don't know how John got through," I recalled. I can still see that lake of reddish brown goo and the angry wake stirred by the Jeep's passage.

"John always said stick to the ruts," Marie said. "The ruts have a rock base."

I don't think there were any ruts visible, but John was usually a step ahead of the mountain when adversity struck. After we had relieved the Jeep of a good portion of its burden, John was able to maneuver it back onto the roadway, and we proceeded up the grade, with half of our baggage left at the mercy of the elements and any opportunistic locals who might chance by. However, Lucas and Polo, who had been sent to help us, picked up the abandoned items intact.

John had met another challenge and won the prize, a few days in his cabin on his beloved mountain. We settled into a comfortable routine, aided by recently acquired amenities: a butane light over the sink, one in the bedroom, and one over John's bed.

Days were spent looking for birds and checking the census tract, with breaks to help with the always anticipated meals. Evening brought domino games while rain pattered on the roof, or full moonlight accompanied the Mottled Owl's nocturnal hunt. We tried not to expect to see Frank Harrison walk down the hillside from his quarters to test our luck at canasta, or to watch his form fade in moonlight, back up the slope, as we pulled the cabin door closed.

On Cinco de Mayo, as dawn announced the sun's emergence beyond cloud-draped lowlands, John steered the Jeep downhill from his cabin, with me holding on in the passenger seat. Years later, Marie expressed to me her feelings at the moment of our departure. "I remember very well standing in John's cabin with Mabel, listening to the sound of John's Jeep crunching down the road to Gómez Farías and home. That is the loneliest sound I have ever heard. It was then that I realized how quiet the mountain could be and how far we would be from civilization; the two of us were really doing this project by ourselves. Frank would not be there."

I had little time to worry after I picked up the Dodge at the box factory and struggled to keep ahead of John and the Jeep as we raced for the border. Ten hours after leaving the ranch we were greeting U.S. Customs officials at the International Bridge in Brownsville.

Marie and Mabel were left in an environment that, superficially at least, had changed little from when Frank was in charge. The amaryllis bed, spread out below his houses in the area of the old walnut tree and the site of the McPhersons' cabin, unfurled a magical carpet of red, pinks, and whites. Frank had been proud of his hybrid amaryllis, and the college was helping fund the ranch project by selling bulbs. The gladioli, in an adjacent tract, had just started to compete for attention. At Frank's plant house, the gloxinias were starting to bloom and the tuberous begonias were budding.

The college campus was not quite the same. Downslope from the cook cabin, a simple cross of pine two-by-fours marked Frank's grave. Dwarfed by sentinel tree giants, the wooden cross nevertheless held the awareness of the passerby. Oddly, the site seemed to be attended by a figure kneeling as in prayer; actually, the form was a fragment of tree stump, which, when viewed from a certain angle, took on the human shape.

The wooden cross was to be only temporary. A "modest headstone" was planned, as explained in a letter dated March 30 sent by Texas Southmost president C. J. Garland to persons whose names and addresses were found in Frank Harrison's papers. Contributions to a headstone fund were encouraged; any money left over would be invested in a memorial bookshelf in the college's new library in Brownsville. A drawing of the planned headstone had been replicated; John Hunter had given a copy to Pancho Rodríguez in Ciudad Victoria, who was to investigate the cost of processing the marker in Mexico while John checked with the local stonecutter in Brownsville.

The census tract appeared much as it had a year earlier. Some of the markers were missing, and the trails needed to be cleared again where vegetation had grown back. The small clearing in progress a year before, near the southwest corner of the tract, had been abandoned; disturbance plants up to six feet high crowded among dried corn stalks. Even birds seemed to avoid the plot, limiting their song to the clearing edge, while in the corn patch the drone and rasp of insects and the muted rustle of brown corn leaves twisting in the wind provided a macabre concert.

The bird population of the cloud forest remained much the same. The Ornate Hawk-Eagle still sailed in exuberant display over the ranch clearing, climbing on powerful wing beats only to stoop with wings closed, roller-coastering, as it were, and at the same time bombarding his air space with a series of wild and maniacal calls, as though in defiance of earthbound bird-watchers. We once observed an adult male perched at close range, a most handsome specimen; we were fascinated by the long, black erectile crest on a black crown and rich rufous feathers that reached from crown to shoulder. (This magnificent raptor had all but vanished from the forest by the 1990s.)

The Crested Guan, though much hunted, was still encountered with some frequency. It sometimes roosted overnight on South Hill or North Hill; its calls at dusk and dawn were wild and challenging.

The Black-headed Nightingale-Thrush, again the forest's most numer-ous songbird, seemed to be nesting everywhere, on trees, on rocks, in sink-holes. The Blue-crowned Motmot, the sleek, darkly handsome bird with the racket-shaped tail, sat upright on horizontal perches, as it always had, wagging its tail slowly from side to side, pendulumlike. Its young were snugly hidden away in their nest tunnel in the clay-sided sinkhole, their presence betrayed by an outrageous chorus of unmusical sounds. A young Mountain Trogon had deserted its nest hole in a lofty stump and sat motion-less and silent in forest shadow, its dark juvenile plumage unlikely to catch the eye of friend or foe, quite unlike the colorful adult male that lingered nearby.

Even though a census study was the professed goal of the trip, Marie and Mabel had no intention of confining themselves to one area. Familiar places called for attention, reexamination, the pleasure of rediscovery. They were places where Frank Harrison had led them in earlier days, sacred ground, scenes haunted by memory. Memory seemed not without companionship. "We feel Frank's presence everywhere," Marie wrote. "It seems as though he is walking along with us."

One locale to visit on any trip to the mountain was North Hill. Easily overlooked beyond a wall of trees if one is near the base, this rocky peak rises just beyond Frank's cow lot, to the north. Like smaller rock masses throughout the forest, North Hill is host to a biotic community unlike that of more level areas. Here we could find rope cactus, cycads, and an abundance of agave plants. The larger trees found no foothold here; those of shorter growth, clinging to the hillside, seemed placed there to help the climber hoist himself, step by step, toward the summit. Off to one side of the worn ascent, and unlikely to be discovered by those who never wavered from the path, was a rock garden that Frank had shown us. Wedged among the rocks were orchids of the *Lycaste* genus, *aromatica* and *deppei*. The former was my favorite. I equated the aroma with that of apricots. The yellow flowers reminded me of ladies in old-fashioned sunbonnets, nodding in the breeze. Another orchid, *Epidendrum raniferum,* flourished here, sending sprays of green-white blossoms from the apexes of long multileafed stalks, with an aroma pleasing but unobtrusive.

Orchid scents, unfortunately, failed to permeate the entire hill on the day that Marie and Mabel made the ascent. Somewhere along the way they were assailed by the odor of carrion. Lucas, who had wished them well as they left on their climb, waited until their return to inform them that "the tigre" (jaguar) had attacked a calf and "carried it off up there." He claimed to have seen paw prints and tooth or claw marks.

On this day there was no indication of a cat of any size, and although the women kept a wary eye out for rattlesnakes and fer-de-lance, no reptile was observed. There was just the effort of the climb, sharp rocks and slippery footing, and a constant search for the handiest tree to grasp.

A climber, having conquered the steep ascent, must be resigned to relax in a vertical position. Rugged limestone boulders, as though strewn at random, cover the crest of North Hill and support a dwarf forest of low shrubs and agave species, which, from a central rosette, fan out aggressively, threatening the trespasser with tooth-margined, spine-tipped leaves.

If one can find a place to stand free of agave, thick brush, and jagged rock edges, the view from North Hill will prove worth the climb. We find it easier to look generally south. To the right (west) we can track West Ridge until it merges with formations at the southern end of the range. More to the left (east) Sierra Chiquita stands out above a hidden Gómez Farías. On a really clear day, the imposing profile of El Abra looms to the far south.

Nearer at hand, South Hill rises modestly at the south border of the ranch. The ranch clearing is too close under North Hill to be seen, so the panorama presents an unbroken sea of treetops, except where squatters have cut patches for corn fields. In May 1966 the only such patch visible was the one adjacent to the census tract. Being remote from any road, such a clearing would remain unnoticed from ground level. Later, the North Hill vantage point would show further human incursion.

Had Marie and Mabel observed the vista from all positions on North Hill (a difficult feat at best) they would have gained a greater appreciation of the extent of the agricultural inroads. Partial revelation came on a hike to San Pablo. "We went down to San Pablo yesterday afternoon," Marie wrote in a letter of May 12, "and were amazed to find the clearing back of Paul's at least 125 acres—this in just two fields that we went into. Corn had been grown there last year."

One of their more ambitious forays was a hike to the lumber camp at Julilo. "May 18, Wednesday, we jaunted over to Julilo," Marie wrote, "leaving here about 8:30 and arriving there about noon." Their walk down the road through the village was observed from behind doorways of the little frame houses, we assume, as no inhabitants were to be seen outside. Perhaps the street was emptied as a precautionary measure, given the nature of the accessories the visitors were carrying, particularly Marie's telephoto camera lens (the size of a small cannon barrel) with a pistol grip. On the other hand, it was siesta time.

At the Morenos' house at the far end of the village, Marie continued, "we called 'Ladislada' and presently Juan peeked out the window and his eyes nearly popped out. We had a very nice visit with Juan and Ladislada—gave her a box of chocolate cake mix to bake for him. They were surprised that we had been here [on the mountain] so long and were staying so long by ourselves. They are coming over Sunday a week and Ladislada will stay with us for a week.

"After praising her flowers, etc., we went up to the grocery (commissary) and bought some Cokes and a kilo of Barro de Coco—the coconut cookies that Papa Frank always brought us back from Julilo." Marie later regretted purchasing an entire box of cookies. It was the custom of the locals to buy a few cookies at a time; one kilo would have lasted the entire village for a number of days.

It was obvious from the visit to Julilo that logging proceeded on the mountain. We never knew what localities were being logged unless one of us came across a new logging road or could trace the sound of activity. We had assumed that as long as pine was being taken out from the higher zones, the cloud forest was safe from plundering. Of course, that concept had been disproved in the past. In reality, the cloud forest seemed always to be existing on the brink of disaster.

Equally troubling to Rancho del Cielo personnel was the possible resumption of squatter activity. My trip notes from the initial phase of the May expedition include a cryptic entry: "Augustín . . . leftist agrarian organization." Typically, I gave no explanation, thinking bird listings more urgent. Explanations and details could wait; they are still waiting, sunk now into the abyss of neglected memories.

Through no fault of mine, Augustín would not go away. Marie wrote on June 2, "Pancho from Victoria came up yesterday afternoon and he, Bob, Mabel and Ladislada went over to San Pablo this afternoon and found Augustín, his corn field, shack, and two dogs. His clearing is west and a little north of San Pablo and well hidden. Mabel and I heard a power saw being used up there one day so evidently he has backing. We think Pablo may come up from Gómez Farías tomorrow and John wants to talk to him."

Lumbering and Augustín were not the only distractions and concerns for Marie and Mabel. "The men have shot at the birds and cattle so much they have run out of .22 shells," Marie wrote, referring to Lucas and Polo.

The college staff, John, and we birdwatchers considered protection of wildlife essential to the preservation of the cloud forest ecosystem. No living creature was excluded, neither the mighty jaguar nor the venomous fer-de-lance. Our philosophy was not shared by all. From the earliest ages, the local people had hunted gamebirds and animals to add needed protein to their diet, and predators were killed to protect domestic animals.

At some point hunting pressure had tipped the scales, with wildlife on the downside. By the time we first came to the mountain, the little brocket deer had been all but extirpated. Down toward the Río Sabinas where the Great Curassow was once a common resident in thick mountainside woodland, we now look in vain for that magnificent bird.

In the book *Wildlife of Mexico: The Game Birds and Mammals* (University of California Press, 1959), A. Starker Leopold shows the following species for the Sierra de Guatemala: opossum, spider monkey, armadillo, eastern cottontail rabbit, gray squirrel, deppe squirrel, coyote, gray fox, black bear, ring-tailed cat, kinkajou, weasel, tayra (a minklike weasel), hooded skunk, hog-nosed skunk, jaguar, ocelot, margay, puma, jaguarundi, bobcat, collared peccary, white-tailed deer, and brocket deer. Of those, spider monkey, deppe squirrel, tayra, margay, and brocket deer are (or were) at or near their northernmost geographical limit.

Domestic animals, if reasonably protected, usually are not bothered by predators. Free-roaming cattle are another matter. When Mabel was interviewing Frank in 1965 regarding ranch history, there emerged the oft-repeated tale of the fatal encounter of one of Frank's cows with a big cat. She recorded the story:

> Several years ago one of my big cows had a small calf. She would come up in the evening, and after the calf had its milk, she would go into the forest to feed for the night. One morning she didn't return. I sent the man who worked for me down to see if he could find her. I gave him a .22 rifle single shot and some shells. About one-quarter mile east of the house he found where the cow had been lying down and had been attacked in all probability by a big jaguar. She had run down into the canyon on the east slope, and he found several pieces of her tail. It seems the jaguar had torn it off with its claws. In the bottom of the canyon the jaguar had gotten her by the nose or head and had thrown her down because the branches and weeds were broken and flattened in a fifteen-foot diameter. The man came back to the house to tell me about it, and he was slightly nervous. I went back with him, and we found where the jaguar had thrown the cow down. There was blood in a small area where they had been fighting. She had gotten loose and started to climb the hill for the house, and the jaguar had caught her again and thrown her down. I followed her trail up the mountainside, where I finally lost it. That day I couldn't find any sign of the cow. Next morning I went out again and found her about 150 yards from the house, dead, with all her tail missing, nose broken, and badly cut up. She must have died from loss of blood and fright. About a year later I heard of an especially big jaguar that some Mexican had killed on the west side of the mountain when it had attempted to kill a cow.

We cannot leave Frank's reminiscences without recounting his bear story. Barbara Warburton never failed to read this story to groups visiting the ranch.

Several years later a bear came into the field and killed a one-and-a-half-year-old calf that I had running loose in the field, but I never got a chance to see the bear close enough to get a shot at him. A year later a bear, and I was positive it was the same bear, came into the calf corral a few feet above the house and attempted to kill a calf. The cow, mother of the calf, jumped over the rock fence and chased the bear off. About four A.M. and when I got out a few minutes later with a twelve-gauge shotgun loaded with buckshot, I couldn't see any sign of an animal, but while I was examining the calf to try and see what had happened, the bear jumped over the rock fence about 30 feet from me to come back and finish killing the calf. Since it was dark, I couldn't see the sight on my gun, so I just swung around and shot from my hip, hitting the bear behind the foreshoulder with a load of heavy buckshot. The bear fell to the ground and rolled downhill like a log, covering his face with his two forepaws. I fired the other double-barrel shotgun and missed him. I had no more shells with me. I ran into the house for more ammunition, and when I arrived where I last had seen the bear, there was nothing but a big bloody spot. I waited until daylight to follow him. I found him lying down in heavy brush about 50 yards below the corral in a slight depression with his forepaws held up above his head and looking very painfully.

Since it was still dark in the brush and I couldn't see to shoot the shotgun, I fired several shots with a .22 revolver, hoping to scare him so that he would get out and I could shoot him again with the shot-gun. Instead I had the misfortune to hit him twice in the head with the bullets of the revolver, cutting him open from his eye to his lip. He rolled over and looked at me and came charging at the distance of about ten feet. I threw the revolver on the ground, grabbed the shot-gun, pulled it up to my hip, and fired. The bear went down, and it gave me an opportunity to back out onto the road about ten feet be-hind me. While reloading the shotgun, I looked around, and the bear was standing on the edge of the road looking at me. I swung around with the shotgun and shot him again. That time he fell, and when he got up he decided to call it quits and started walking away from me down the road, falling dead about twelve yards from me. He was an old male that must have had difficulty in finding other kinds of food, and on skinning him I found an old .38 revolver bullet embedded in the knee joint of his right hind leg.

Lucas and Polo had been shooting at squirrels and birds that raided the orchard. The fruit and nut crops were not considered commercially important to the college people, but protecting them from all marauders was a way of life on the mountain. Marie and Mabel had no authority to stop the shooting. John Hunter did.

The resolution to the problem came about in an unexpected manner. "Mabel and Bob had gone into the census area one morning for the dawn chorus when they saw one of Lucas's friends shoot a squirrel. They took him to Lucas and both to John. John laid down the law about shooting around here, and I am sure it is all over Gómez Farías by now," Marie reported.

Spot-crowned Woodcreeper

18

A FTER John and I left the ranch on May 5, 1966, Marie and Mabel were sole occupants of the cabin until May 23. No one drove up to use the college buildings and the other private cabins, nor did Frank's many friends from Tampico and other towns come up to visit as they had when Frank was alive. I was convinced that the women relished their privacy and freedom. The two families staying in Frank's guest house typically kept to Frank's clearing; however, Marie and Mabel occasionally visited with them, and Lucas supplied the women with milk.

Despite glowing accounts of their adventures, Marie confessed to missing me, and I thought it best to alleviate the problem. John, who had been unable to go back to the ranch, was quick to encourage me. I would have to drive the Dodge, and I indicated to John that I would leave it at Ciudad Mante, catch a bus to Gómez Farías, and walk up.

John thought it would be better for me to leave the Dodge with one of the shopkeepers at El Encino, or if the road was dry, drive to the patio of Carlos Gutiérrez, catch a truck ride to Julilo, and walk to the ranch. As John wrote to his birdwatchers, "I may send some rat poison with him, but, otherwise, he is going to travel very light and expect to live on the people at the cabin. If he goes by Julilo, he could pick up a couple of dozen eggs from Ladislada, which might help out. I will bring down fresh meat and vegetables when I come."

Of course I refused to take John's suggestion. My way seemed simpler, and I wouldn't have to carry eggs. So, it was Ciudad Mante and Los Arcos courts for the evening of May 22. I had enlisted two traveling companions. Jay, from Austin, was a young photographer; David, from Brooklyn, was a birder. It was pleasant at Los Arcos, and we enjoyed our dinner. I was convinced I had made the right decision.

On the morning of May 23 we had a leisurely breakfast in the palm-shaded courtyard at Los Arcos before going into town and the bus terminal. The station was small and crowded with milling transients, but despite the confusion we succeeded in purchasing tickets and were steered to the Gómez Farías bus. David, who had experience jostling among New York commuters, pushed his way to a seat near the front of the bus. Jay was somewhere toward the back. I sat with David.

The bus was a local, a far cry from the big cross-country models, and I doubt that it would have survived a longer trip than the Mante-Gómez Farías run. It creaked and groaned with age and abuse, and like others of its kindred traveling the back roads of Mexico, it was held together as a single entity by baling wire, duct tape, and the determination of the operator. I was reminded of John Hunter—his faith in the final outcome and readiness to overcome any obstacle along the way.

I envied John's attitude but was unable to embrace it. I worried. I tried to hurry our bus along mentally; I pushed with my mind; also I braked when I thought appropriate. I had a sinking feeling when the old machine sputtered to a halt. The driver dismounted and lifted a trap door onto the vehicle's internal organs. The driver appeared unconcerned; the passengers seemed unconcerned.

"It's not that far. We could have taken a taxi," David said. He and his baggage were jammed into the seat next to the window. The window was open; if he saw a bird he could lean out.

"This is routine," I said. "You'll get used to it."

David did not seem to hear; he was looking out and up. At that moment the driver slammed the trap door shut. "There it goes," David muttered. "Bird on wire. Probably Tropical Kingbird."

The driver resumed his seat. The passengers showed little reaction; they had expected the bus to start.

Since Gómez Farías was our destination, I concluded that most of the passengers were residents of that town or some village back up the mountain. In appearance, they were the people we waved to as we drove through Gómez Farías with John Hunter. The women had changed to their Sunday best, neat but not garish, whereas the men were dressed much as they would be on the trail. I wondered what they thought of us, outsiders of another culture, with interests foreign to them. Our entire experience in Mexico was lacking in one major respect: we had no opportunity to know the local people other than the Morenos and the ranch workers. The lives and culture of the people were viewed at a distance and fleetingly; our schedule and the remoteness of the ranch from other settlements were to blame.

Not long out of Ciudad Mante we passed El Limón, the only town of size on our route. Here Frank Harrison had picked up merchandise shipped to Xicoténcatl, the area's railroad station, a few miles to the east. North of

El Límon, pointing west, a paved road intersects with the Pan-American Highway.

I remembered how John Hunter spiced his travels with a recitation of regional history. I decided that David needed enlightening. I pointed. "That road goes west to Chamal. That's where the North Americans first settled. That's where Frank Harrison lived before he went up the mountain."

"The man who got murdered?"

"Yes." The conversation would have ended there, but I was insistent. "I've often wondered just where Frank Harrison's place was in Chamal."

The side road, a narrow strip baking under the morning sun, diminished westward across low country toward an isolated hill, beyond which lay Chamal. The land known as El Chamal encompassed a valley about eight miles north-south and twenty miles east-west, bounded by mountains or foothills except on the south. The Chamal hacienda or farm lands were granted the original owner by the king of Spain between 1613 and 1617. The Blalock Mexican Colony obtained title deed from the International Mortgage Bank of Mexico, date March 21, 1903. Chamal cost $55,000 gold, of which $30,000 was paid in cash. The remaining amount, plus interest, was paid by March 1905.

A newspaper started at Chamal in 1912 was published twice a month. The second issue of the *Chamal Record* carried an account of the founding of the colony:

On March 3, 1903, two special immigrant trains pulled out on a switch and stopped at a little station called Escandón, on the Monterrey and Gulf branch of the Mexican Central railroad in the State of Tamaulipas, Republic of Mexico. The first one that landed contained men, women and children besides their beds, baggage and lunch baskets. The second one contained mules, horses, hogs and chickens, and various household goods, wagons and farming implements, and a few men to look after the livestock.

This bunch of people and their worldly belongings had come all the way from Mangum, Okla., and were destined for Chamal, the newly acquired lands of The Blalock Mexico Colony. There were 33 families, besides some bachelors, in this bunch of humanity. The occupations of the men were put down as follows: 1 merchant, 1 M.D., 1 cowman, 2 blacksmiths, 2 carpenters and 35 farmers.

Having been on the road since February 20, they were certainly tired, and greatly enjoyed the stop.

The work of unloading the cars took 2 or 3 days, the things being strung along the track for over a hundred yards.

The trip overland from the station to Chamal, was tiresome and tedious, and it seemed that the distance was twice as far as it really was, on account of the roads being so rough, they being merely trails where the burro and mule trains traveled from one village to another, though they were cut out sufficient for the wagons. In those days, wagons were about as great a curiosity to the natives as were the Americans themselves.

About 2-fifths of the distance out here is a village of natives, called Xicotencatl, containing a population from 3,000 to 4,000.

Three miles this side of Xicotencatl (he-co-tin'kle) is a big wide flowing stream bearing the name Forlon. It has large Cypress trees growing along its banks. Just on the other side of the mountains which form the eastern border of Chamal, is a clear, deep, fast running stream called the Río Frio. It is not as wide as is the Forlon river. Río Frio is spanned by an antiquated bridge, supported mainly by Cypress stumps cut off at just the right height for piers. The road over the mountains seemed to be a curiosity to most of us. It is a government road and a real good one when properly kept up. We had seen mountains before, but no good roads running over them. On reaching the top of the mountains, the promised land lay just before us, in fact, our vision could rest on the palm valleys stretching out in front of us. It was a very hot day and most everybody and the chickens suffered for lack of water.

The headquarters of the ranch being located at Old Chamal, we naturally pulled for that place.

At that time, there had been no surveying done, and no one could point out a piece of land and call it his. Since that time, the village of Chamal has been laid off and settled, the 20 acre blocks laid off around it, and all of the valley cut up into sections and title deeds made out and turned over to the various owners. Verily, things have changed very much on Chamal since those days.

Most of the first colonists reached Old Chamal on March 7. Eventually, a certain hill was selected as the new town site; this community was called Chamal.

I related to David what facts I could remember from the newspaper accounts. I could not tell to what extent he was receptive. He was looking out the window, naming any bird that he could identify. As for me, my commentary was a way to lessen the discomfort of the ride, the bumping and swaying, and the hot wind and dust blasting through open windows.

I could not put the Chamal settlers out of my mind. The Oklahomans were a world apart from our fellow bus passengers. The newcomers did not need to adapt to the native culture or life style, but certainly to the environment. Their dependence on natural resources readily available is well illustrated in the construction of their homes. As described in the *Chamal Record:*

> Most all of the houses built by the Americans at first were mere sheds. They were made by putting up hard wood forks at the corners and other forks along the sides as the length of the building might require, and most of them had tall forks at each end to hold up the ridge poles. For rafters, large bamboos were used; poles were used for joists and plates; small bamboos were used as lathing, and palm leaves took the place of shingles. Another curiosity about these houses was that no hammer, nails or saw were used in their construction. The forks and poles and bamboos were all tied together with a vine called "bajuco" (ba-hoo'ko), and the palm leaves were tied on by the stringy outer edges of themselves. ["Bajuco" may refer to *Petrea volubilis,* purple wreath.] The walls were usually made by putting bamboos horizontally and tieing palm leaves onto them. The floors were composed of dirt of the particular kind wherever the house might be located. About the first floors that were put in were of rock, and made by fitting rough, flat rocks together as best they could. The principal reasons for making houses in this way were that the cost was very small, and they were very cool.
>
> But soon they began to build houses out of palm logs, in regular old log house fashion, with one log laid above another while others used split palm logs by standing them on end for a wall. Some of these palm log houses have been chinked and fixed up till they make real

nice homes. Most all the Americans now have lumber floors in their houses—a few native lumber, but most of them are pine.

I recalled the old yellowed photograph of what, we assume, was Frank Harrison's house in Chamal in 1930: palm thatch roof and sides, supported by poles.

Frank had traveled our highway countless times, as related in his journal. It would have been interesting to see it through his eyes, in the 1930s when the highway was new—only three decades before, but how many of our fellow passengers even existed then! I glanced at those seated nearby; for a moment they seemed detached in time, and the ghosts in my mind were contemporary and urgent.

"We're turning off," David said.

I thanked him for the observation. We were at San Gerardo, then onto the old road up to Gómez Farías. There is a new road now, surfaced and smooth and fast (the old road was dirt and rock, rough and slow), but the routine is the same: past flat agricultural land, a few remnant palm trees scattered about, then tropical deciduous forest and a gradual ascent to Gómez Farías.

David was beside himself, attempting to spot new birds in a new environment; they, on the other hand, were fleeing the road monster.

The bus struggled up the grade, reached the "Bienvenidos a Gómez Farías" sign, and then, like a horse heading for the barn, sprinted, wheezing and clattering, to the plaza. It was high noon. Passengers disembarked and scattered homeward, carrying shopping bags from the markets of Ciudad Mante. The bus driver vanished.

David and Jay joined me by the plaza wall. The municipal building was across the street, Pablo Cordova's home base. Other than an old man sitting in front of the structure, no humans were to be seen.

The day was cloudy, hot and humid, typically May in the lowlands when all of nature awaits the onslaught of rain. There would be little activity on the streets during the next several hours. The plaza, throbbing with life in the evenings, was in a siesta mode. As there was little movement, so was there little sound. An Inca Dove delivered its monotonous "cooo-coo" endlessly, and insects buzzed at intervals from the big tree on the plaza. Mariachi music, muted by distance, reached us on the breeze, rising and falling in volume, from a radio in some house nearby. I recalled, with a touch of nostalgia, Saturday nights at the ranch when a southerly wind brought whiffs of music up the slope from Gómez Farías.

I forced myself to action. "We should eat before we start walking," I said. "We'll need all the energy we can get."

The tree on the plaza offered refuge from the noonday sun, and we occupied the bench under its thick shade. My idea of a picnic lunch (Marie not being present to set me straight) was a package of cheese crackers, a small can of V-8, and a now very limp chocolate bar. For David, food was not a priority. He had spotted a bird and spent the next few minutes pursuing it around the plaza.

"That was a lifer!" David beamed when he returned to the bench.

"What bird was that?" Jay, I felt, was trying to understand the birder's ways.

"Masked Tityra." David scribbled in his pocket notebook. We usually found this strange songbird (pink, featherless face framed in black, and with red eyes) in the heart of town, perched in full view.

If I had entertained any reservations, I was convinced now that it would be a long hike to the ranch. Accordingly, I gave marching orders as soon as David finished a fruit bar.

We picked up our gear and headed down the dirt road, past dooryards ablaze in bougainvillea and hibiscus, past Don Félix Burgos's house up on its dirt bank, to the fork in the road where the right branch dead-ends and the left plunges into the valley separating village from mountain. Suddenly, the range looms unobstructed, rounded peaks forming a scalloped horizon; today it was forest green against blue.

Even in early afternoon, birds were active in the brush and in cultivated fields, small birds such as Yellow-faced Grassquit, White-collared Seedeater, Olive Sparrow. A big Boat-Billed Flycatcher eyed us from a treetop, emitting unmusical, rasping sounds. David might have been a kid who discovered a new candy store. Jay showed polite interest.

We reached Lucas's Bottom slowly. I would have pointed out Lucas's house, but Jay had walked out of earshot by this time, and David was scribbling frenziedly. He looked up and saw the big strangler fig that had encased the host tree with its multiple ground-seeking roots. He jotted another entry in his book.

The road started a gentle incline to Fred Blesse's corner and the shrine. Trees overhung the road, cutting off any breeze. A Black-headed Saltator projected weird vocalizations from thick brush. David tried in vain to lure it into view, finally turning to me in disgust, perspiration beading his face and forehead. He took a long drink from his canteen.

"Not too much at once," I cautioned. "You overheated your engine."

David smiled faintly. "How much farther?"

"We haven't started yet. You slept through the briefing."

Disbelief flashed across his face. Then he grimaced, shifted his backpack, and resumed walking, heavy boots grinding against loose rocks.

Jay was waiting for us at Blesse's corner, rested. David and I found convenient rocks to sit on and shed our gear.

"It's uphill from here?" Jay pointed to the first steep grade.

"It's been uphill," David panted. He drew a sleeve over his face.

I was beginning to worry about David's stamina. Although he appeared not to have missed any meals, he was not obese, but I suspected that he was sedentary. Jay was much heavier than David; in his case, muscle outweighed fat. We sat for a while without speaking. Nature had gone into limbo, as though waiting for us to make the first move. No breeze made it down or up to where we languished. The sun, I was positive, was stuck above the canyon rim, refusing to move, heating the rocks on the roadbed. Finally, a bird began to sing on the slope above us.

David became mildly alert. "You have House Sparrows out here?"

"Yellow-green Vireo," I said. "Sounds a bit like a House Sparrow."

David raised his binoculars.

"John Hunter always stops here to listen for trucks coming down," I said, "a tradition that started with Fred Blesse."

My statement failed to impress the others. I decided that further pontification would be a waste of time, as would a prolonged rest stop. Accordingly, but lacking in enthusiasm, I ordered the march to resume. We had just risen and adjusted our gear when Jay nodded in the direction we had traveled.

"We have company."

A male figure was walking briskly toward us, still at some distance. Odd that we had not noticed him until now. I turned away, self-conscious because I knew that we would be overtaken quickly. "They all walk here. They could walk all day and not break out a sweat." I think I sounded a bit resentful. I did not look back until I heard footsteps directly behind me.

"Buenas tardes," I greeted, glancing sideways at the walker. He was a young teenager, probably fourteen, neatly dressed. His name was Esteban. He had been at school and was going home to San José, on up the road. He indicated that he had been on the bus with us. After the initial exchange of information, we lapsed into an awkward silence as we trudged up the grade above Blesse's corner. Esteban adjusted his stride to ours.

David called a halt halfway up the grade and reached for his canteen. He was breathing hard. Esteban, who carried only a cloth shopping bag, at that point insisted that he take David's backpack as well as mine. David looked relieved, and I did not wish to hurt Esteban's feelings, so we proceeded in that manner to the Aguacates junction, making fair time.

Esteban parted company with us at the junction. I offered to compensate him for his assistance, but he graciously declined and went on his way at a quickened pace. A short walk would take him to Alta Cima, then a steep climb up the next ridge to the beech zone and a further hike to San José. He should have no trouble being home by nightfall, I thought.

"I didn't see him on the bus," David said, backpack in hand.

"You didn't see anybody on the bus," I reminded him.

"He didn't start walking when he got off the bus," David observed.

"Lucky for you," Jay said.

I glanced up the road toward Alta Cima, but Esteban had vanished as quickly as he had appeared below Blesse's Corner. "Some people swear they've had angels appear and help them," I said.

"They would speak English," David said.

It was time to change the subject. "This ground you stand on is called the Aguacates. Dr. Cameron settled here when he left Ciudad Victoria. Later he moved up the road there to Alta Cima."

David had his binoculars fixed on a bird perched on a dead tree trunk. "Sulphur-bellied Flycatcher," he announced.

I did not bother to look. "Streaked Flycatcher; this is their habitat. They sound different, and this bird's bill is smaller."

"Another lifer." David reached for his notebook.

"You can still find the foundations of Dr. Cameron's house, back there in the woods," I advised. No one volunteered to leave the roadway, and shortly we started the grueling climb up the Aguacates grade. We took the grade in short spurts, walk and rest (sit if possible, but avoid the mala mujer). About halfway to the crest I noticed that David had stopped perspiring. Alarmed, I insisted that we stop as soon as we could find shade. We had been resting only a few minutes when a man appeared around a bend below.

"Another angel?" Jay was amused.

"Not unless Pablo Cordova passed on recently," I said.

The Gómez Farías police force was on his way to Julilo to deliver a paper, we learned. Sensing our predicament, Pablo offered his services. I wrote a note to Marie, requesting that Lucas bring food and water. Thus authorized, Pablo took my backpack and David's and continued on his way. I was thankful for myself as well as for David; my pack had become increasingly burdensome, and I was questioning my decision to carry the added weight of fresh bed sheets up to the ranch.

Later, we reached Frank's red gate. To realize that we were in the cloud forest was some incentive to continue. There was a slight breeze now, and it was a bit cooler. The forest trees were casting longer shadows as the sun slipped westward.

Meanwhile, Pablo had arrived at Rancho del Cielo. Marie and Mabel had gone to the Indian caves, some yards off the ranch road, and would have missed Pablo had he not been smoking a cigarette. Thick foliage was no barrier to tobacco smoke.

Sometime later, Pablo and Polo met us with the requested food and water. After we had satisfied our needs, they led us through a forest short-cut to the ranch road, where the women met us. By this time the sun had dropped over West Ridge and dusk came quickly. A few birds still called, but David seemed unmoved—he was reviewing his notes.

Our visit was of questionable value to our hostesses. Jay was helpful, but David proved to be more of a burden, spending daylight hours pursuing birds and evenings recording his exploits. "Mabel, Marie and Jay played canasta with Fred one night," Marie wrote in John's trip log, "while David wrote out his life list, Mexico list, year list and his wish list. While listing he talked constantly to Fred, so that he didn't know what his canasta hand was doing."

I suppose my principal contribution during the period was keeping David entertained in the field, hence away from the cabin.

Marie summed up the situation well, in a remarkably understated log entry. "Since Marie's camera had been on the blink, she was overjoyed to see Jay, who fixed the thing. Fred was in a daze he never came out of, and David said the cloud forest reminded him of Brooklyn."

19

"DAVID had a one-track mind, all birds," Marie said in retrospect. I could understand. The lure of birds had drawn us to the ranch in the beginning; mainly, it was my own obsession with the feathered creatures. Marie had assured me of her interest in tropical plants, butterflies, and other creatures, "long before I had a chance to go to the ranch." Finally, I conceded that nature offered more than just birding, and in coming years when we would guide birders through the forest, it was never solely for the avifauna. We were pleased to point out plants, insects, and whatever other interesting features we encountered on our walks, so that our guests would return home with a feel for the total experience. Perhaps it was so with David; it just didn't show.

The forest affected people in different ways, and only a person with zero perception could leave untouched. Frank Harrison, over the years, had in a sense tamed the wilderness; nevertheless, he respected its power to overcome the faint-hearted, and to regenerate itself from adversity. For Frank, competing with the environment had led to an intimacy that we could never fully comprehend. Marie and Mabel felt that particular love flower during their extended sojourn at the ranch. Marie has a special glow when the mountain comes to mind.

John Hunter experienced the forest somewhat vicariously, but no less intensely. John drank of its essence through sight and sound and smell. It was his joy to sit on the cabin porch of an evening, facing east, watching thunderheads build up beyond the tree tops, when the scent of rain came on a south breeze and birds voiced regret at parting day.

The porch was special. Its floor slanted to a short board retaining wall topped by a plank laid flat, a handy rest for the feet when leaning back in John's old rocking chair. We shared the porch with stacked firewood and John's nemesis, the refrigerator, the eccentric behavior of which often lured John to a nocturnal contest of wills. But the porch was ideally suited for the contemplative.

Viewed from the porch, the forest fell away to infinity, an oak-sweetgum woodland whose uniqueness had been announced to the world beyond only after scientists had explored the region less than two decades before our first visit. In the 1960s, the region was still little known to the outside world. Al-

Mountain Trogon

though publications were available that detailed the investigations of such as Paul S. Martin and Aaron J. Sharp, most copies were gathering dust in the libraries of academia.

In a way, Marie and Mabel must have been relieved when we parted company on May 28. We had upset their routine and precluded any serious work in the census tract.

Days later, I received a letter from Marie. "It seems that I was running in circles, and hardly got to see you after all the effort you went to to get up here." Our intrusion into their routine was only the first of a series of distractions, as far as pursuit of the bird study was concerned. We left them on a Saturday. The following day Juan and Ladislada Moreno walked down from Julilo to have dinner (lunch), as they had done with Frank on alternate Sundays. Ladislada stayed until June 4, much to the delight of Marie and Mabel. Barbara Warburton and the college group, and Bob Deshayes, had driven up even before our departure. The presence of the college people provided opportunities to join field excursions farther into the mountains, an invitation Marie could not refuse. Perhaps, in light of the extracurricular activity, it was fortunate that we had agreed that the women should stay at the ranch for two additional weeks; by doing so, they were able to work on their project as late as June 15.

In due time the bird census findings were summarized and analyzed by Marie and submitted to *Audubon Field Notes*, to be included in the Thirtieth Breeding Bird Census issue (December 1966). The following are excerpts:

> The severely dry spring of 1965 was not repeated this year. The rainy season arrived on June 12, with 16.70 inches of rain measured from that date through June 20, as contrasted with 11.85 inches measured from February 17 through June 11. The natural pot-holes were dry for only a few days in early June, whereas last spring there was no standing water for months at a time. . . .
>
> An increase in bird song and other breeding activity was quite evident at an earlier date in this comparatively wet year. The Least Pygmy Owl called almost continually daily for about a week following a good rain at the beginning of the census. Singing decreased as the forest became drier. An increase in shooting in the inhabited clear-

ing adjacent to the northeast corner (for the protection of cultivated plants) may have been an added reason for an increase in the White-fronted Dove and the Clay-colored Robin, species which frequented the orchard and gardens. At the same time, elimination of hunting pressure by the neighboring agrarians—who apparently killed and ate any bird large enough to justify the effort—may have contributed to a general population increase.

Although agricultural encroachment had ceased after Frank Harrison was murdered, the hiatus was only temporary. The man named Augustín, previously alluded to, apparently was the principal operative. His presence on land nearby failed to deter Marie and Mabel from the business of the bird census and other activity at the ranch.

About two weeks after the women left the ranch, we received a letter from John, enclosing a letter he received from Lucas. It read, in rough translation,

> The following goes to bring you greetings and inform you that I went down to Gómez Farías to look for men to work, and the first day we went to work it began to rain and it hasn't stopped even for an hour ever since. Because it has been raining day and night, the road is practically impassable because of 3- or 4-feet-deep ruts full of water on the road. I am, therefore, going to stop work on the road until it stops raining. I will just go ahead and clear the road of the fallen trees, branches, and all the big rocks on the road, but I will not begin until after July 1.
>
> There is something else I want to tell you that has me worried more than the road, and that is that I was looking for a lost calf and found Augustín Esqueda, the man who works in San Pablo, and I asked him several questions. First of all, I asked him how many men worked there, and he said two men and that he also has a brother who is coming to work there. This makes three men working there, and he said that they would never leave, even if they were put in jail for working there.
>
> The damage that the cows caused was to another man named Guadalupe Alvarez, and I understand he got very angry. Then, we

started back home, and after about 20 minutes of walking, we met a pickup with an army captain and two policemen. I told them about Augustín, and they said they would catch up with him. The next day, the police came back and said they were not able to catch him because he took to the woods. That is why I am writing you now, because I am worried that they might want to harm us.

Despite that warning, reports of the trip of July 7 to 14 failed to mention the agrarians. It was a trip John called "indescribably rough." Eighty inches of rain had fallen between June 1 and July 10, making the road from the highway at El Encino to the Río Sabinas impassable. After meeting a small delegation of college people at El Encino, both parties proceeded to Gómez Farías.

"The road between Gómez Farías and the Aguacates is completely destroyed," John wrote. "There were holes that you could drop a jeep into; in fact, I did." Three times the winch on the college monster (as the weapons carrier came to be called) pulled John out. One reason he had dropped into holes, John explained, was that he had no brakes due to a break in the hydraulic line "before I got on the ledge at Gómez Farías." John drove ahead, reaching the cabin after dark. With no brakes, the jeep slipped back against a tree on the slope below the cabin, and John was unable to move it from there.

Meanwhile, the fan belt on the college truck had broken on the Aguacates grade, and the boys decided to wait until daylight to work on it. Consequently, Caroline Hunter, Barbara Warburton, and two other teachers had a rain-drenched walk to the cabin, arriving about 10 P.M. Elizabeth had accompanied John, but Caroline had ridden with the college party because John's driving "made her nervous."

"The days in the cabin were beautiful," John wrote. It rained every night, two to four inches. "We canned plums. Also crab apples and mangoes. . . . I fixed my brakes by cutting line to rear left wheel and closing it off. Hope it works on the way down."

Augustín was not the only concern for college personnel. The men who had killed Frank were still in jail, but there was no assurance that they would stay locked up. With that in mind, John went to Xicoténcatl in early August to see "the lawyer there and also the judge. I think they are getting ready to turn our men loose. They say they have got to get more evidence against them, if they hold them. At present, they plan to send two detectives up to the mountain with a college party on August 26th. I hope I will be able to go with them."

John's wish was granted. On August 26, John, Mabel, and I loaded onto the Jeep and headed for the International Bridge. We cleared customs two hours before sunrise and were in Ciudad Victoria by mid-morning. The usual visit to the McCollum residence and gas and market stops were supplanted by calls at Pancho Rodríguez's house and the McCollum box factory to check on the monument for Frank Harrison's grave, a project Pancho had supervised. Also, we visited Lic. Zorilla, who handled legal matters for the ranch. We were out of Ciudad Victoria by noon.

At El Encino we pulled off the highway and were greeted by a uniformed officer, wielding an automatic rifle, and two plainclothes detectives, as promised by Jesus Chávez Palmares, jefe de grupo de la Policía Rural. Whether or not the uniformed man was Sr. Chávez I do not know, but his presence must have made a lasting impression on the local people. The two detectives boarded the Jeep, and we nosed between the roadside stands onto El Encino's main street, westward. Juan Moreno joined us at the lumber patio.

The Río Sabinas was at flood stage; a rush of clear water poured over the low-water bridge. I waded into the torrent to check the water's depth, and seeing that I was not washed downstream, John coaxed the Jeep across. Remarkably, the crossing was the most challenging aspect of the trip, and we reached the ranch before sunset.

The detectives were housed in the Keller cabin. Nothing has been recorded of their activities while at the ranch, but we must assume that they were there to check on the agrarians. We had been informed that by order of the government, no ejido was to be established on forest land. While we were at the ranch, Mabel led the detectives to Augustín's corn field (where the crop was well along) and to his little wood-frame shack. Augustín was absent, and the building yielded nothing of interest.

We found as many as 30 cows and calves in the old clearing at San Pablo, presumably Frank's animals; grass had taken over and provided good grazing, in contrast to the meager fare to be gleaned in the forest. The presence of the cattle provided an ongoing source of friction with the squatters.

Oddly, John again made no mention of Augustín in his trip log, and my notes contained little on the subject. I did note that Augustín and his dog appeared at John's cabin, in company with a man who sought to buy a calf to be butchered. The man "was better dressed than Augustín," I wrote, then gave a less than exhaustive description of Augustín: "round head and much hair. Clean-shaven. Rough features. No hat, etc."

Mrs. Warburton and a college group, riding two monsters, had come up the mountain with us. In addition to making the usual field trips, they set about cleaning up Frank's cook house.

John recorded in his trip log, "Wednesday we sent Geoff [Mrs. Warburton's son] and a monster to Victoria to bring up Frank's tombstone and Pancho Rodríguez." While they were gone, Alfred Richardson and "other boys" poured the concrete base for the monument.

John wrote on October 7, "The stone is set on a concrete base on Frank's grave, and it looks very good. They turned the apex of the stone parallel with the grave so that the dates, etc., can be read from the college building side and the cross is toward our cabin."

The cross is of the Latin model, except that arm and shaft terminate in a trefoil (like a three-part cloverleaf) at both ends, after the pattern of the botonée cross. The inscription, in block letters, reads:

John William Francis Harrison
Born Baysville Ontario Canada June 21, 1901
Murdered Rancho del Cielo Mexico Jan. 29, 1966
A sincere student and gifted teacher
To him who in the love of nature holds
Communion with her visible forms

Nowadays the grave is surrounded by agapanthus (a lily plant native to Africa); its pale blue blossoms, blooming in early summer, are a favorite of hummingbirds.

The setting of the stone compensated, in John's opinion, for "a plenty rough trip." John's visit to the ranch was cut short by a foot infection, which put him in bed, and when fever developed he knew it was time to leave. Pancho drove the Jeep to Ciudad Victoria, where I and John Arvin (a birding friend who had come up with the college) took over the reins. It was a nerve-wracking night drive, complicated by trouble with the fuel line, but we made the border by midnight.

Blue Mockingbird

20

JOHN'S trips to his mountain retreat were seldom without setbacks of a mechanical nature or otherwise. Certainly the most harrowing of all adventures was spawned by an act of nature rather than man or his inventions. How John survived the ordeal mystifies me; it must be a tribute to his determination and a little help from the Almighty.

A late-season hurricane hit the east coast of Mexico in the fall of 1966. Most Texans are prone to dismiss hurricanes that go ashore in Mexico as of little consequence, perhaps wreaking havoc in unpopulated areas before breaking up over the Sierra Madre. The Brownsville people are more realistic, and certainly those associated with Rancho del Cielo cringe when a storm disappears into nearby Mexico.

We heard of Hurricane Inez through the *Austin American-Statesman* of October 11, 1966. An article by the Associated Press out of Brownsville reads:

> Hurricane Inez, erratic to the end, veered away from Texas and laced into the northeast coast of Mexico Monday, damaging at least six small villages and threatening Mexico's sugar center.
>
> The rugged brush country north of Tampico quickly took the steam out of the giant storm's vicious winds, cutting them from 135 miles an hour to 100 some 10 miles inland.
>
> The New Orleans Weather Bureau said Inez was "breaking up rapidly" in the hills west of Tampico by midafternoon. Highest winds were down to an estimated speed of 80 miles an hour near the center.

John was anxious to know how the ranch had fared, but it was more than two weeks before he could get away with a delegation of men from the college. His experience is best related in his own words, in a letter to "Bird-watchers, *et al.*," dated November 5, 1966.

> We got up about three-thirty Friday morning [October 28] and got out of Matamoros about six o'clock. We made excellent time to Victoria; ate lunch in the cafe and got out of Victoria about twelve-fifteen. We had very little bit of trouble getting to Julilo; we met three trucks on the road. The Sabinas was just over the bridge but not at

all difficult to cross. We saw evidence of many trees cut out of the road on the way to Julilo. We got to Juan's house about five o'clock and lost no more than five minutes there. He told us he thought it was impossible to make the trip to the ranch, but we started. About a half mile out of Julilo, we met Augustin and his dogs, and he told us Lucas was in Gómez Farías and that he thought it was impossible to go through. We had a borrowed chain-saw from Brownsville, and we hit our first tree about a half mile out of Julilo.

We couldn't get the chain-saw started there, and, while we were fooling with it, the boys chopped this one out with an ax. We had two axes and my cross-cut saw, and this tree wasn't over about ten inches in diameter. The next tree we hit was a big sugar maple about three-foot in diameter at the base with two trunks. We worked and worked trying to start the chain-saw and finally sawed it out of the way with the cross-cut saw and pulled the logs out of the road with the winch. When we hit the third tree, I decided I had better walk in to camp and get Lucas to bring back the chain-saw to help them. I was the only one who knew the road well enough to walk it at night.

I got Jim Garland's brother-in-law to walk with me. He was about fifty years old and a man who had been a Drill Sargeant in World War II and a real walker. I thought, surely, I could walk a mile an hour, at least. It got dark on us, and I was having to stop and rest every couple of hundred yards. We finally passed the Malacate road; I never did see the mine turn-off but recognized the grade into the old lumber-camp yard. By that time, my legs were buckling on me, and I had to stop every hundred yards and rest. The moon came up and was good and bright, and I took the road off the lumber-camp to the clearing, and it took me three hours from there to the cabin. I was completely played out. We counted the trees until we counted forty of them, and we figured it would take a half hour for each tree, even with a chain-saw. We finally hit one that had the whole top down in the road with at least four or five big branches, and we couldn't see any way through it or around it; so we laid down and went to sleep thinking to spend the night there; but it was too cold to sleep. After a few minutes, I got down on my belly and wiggled through it like a snake and over the rest of it like a squirrel.

We could hear the dogs barking at the camp, and, when we got about 300 yards away, I was completely played out and asked Mr. Dunham to take the flashlight and get Lucas to bring me a drink of water and maybe I could make it in. He walked up to the cabin, couldn't raise anybody and then went over to the college campus looking for something to bring me back some water. He couldn't find a thing, so he came back down. I don't know whether it was being mad because Lucas and Pablo were not there or what, but some way I managed to make it in. You ought to try to walk from Frank's pila to his house; I never saw such a piece of rocky, rough ground in my life; if there is a trail there, we couldn't find it.

I had left my keys at the jeep, so we decided we might just as well try to get in Frank's house and sleep as going down to our house. We tried to break in Lucas's house; I heard a baby crying and, of course, Lucas and Pablo were both there, but Dunham hadn't made enough noise to wake them up. Lucas got us some water and got us down to the cabin, lighted a lantern, and we went to bed about 2:00 A.M.

Lucas and Pablo then loaded the chain-saw on a burro and got back to the trucks about daylight. They [the college men] had gone down the Malacate road quite a ways, finally decided they were wrong and came back and camped at the junction. They had a flat tire on the weapons carrier and the battery was down; but they got the tire repaired and the car started by pulling it with my jeep. With the help of Lucas and our chain-saw, they made it to the camp by about noon.

Storm damage at the ranch must have been minimal. "The plant house had the roof taken off it, and we are ordering lumber to rebuild it," John wrote. A later hurricane did extensive damage on the slope east of the ranch but blew up and *over* the ranch itself.

"Monday we sent a truck down the road to the Aguacates and cut out six more trees." The party left the ranch the following day. The road down to the Aguacates junction was "terrible." The road was better from the Aguacates to Gómez Farías; the "Municipales" of Gómez Farías had been running trucks on this stretch of the road every day as they worked on their water system, bringing water down from Indian Spring on West Ridge. It was smooth sailing from Gómez Farías to the Pan-American Highway, as the new paved road had just been completed.

"It was quite a trip," John said in summary. "I don't want to ever have to walk into that place again. I decided I won't die of heart-failure, or I would have died on one of these rests. However, I am about to recover from it. . . . I did not fall a single time and did not get into the 'mala mujer,' so I think that is a record."

Lumbering continued on the mountain. Tracking the woodcutters was difficult without adequate transportation and time to waste. Operations moved from site to site as the supply dwindled, new roads were cut and abandoned, and lumber camps appeared and disappeared. Most work was done in areas off the main trails, areas uninhabited before and after the lumbermen left. Little old trucks top-heavy with a few logs crept along serpentine, roller-coaster roads and disappeared toward some sawmill that was never in place long enough to appear on a map.

The camp at Julilo was in transition in July 1967 as the company finished harvesting its prescribed area. Marie noted that there were fewer people in the village, although logs were still being brought in. In March 1968 we received a handwritten letter from Juan Moreno; he and Ladislada had moved to the state of Zacatecas. Juan closed with, "Now we put our house to your orders, even if it is not much comfortable, but anyhow we hope to see you here some day."

We were more preoccupied with agrarian operations than with logging in 1968. The squatters were making no effort to hide their handiwork. I had an opportunity to inspect the area firsthand on the college's Easter trip in early April—a good time, as apparently most of the people had gone to the lowlands. Barbara Warburton lent me one of the students, Rodney Wilson, as an aide. We walked the Gómez Farías road from Frank's red gate to San Pablo, making a particularly thorough inspection of San Pablo and the clearings on the north side. The grassy portion of Paul's Field at San Pablo had been plowed, and there was evidence that Jacinto Osorio's house was being used.

More distressing was the work being done at the junction. An area at the northeast corner was being cleared for an undetermined distance. Removal of large trees had transformed the corner from deep shade to open sunlight. On later trips, I never passed this place without remembering the thick canopy that had been and the feel of the primeval forest. In time, the corn field and the shanty that had been put on this tract disappeared, and mala mujer invaded the clearing along with low shrubs. For a while it was a great place to view the Wedge-tailed Sabrewing, a hummingbird that claimed the white blossoms of the mala mujer and entertained us with its frenzied vocalizations. Later, second-growth forest began to reclaim the land.

A month after our snooping expedition, John reported a new development. "I understand they have an order to have all the cattle on the mountain rounded up and impounded at Gómez Farías," John wrote. "As far as I am concerned, I hope it's right. It will get the cattle off our hands and probably force them to be sold for something; even if the money is impounded by the court." Considering the trouble Frank Harrison had keeping up with his cattle, it would seem that the squatters would have their hands full herding cattle down the mountain. Indeed, no immediate action was taken.

Alfred Richardson, who spent most of June on the mountain collecting plant specimens for the herbarium at the University of Texas in Austin, related an incident that occurred some time after Frank Harrison's alleged killers were released: "I guess not much more than a year after Frank was killed, the agrarians, about three or four of them, came up the Hunter hill all carrying machetes with the blades finely sharpened, and they were fingering the sharp edges of the machetes. And I didn't know who they were. Lucas was there, and he was grinning at them and trying to be friendly, and was very secretive to them. And they started complaining about cows, about Frank's cows getting out and eating their corn. John knew who they were—one of them was one of the guys who killed Frank—and John shook his finger at him and said in Spanish, 'You killed the owner of those cattle, and it's your fault those cattle are loose to get in there, so you get off this place, and don't you ever come back!' And they left. We didn't have a thing to defend ourselves with, but they did what John said. That night was pretty tense, just waiting for somebody to jump in the window with a machete, but nothing happened, and they never came back."

"Didn't John have his shotgun?" I asked.

"Not when the men came up; it was on his bed. He made sure it was loose in the holster that night."

"You closed the shutters?"

"No. I wanted to close them, but John wouldn't do it. Caroline was there too; she was at least as upset as I was. Not upset—scared."

By July, responsibility for disposal of the cattle seemed to have been dropped on the college. "I am in hopes we will get the order through to sell the damned cows on the mountain," John wrote on July 20. "We will be lucky if they bring the cost of settling the suit and their sales cost. I got a bill from the lawyer for $380.00 in the matter of the Estate, and we have a bill against them of about $300.00."

On August 9, John and party embarked on a trip to the ranch. The customary visit was made to the lawyer in Ciudad Victoria. "Saw Lic. Juan Zorilla and Mr. San Miguel," John wrote in his trip log. "And they are sure they will have permit to sell cows next week. How in the hell we are going to gather and get the cows down I don't know and how many there are is a totally unknown figure."

21

BY 1968 the college ranch schedule had settled into a routine of sorts. At the helm was Mrs. J. O. E. (Barbara) Warburton, instructor and chairman of the Biology Department. Barbara was not an imposing figure physically (middle-aged, short of stature, and of medium build), but she was ostensibly a person to preside over an orderly biology laboratory. She was that and much more, a strong-willed disciplinarian, a take-charge person.

Barbara could be stern and outspoken, and the erring student might well quake if those blue eyes, peering from behind thick lenses, should turn his or her way. But she had a compassionate side, available particularly to her charges, and a sprinkling of British humor.

At home, Mrs. Warburton was *numero segundo.* Husband Joe was incontestably the head of the house. He gave orders, and they were carried out. Joe was a successful lawyer, despite the polio that struck him down temporarily at age fifteen. The old disease haunted him thereafter, but determination kept him on his feet during an active career.

Joe was opposed to Barbara's going off to Mexico periodically, but he conceded that her work was important for her and the college. Barbara, on the other hand, harbored an uneasiness that was not usually evident. Joe's health was a constant concern, and she would have left the ranch on an instant's notice if needed at home. It was some comfort when a relatively flat, grassy area in Frank's clearing was designated a helicopter pad.

Someone in Joe Warburton's family had access to a helicopter, and it was agreed that should there be an emergency involving Joe, the aircraft would be sent to the mountain. Barbara must have been alarmed when a forestal helicopter appeared over the ranch on August 5, 1972, and relieved when it did not land. Three days later one did land.

The college had been hosting a group from Pan-American University, and no one was in a hurry to get out of bed on August 8. Barbara, in nightgown and robe, was enjoying a cup of tea in her favorite chair while the crew fired up the cook stove, Marie recalled. "Then we heard the helicopter. It was close, circling. We could see that B.W. was alarmed. She put her cup down, jumped up, and started running—uphill to the helicopter pad, long

White-throated Robin

red robe flying, and seven or eight of us at her heels. It must have been a sight!

"The helicopter landed about the time we got to the crest of the hill, and out stepped this World War I flying ace, a tall man with a white flowing scarf about his neck, flight suit and boots. The flying ace introduced himself and his assistant and explained that they were surveying the forest—roads, soil, minerals, and all—and there were too many clouds, so he decided to put down in this nice open spot. The pilot spoke very good English; he was educated in California and had been flying helicopters for twenty years.

"B.W. generously suggested that the girls would fix the men a real American breakfast, so they did. And we had conversation, pancakes, and I don't remember what else. Then we gave them a tour of the ranch, and they took off."

The biological station came into being, appropriately, at a time when emphasis in schools of higher learning was shifting from strictly laboratory work to supplemental fieldwork. Texas Southmost was just a two-year college, but it now was in a position to develop a field program that would be the envy of many senior colleges. The continued success of the program at Rancho del Cielo would be due largely to the foresight and direction of Barbara Warburton.

The cook house was the first building to be completed on the mountain campus, followed by two dormitory cabins to either side and a little upslope from the cook house, against the forest edge. Cabins were set on a rock base and constructed of pine lumber, topped with a tin roof. The unpainted exteriors gave a rustic appearance, in keeping with the woodland setting. As for the dormitories, one main sleeping room occupied most of the rectangular structure; a partitioned area enclosed bathroom facilities. Windows, wash basin, sink, and toilet (fixtures discarded from old Fort Brown in Brownsville) had been in storage at the college.

Amenities were scarce at first. Hot showers were available but required some effort to prepare. Water was hauled from the spring and transferred to an elevated metal drum outside the cabin. A fire was built under the drum and water piped into the cabin by gravity flow. "Nobody wanted to take the first shower," Marie recalled. "It was always cold, and the last shower was too hot. You wanted to be somewhere in the middle."

It was not long before tanks from an aircraft carrier (Korean War surplus, again) were hauled up the mountain to catch rainwater from the cabin roofs, and butane water heaters were procured. Before the latter acquisition, however, the most sophisticated equipment could be found in the cook cabin: a butane refrigerator as well as a water heater. The latter stored water that passed through coils of copper tubing inside the two wood-burning stoves on which meals were prepared. The dining tables were reconstructed pin-ball tables that had been gathering dust in Fort Brown storage. Wood tops attached to metal frames made quite sturdy pieces of furniture.

The sleeping area in the dormitory cabins accommodated about ten metal double-deck bunk beds, with mattresses. An ample supply of blankets was available. The space was heated, at least partially, by a pot-bellied wood-burning stove. A system of overhead butane lamps was donated by Oscar Kieswetter and the gas company in Brownsville.

With the three cabins in place, about five student trips were made during the year. Student participants were selected on the basis of several criteria: his or her classification, degree of interest, and participation in activities of the Gorgas Science Society, the college's science club. Even more important to Warburton was the lasting benefit a student would gain through his or her contribution to the project, the ability to cope with the natural elements, the capacity to live harmoniously with others through trying circumstances, and the young person's general excellence as a student of science.

About fourteen students were taken per trip, which lasted from a week to ten days. Trip expenses were paid through various projects, including sales of amaryllis bulbs and candy. Frank's hybrid amaryllis were a popular item with the general public. One Florida buyer ordered 3,000 bulbs at about a dollar each, but most sales were of relatively small numbers.

A trip to the ranch was eagerly anticipated, but students were assured that this would not be a leisurely vacation; each trip was a work-study adventure. Students performed the work and were held individually responsible for the success of the venture. Boys who were good drivers and who showed mechanical aptitude were trained in mountain driving and truck maintenance and cautioned that the vehicles must remain serviced at all times. Girls prepared meals and were expected to have food on the table on schedule. Both sexes shared kitchen duty and such chores as housekeeping and hauling garbage. Warburton was adamant in regard to a spic-and-span venue. Housekeeping duties included a thorough scrubbing of the cabins at the end of each trip and, once a year (in rainy August) scrubbing of the floors with lye soap and water. Finally, there was the cleaning of the cook stoves, a formidable but necessary task.

The ranch experience was for many students the first opportunity to leave home without parental escort, and possibly the first time that they, as individuals, were responsible for the success or failure of a common project.

Equally important to the experience of working together in harmony was personal contact with the natural world, where laboratory specimens come alive and concepts gain clarity. Here all branches of natural science could be viewed in interrelationship, and botany, zoology, geology, and other disciplines began to make sense as part of the whole.

"The students gain practical experience in field study techniques and receive valuable instruction in identification and taxonomic practices," Warburton wrote in a presentation of the ranch study program. "Students also feel the excitement of scientific discovery in finding specimens which contribute to scientific knowledge by extending the range of distribution of certain species and providing a challenge to identify new specimens found in the forest."

Students, in the course of their study at the ranch, gained valuable insight into the lives and customs of the people of the region, through lectures on history, cultural anthropology, and archeology.

A number of students were so inspired by their experience at Rancho del Cielo that they went on to pursue scientific careers at four-year universities. Some would come to the ranch for extended periods of graduate research. Warburton was proud to point out that the attraction of the ranch program had led more students to enroll in science courses and to join the Gorgas Science Society.

Students and volunteers had played a major role in construction of the buildings on the ranch campus, and they were counted on for repair and maintenance. Special work trips were organized as needed. An excellent example was the pila trip of January 1968. The need for a dependable water supply had become painfully apparent; a storage reservoir such as the pila that served John Hunter's cabin was the logical solution. This one, however, would be larger, with a planned capacity of 50,000 to 60,000 gallons.

On Friday, January 19, Barbara Warburton and Gonzalo Garza set out with fourteen students and two college workmen in three trucks (weapons carriers); the same morning, John Hunter's party, with Marie as guest, departed Brownsville for the mountain. Cement was added to John's usual shopping list in Ciudad Victoria; it was transferred to the college trucks when the college party caught up with John at Félix Burgos's house.

"We had a good trip up the mountain," Marie wrote. "John didn't stop or kill the engine a single time."

Excavation for the pila had been mostly completed on previous trips. It was dug "to a depth over John's head," which would exceed six feet four inches. (We have no record of John getting in the hole, nor is it likely.) The next move would be to cement the floor and construct walls. To accomplish that, the boys were assigned these duties: haul sand and cement up the mountain, drive trucks, service trucks. The work occupied them fourteen to sixteen hours a day for nine days.

The girls prepared meals and kept a pot of coffee on the stove, in addition to housekeeping chores.

Every trip was an opportunity to add to the ranch inventory. This time it was a stove for Pablo, whose family was living in Frank's cook house now but had to go to the guest house and share cooking facilities with Lucas's family. Also, a water heater was brought up for the boys' cabin.

The latter appliance could not be utilized immediately. Because of a water shortage, showers were taken at the John Hunter cabin. John's shower arrangement was a stall under the bedroom, formed by rock walls on three sides and a shower curtain on the fourth (outside). The walls were only about four feet high in places, permitting a view of the open space under the house. One always envisioned vinegarroons (whip scorpions), tarantulas, or venomous snakes lurking in the shadows, whereas the shower curtain was a more likely cause for concern—it responded to the slightest breeze.

Student Randy Price gave his impression of John's shower in *The Collegian* of Texas Southmost College (no. 6, February 28, 1968): "Besides all the trouble you have to go through in order to get a shower it's fine. Like you have to close the shower curtain to keep the bats from showering with you, and you have to open and close the cold water faucet to keep from scalding to death. Then you have to shake into your wet clothes 'cause it's so small you can't even turn around."

On Sunday, Marie tagged along when Barbara took three trucks and seven boys down the mountain to purchase sand and cement. They drove north on the Pan-American Highway, then turned left to the town of Llera and to the Río Guayalejo. The boys were spared the job of loading the truck, as the sellers did the shoveling. The expedition left the ranch at 7 A.M. and returned by dusk.

With a supply of sand, it was possible to start mixing concrete for the floor using water from John's pila, after which the rock walls (at least a foot in depth) could be built and cemented. Tuesday through Sunday the boys mixed concrete, and two boys and the two college workers (with Pablo and sometimes Lucas) built rock retaining walls and poured pillars. The other boys and Garza made five more trips with two trucks for sand.

"They are using sand as fast as two trucks can go down to Llera and bring it back," Marie wrote. "The drivers said they knew where every rock and tree was."

John's party had left the mountain on January 23, but Marie remained as a guest of the college, sharing John's cabin with two students and assisting the staff. In addition, she was designated guide to two visiting scientists who had been brought up from Ciudad Mante on January 22, Lucerne Sorenson, head of the Science Department at Pan-American University, and Pauline James of his teaching staff. Dr. Sorenson was interested in bringing his graduate seminar for teachers to the ranch for three weeks of fieldwork.

Barbara Warburton had never before supervised construction of a pila and had not correctly judged the amount of time, labor, and materials required. The original plan had been to return to Brownsville on Sunday, January 28, as classes resumed on Monday. It became apparent that the pila would not be completed by that time, nor was there enough sand on hand to finish the job. A compromise was decided on: two trucks would take six students and the visiting scientists down the mountain, leave them, and return with sand. The work trip would be extended for only a day or two.

Marie wrote, "Just as we finished lunch at 1:30 P.M. one truck came back with sand and said that the other had broken a spring at the shrine and water station and had gone back to Gómez Farías. That would have meant a day's delay in getting it fixed. It had rained all night the night before and most of the morning and they couldn't mix any more cement."

Barbara Warburton reluctantly admitted defeat, for the short term.

"We left the ranch at 3:30 P.M. . . . . We met the other truck at Lucas's

Bottom. Mr. Garza and Bobby [Bryant] had it chained to a branch of a large tree. They cut a tree and fitted a piece of wood in there and we came on. One truck had bad seals in the back tires—which made the load uneven (the people rode in that), and the third (which I was in) had weak brakes and one crooked dim light so we had to use the high beam all the time."

Vehicles traveling the mountain roads take an incredible amount of punishment. Various and ample spare parts are a necessity for any trip. A good winch is indispensable. Aside from actual mechanical equipment, every traveler should have access to a chain saw, an ax, and a machete. One should always understand that progress may be stalled indefinitely and so carry provisions for an overnight stay in the vehicle.

Vehicle maintenance is a drain on the college's ranch budget. After purchase, a vehicle has to be refitted to meet specific needs, such as a metal framework on the bed, over which a tarpaulin can be secured; padded benches on either side, seating a total of ten average-sized persons; and various mechanical adjustments. Add the cost of fuel and frequent tire replacement, and ownership of the vehicle is a major expense.

The first vehicles enlisted for ranch service were retired Korean War Dodges, which had been used as weapons carriers; at $250 cash they were a bargain. A dealer would have put the vehicles out to pasture, but they were ideal for the college program. The flathead straight six-cylinder engine worked like a charm, most of the time, and the short wheelbase gave ease of maneuverability on the steep hairpin curves. In 1969, new Dodge Power Wagons took over primary duties, although one of the old monsters was retained.

After supper at Turner's in Ciudad Victoria, and some deliberation, Barbara gave orders to proceed. The caravan arrived at the border at first light.

Exhaustion and rain were reported to have terminated the trip. There is no doubt that fatigue was setting in, and some may have embraced the excuse of a mechanical breakdown, but once a person has come under the spell of the forest, hardship becomes merely a temporary nuisance.

Linda Augustine, a student, speaks in *The Collegian* for those countless young people who have labored with love at Rancho del Cielo: "I love Rancho del Cielo; it's a part of me now. Its pitted roads, woody paths, the wood stove I slaved over, even the hurry-house — they are all a part of a wonderful *experience*. I'd go back and do everything over again so that I could be with that little part of me that's way up there on that mountain."

White-tipped Dove

22

OVER the millennia, nature has buffeted the forest with wind and fire, flood and drought. In time the crisis passed, wounds healed, the forest regenerated. But there is an agent—humankind—that now has the know-how and power to alter forever the forest's environment, transforming woodland into wasteland. This was not always so. The earliest human inhabitants of the region existed in a manner compatible with the land, leaving little to recall their having been here: pottery shards and other artifacts from caves and Indian house mounds.

The ancient people were of the Huastecan branch of the Maya. Extensive settlements, even a few small pyramids, have been identified in the lowlands, and judging from the remains of house mounds, a considerable population lived on the mountain. Those settlements all had disappeared before the period of conquest; the forest was left largely as it had been found. Destruction of habitat on a large scale came in more enlightened times and from two major sources: lumbering and farming.

Lumbering was by its nature destructive. First, roads wide enough for a truck to pass were cut to desirable sites. Where the terrain was too steep to drive a truck in, a swath was cleared to the width of the logs. Oak was cut to form rails, and the logs were rolled down to a pickup point.

A large tree felled by natural causes or human effort is likely to take several adjacent trees down with it. If not moved, the tree remains to furnish, eventually, rotting material for the forest floor. Old forest giants are a microcosm when standing, host to millions of living organisms, including bromeliad, orchid, fern, moss, lichen, which in turn offer habitat for various amphibians and insects. The fallen tree retains some of its adornments, although losing the tank bromeliads and orchids that prefer loftier perches, and will in time be home to fungi and creatures that thrive on rotting wood.

On the other hand, the tree reduced to a commercially valuable log leaves a pile of trash that provides temporary refuge for brush-loving birds and mammals, then gradually adds material to the soil. In either case, ground cover responds as sunlight penetrates the canopy, disturbance plants such as mala mujer appear, and saplings of the tree species reach for the sky. Although the forest opening represents a dramatic change, the soil retains its substance and vitality. The forest heals itself over the years, and the casual visitor of the future does not suspect that a cycle has been completed.

Enrique Beltrán, in the foreword to A. Starker Leopold's *Wildlife of Mexico*, wrote, "We are accustomed to thinking of forest protection chiefly in terms of regulating excessive logging, as though this were the only or the principal cause of forest destruction. Yet the clearing of trees and brush from the land to make it suitable for farming, or the inadvertent clearing by burning or overgrazing, may be even more significant."

Agriculture, if intensive enough, can be deadly to forest life. The local people, as is the custom throughout the Americas, practice the slash-and-burn method, laying the soil bare, at the mercy of driving rain and burning sun. After a few years of sustaining crops (primarily corn), the soil has leached so badly that further agricultural attempts are futile and the farmer must clear another plot. Surrounding forest, if any, will gradually encroach on the abandoned field, but recovery of the soil will span generations of humankind.

Frank Harrison was able to overcome soil nutrient loss. His land, originally cleared by the McPhersons, was one of the more arable spots on the mountain, and he maintained it by constant fertilization (cattle manure and bat guano particularly) and crop choice. Rancho del Cielo's gardens and orchard were small and ringed by forest, negating climate change.

The tropical deciduous forest and the palm forest of the lowlands had been largely cleared during the twentieth century, planted mainly to sugar cane and orchards. The land below had been sufficient to support the local human population, and except for the colony at Alta Cima and a few other small settlements, the mountain was spared the machete and the ax until mid-century. Although there were areas on the mountain where crops could be planted without walking amid a field of boulders, the soil was thin and soon depleted, unlike in the fertile valley of the Río Sabinas.

As related earlier, members of the scientific community, having recognized the uniqueness of the oak-sweetgum cloud forest surrounding Rancho del Cielo, attempted to raise funds to buy forest land. The effort failed. The mantle then fell on a new generation of concerned individuals, who saw the value of preserving the forest as a study and research opportunity and, practicality aside, realized that they held a small part of a natural treasure in their grasp.

It may be difficult for the outsider to understand the importance of preserving this particular piece of land in its present form, and the urgency to do so. In one sense, the forest is a key that unlocks the history of North American vegetation back to the Tertiary Period (65 million to 10 million years ago). Flora of the cloud forest is a mixture of northern and southern elements similar to certain Eocene fossil flora. (The Eocene Epoch goes back beyond 40 million years.) Beyond those facts, and taking in the lowlands and the entire mountain range, this diversification of biotic communities within a small geographic area is rivaled by few places on Earth.

If eroding activities could not be curtailed, the people of Texas Southmost College reasoned, the only recourse was to purchase more land, from which the destructive elements could then be excluded; hence, much time and effort was channeled in that direction. In the beginning, the burden fell on John Hunter; he carried it heavily on his broad shoulders.

During Marie and Mabel's raid on the Julilo cookie supply, Juan Moreno indicated that Arturo Arguello would sell 1,000 hectares or whatever John wanted to buy if John contacted him personally.

Meanwhile, John was off on another tack. In an August 1967 letter to us he wrote, "I have finally gotten a young lawyer in Victoria who is sort of an assistant to Zorilla to working on getting the State to take the two pieces of Paul Gellrich's land and sell them to us. A title from the State would be good."

If land could be bought, money would be needed, and funding for the biological station alone was a continuing challenge. In October, Barbara Warburton led a trip to the ranch with a representative of the "Educational Agency" as a special guest. It was hoped that the agency would "give us a grant on the rancho," according to John.

For a period before 1968, farming activity near the ranch ceased. Finally, San Pablo was deserted; the few frame buildings that the squatters had built up against the woodland, toward the census tract, had been abandoned. Nor was Jacinto Osorio's house, in the clearing, being used. Whatever was transpiring around Augustín's field went on beyond a screen of trees, in the shadow of West Ridge.

As if land acquisition, station funding, and Augustín's presence weren't enough, a new and disturbing situation had developed; the men jailed for

Frank Harrison's murder had been released. John reported the matter in a letter to us, dated May 6, 1967, following a trip to the mountain. In Ciudad Victoria he had gone to see Lamarque. "Mr. Lamarque had the packages that were brought down from Frank's and, unfortunately, they contained nothing which could carry a fingerprint. One package was made up of the old clothes that we had taken down to Frank during the Fall before he was killed; the other package was made up of blankets and bedding which the murderers had stolen from Frank's cabin." (One of the Southmost students had found a suitcase containing some of Frank's belongings "hidden" in a tree in the forest; we do not know if its contents were included with the foregoing.) "Both of the men are now out of jail and are in Gómez Farías. Mr. Lamarque has asked the chief of police there to keep close surveillance on them. I don't know what this will mean, but I hope it means they won't be allowed to come up to the mountain."

Within a few months the squatters were noticeably active. On March 30, John reported, "I just got back from a trip to Rancho del Cielo. . . . The agrarians are really crowding around us, both at San Pablo and on the section between the red gate and San Pablo. I would judge there are not less than fifty people in the area now. I am doing everything possible to get them moved, but I can't do much in either Gómez Farías or Victoria. I am trying to get contact with Arguello and see what can be done there."

We shared John's concerns but felt helpless to render aid in any practical fashion, until we had an idea. We had talked casually with John and Barbara on numerous occasions about ownership of cloud forest land. Since the college was making no headway in purchasing additional land, there might be others who could, and toward the same goal: preservation. We were aware of the ongoing and escalating efforts to conserve the planet's natural resources, and we knew of various agencies involved in this movement. While we had no direct clout with any group, we knew some of the people involved. Our idea was to sound out a birding friend, Edward C. Fritz, on the matter. Ned Fritz was a Dallas attorney who was dedicated to the conservation movement. At the time, he was president of the Texas chapter of The Nature Conservancy; as such, he was in touch with other like-minded organizations.

John Hunter visited us in Austin in early March. His report on farming activity prompted me to write to Ned without further delay. I stated that eight or ten men, including one or more of the men accused of killing Frank

Harrison, had made three clearings along the main road through the cloud forest. According to John, the forest service would make no attempt to remove the squatters without a complaint from the landowner, who lives in Mexico City and lumbers in the pine-oak zone.

"John anticipates trouble when the agrarians' corn is up. Frank's cattle still roam the woods at will, and will eventually get into the corn fields. Apparently the agrarians have anticipated trouble with the cows; John reports they found a dead cow with its tongue cut out, and two cows with their tails cut off."

Also, I expressed concern about current lumbering of oak and sweetgum in the northern portion of the cloud forest, within three miles of Rancho del Cielo.

"I asked John about purchase of land adjacent to the rancho. He has no prospects at present. He thinks the land could go for as little as $10.00 an acre, if available. Southmost College has a new administration, and I don't know if they will adopt an aggressive attitude toward expanding the college holdings."

Ned Fritz began to make inquiries, and if land acquisition in the cloud forest seemed to be moving forward, it was mainly through his efforts. In early 1969 he wrote to the World Wildlife Fund regarding that agency's qualifications for holding land in Mexico should a tract be donated.

C. R. Gutermuth, treasurer of the World Wildlife Fund, replied in a letter dated January 31, "Foreigners and foreign corporations cannot hold title to property within approximately 300 miles south of the United States border. . . . The World Wildlife Fund could buy the land, and convey the title to the Instituto Mexicano de Recursos Naturales Renovables, a private Mexican organization that is headed by Dr. Enrique Beltrán. While we are not absolutely certain as to the kind of protective arrangement that might be worked out under Mexican law, it would seem some satisfactory provisions could be made."

It was suggested that money could be donated to the World Wildlife Fund on a tax-exempt basis for acquisition of land in Mexico. The title would then have to be conveyed as above.

Beltrán, as Fritz pointed out, was probably the leading conservationist in Mexico, was politically influential, and as such should be able to protect land designated as a reserve. With that assurance, we were urged to obtain an option and raise pledge money toward land purchase.

I considered myself a go-between, while pledging support in whatever way compatible with our means, but Ned Fritz's approach had a sobering effect. Was I ready to volunteer as a solicitor of funds for the project?

In more optimistic moments I could imagine a multitude of people willing to contribute financially on some scale toward preservation of the forest. The scientists who had worked with Frank Harrison came to mind first. George M. Sutton had expressed willingness to do what he could to promote the ranch project. Certainly the cabin owners would be sympathetic, and perhaps the friends they had hosted from time to time, and the college people, and cavers and birders who had come up on their own. The forest had influenced a multitude of people.

I felt that we could trust Beltrán, but we knew that policies change with administrative changes. I consulted with John Hunter.

John replied promptly, and my inclination toward caution was vindicated. "I am getting a letter off to my lawyer friend in Mexico City, a copy of which is attached. I would like to get his frank opinion of the thing before we get in too deep. I know he is very suspicious of anything that has to do with government organizations, and you will recall he advised us to stay clear of expansion a couple of years ago."

John's letter of February 11 to Burnell Goodrich follows, in part:

Both of the lumber companies who own the land are encroaching legitimately, cutting out maple at this time; but, in time, they will cut out all the gum and most of the oak and probably the magnolia. Also, the Mexican Agrarians are encroaching on us from every side. They have not made any attempt to take any of our property, and I don't think they will. We have disposed of the cattle which Frank left, and this has gotten that irritation out of the way with them.

I understand that an *ejido* cannot be granted in land that is under the control of the Forestal Department of Mexico. If this is true, they are illegally on the land, but no one in the State of Tamaulipas wants to throw them off it. They are encroaching on the bird and animal life; and, in time, they will materially clear out the forest area. They do it in small patches of an acre or two here and an acre or two there. The pieces of land that are flat enough and suitable for farming are very fragmentary, and I don't think that in a thousand years the land would support an agrarian settlement.

Goodrich was asked to check on Beltrán's organization and the advisability of dealing with them.

> I well remark the advice you gave me the last time I asked you about buying the land at that time by private individuals, and you pointed out the possibility of losing the whole area to some Mexican Government Agency. . . . In time, we may have to go with someone, and the World Wildlife Organization in the United States has been very devoted to the maintenance of the property which they control; and, if the Mexican organization is anything like them, it might be well for us to tie up with them now.
>
> Do you have any idea of what the going price is for unimproved, cut-over Mexican forest land? The land is really not cut-over land in the sense that all the trees have been taken out, but a great many trees have been taken out, and the ones that are left are in places where it is almost impossible to remove them with the equipment the Mexican lumber companies have now; but, if the price on lumber goes up and it becomes more scarce, naturally, they will develop means for coming back in and taking out trees that were impossible a few years ago.

The people at Texas Southmost College, while endorsing the concept of protected land, took a cautious approach. Lic. Zorilla should be consulted, was the opinion of Quentin J. Bogart, who succeeded C. J. Garland as president of Texas Southmost in August 1968. Such a meeting, in Barbara Warburton's opinion, should include Mr. Champion, who was replacing John Hunter on the Rancho del Cielo board.

We reported developments, or lack of same, to Ned Fritz. Ned stressed the respect that the World Wildlife Fund enjoyed across the planet through working with private agencies and governments; its prestige would be an invaluable asset in dealing with Mexican officials. Further, Ira Gabrielson, U.S. head of the World Wildlife Fund and a leading conservationist, knew Beltrán personally and was impressed with his ability and influence.

Goodrich's reply to John's letter was encouraging. On February 25 he wrote, "Your thought of having a sanctuary conveyed to the Instituto Mexicano de Recursos Naturales Renovables is sound and in keeping with my own thoughts. I would suggest that the appropriate people in the World Wildlife Fund be approached about helping to set up a bird and/or wildlife sanctuary in your area. . . . It would then be up to the Fund to send a representative to Mexico for discussions with the institute outlining the extent to which the Fund would go in helping the Instituto to create a sanctuary. After that, it's up to the Instituto."

Goodrich advised against any private individual or organization, Mexican or foreign, buying land and donating it to the Instituto. "I should think that the government here could expropriate the necessary area for a public park and sanctuary. The fund could contribute to its operation and maintenance."

Shortly thereafter I received a letter from President Bogart, of Texas Southmost College, dated March 4: "Your interest in the preservation of the Rancho del Cielo area of Texas Southmost College is most appreciated. Mrs. Warburton and Mr. Hunter have shared your interest in encouraging the World Wildlife Fund to enlarge the undisturbed area of our mountain property. Of course, we are not in a position to encourage or discourage this fine group at the moment," one reason being that Goodrich was "out of his office" and it would be two or three weeks before the college people could expect to hear from him.

"I personally had occasion to make a trip to Cuidad Victoria last week," Bogart continued,

and discussed the matter with our attorney there, Sr. Juan Zorilla. Mr. Zorilla could see no reason why the Mexican authorities would have any objection to the World Wildlife Fund securing property around the Ranch—however, he felt that a much more effective way of protecting the region would be for the Fund to buy the property and assign it on a natural preservation basis to the University of Tamaulipas. Apparently the Mexican institutions of higher learning are highly protective and no individual or group of agrarians, etc., are permitted to interfere with University lands. I respect Mr. Zorilla and his opinion highly and, therefore, feel that there is no ulterior motive in this suggestion.

This postscript was added: "I believe that as the proposed purchase becomes an active project that we will need to anticipate an expenditure in the amount of about $10 an acre including attorneys' fees if we are to acquire the needed amount of property."

"Have you ever raised money for anything?" Marie asked me, waving Bogart's letter.

I couldn't think of any such incident. "I had a cold drink stand once when I was a kid. It lasted maybe two days. But we're not talking money yet."

"I just hope you know what you're getting into."

I made the expected retort. "Don't you want to save the forest?"

Marie's look conveyed more than words; I was suddenly reduced to a lower lifeform. I changed directions.

"I thought we were making some headway, now this University of Tamaulipas thing. I can just see a bunch of student game wardens."

"You're jumping to conclusions. Besides, game wardens don't need to be gun-toting bullies. A student could be alert to what's going on and establish rapport with the local people."

"I suppose so."

"And let me remind you that the University of Tamaulipas and other area schools have been using the mountain as a living classroom for as long as T.S.C. has been here. Students can be quite sensitive to environmental problems. And I'm sure they have qualified biologists at the university."

Reason had triumphed again, I conceded.

"How would Dr. Beltrán's group run it?" Marie asked.

I pleaded ignorance.

"Either way, it wouldn't be a public park," Marie added. "You remember what Irby Davis said about public parks in Mexico."

I groaned. "The public figures the public owns the public park and the public goes in and does whatever the public wants with it."

"Well, calm down. Wait and see what works out."

I had little time to fret. John Hunter was anxious to take Ned Fritz to Rancho del Cielo and suggested a trip as soon as Ned could work it into a busy schedule, which turned out to be sooner than I had anticipated. Consequently, I made hurried preparations and drove to Brownsville on March 6. We cleared Matamoros customs by 6 A.M. on March 7, a Friday, and were at the ranch by 6 P.M.

It was a long weekend but seemed a short time for introducing Ned Fritz to the cloud forest; however, the weather was cooperative and we made the most of the opportunity. We climbed North Hill and South Hill, walked the short trail for some distance, and approached San Pablo—and talked a great deal.

Ned later wrote eloquently of his experience in the January-March 1969 issue of the *Bulletin of the Texas Ornithological Society*. It was apparent that he had absorbed a vast amount of information by observation and conversation and had a solid understanding of the situation on the mountain. Unfortunately, oral transmission can lead to distortion of facts if not clearly presented and if recalled imperfectly, so it is not surprising that some inaccuracies occurred in Ned's report, as well as in a letter he wrote to Enrique Beltrán, dated March 12:

> I have just returned from an inspection of the cloud forest above Gomez Farias. The forest is still in excellent condition except where the agrarians are illegally moving in and clearing areas for habitation. Attached hereto is a list of birds we saw in two days.
>
> Enclosed also is a copy of a Project Proposal which I shall appreciate your approving as a project of your Institute. You will note that the area is stated as 2,500 acres. 1,700 or 2,000 acres would furnish a sufficient sample of the ecosystem. I enclose a Xerox drawing indicating the area in question, the location of agrarian clearings, and the location of the 62 acres, called Rancho del Cielo, used as a biological station by Texas Southmost College. . . .
>
> The main problem is getting rid of the squatters. . . . Squatters are constantly coming into the forest from the region of Guanajuato and Michoacan and are clear-cutting and burning the trees on a line heading northward through the cloud forest. There may be fifty living in the colony by now. They rove the forest, walking a couple of miles to a water-hole and killing birds and animals. . . . It is speculated that some outside political force, possibly opposed to the government, is supporting this colonization. I am advised that the squatters have not applied for recognition as an *ejido*.
>
> . . . I suggest that if the Institute receives the surrounding land, it enter into an agreement to permit Southmost Texas College to conduct biological studies on Institute land and that the Institute may use the facilities on Southmost's 62 acres at certain times.
>
> If the Institute is interested in this project, would you be good enough to contact Arturo Arguello and ascertain what price he would sell the property for. If he will sell it, contributions will be sought by a Texas project committee in the name of World Wildlife Fund if World Wildlife also approves.

We do not intend to launch any fund-raising drive unless your Institute indicates a willingness to receive a sufficient donation of monies to purchase the area, and to attempt to have the agrarians removed by the government.

We examined Ned's "Natural Area Project Proposal."

"Ned doesn't fool around," I mused. "It's like setting a match to gasoline."

"You, on the other hand, think things out a long time before you do anything," Marie observed. "Or else you go off like a firecracker."

I pointed to page 1 of the proposal. "Arturo Arguello lumber and sawmill operator Mexico City. Now ill in a sanatario."

"You knew that."

I didn't remember. "I like this, under Description of Area: northernmost cloud forest in Mexico, including areas never disturbed by man."

"Northernmost *tropical* cloud forest"—Marie insists on correctness in describing the forest—"and we don't know what the Indians might have done way back then."

"Under Special Problems," I continued, "A group of *tough* agrarians, clearing 200 acres per year and taking over illegally. I shouldn't have let you stay up there with Mabel."

"Hah!"

I knew what "Hah!" meant. I turned to the last page. "Availability of local people: for project committee he lists John Hunter, Bob Deshayes, and Fred Webster."

"Are you sure? He wrote 'Fred Webster' between 'availability' and 'fund raising'; it could mean either."

"It's only a proposal." The gravity of the matter was beginning to get my attention.

John Hunter's letter of March 14 contributed to a sense of gathering momentum. I was beginning to feel like an onlooker, which was not all bad.

The day that Ned Fritz and I left Brownsville, two of Arguello's men visited John. They sought help in raising 50,000 pesos, the agrarians' price to get off the land. John would have nothing to do with what he considered a bribe.

"We wound up paying a thousand dollars for lumber," John wrote, ". . . and they are going to use the money along with some other they hope to raise to get the Agrarians off the place; and they hope to have them gone by April 1st. The Agrarians have now filed a formal application, and the Arguello people say the only way that they can get rid of them is to pay them off so that they will leave voluntarily."

John attached a crude map of the Arguello land, which the men had drawn for him.

> If we bought a strip 2 kilometers square using the north line of the Ejido Alta Cima as the south line of our property and the tract (Arguello) line as the east line, we would have approximately 400 more hectares and control the land from the east line of Arguello's property from the Malacates to the Aguacates corner and extending west almost to the cave road. . . .
>
> I know there is no chance of buying any land from the Ejido Alta Cima. . . . If we buy other land, we ought to buy it east of the Arguello land; and, as yet, I do not know who owns this land. They tell me that this line is approximately 250 meters east of our east line. The place where the east line of their property crosses the Encino to Julilo road is the corner we used to call Rudolph's corner. You remember it had an old fence and a small spring there.

I was a guest of the college on a trip the first week in April, the Easter outing. John Hunter and party were present also. Although it had been less than three weeks since I had been on the mountain with Ned Fritz, I was eager to check on the situation firsthand again.

We went up the mountain the long way, El Encino to Julilo. I was looking for evidence of logging or other disturbances. As to the former, we were nearly to Julilo before some logging signs appeared. Julilo is higher than Rancho del Cielo, in transition between cloud forest and humid pine-oak forest, but I could not tell what species had been logged. Julilo itself was a surprise. The sawmill and the store had been dismantled, but several houses were still occupied. The Morenos, of course, had moved out. As usual, little activity was evident. A herd of goats eyed us suspiciously. Someone had planted corn behind a high fence of posts and boards, presumably excluding the animals. As always, Julilo projected an idyllic life style, simple and informal, a scene rimmed by forest and topped by clear, cool sky.

The ride between Julilo and the ranch was uneventful. We encountered two cows but no humans. Two trees fallen across the road provided the only diversion.

Participating in the college program left little time to dwell on other matters. We did walk to San Pablo. The east exit (or entry) to the area was blocked by fallen trees. The framework for a house (shack) stood to one side. A rock house had been built on the slope by Paul's Field; this was occupied. The man living at the ranch road junction was planting corn. He would poke a stick into the ground and a boy would drop a kernel or so in the hole. (Sometimes bean or squash seed are added.)

One day Humberto Manjares, head man at La Perra, appeared on the campus. Quoting from a letter I wrote to Ned Fritz: "He indicated sympathy on his part and the boss's part for a preserve. He said that the ringleader of the agrarians had been paid off and had left the area, leaving his followers holding the bag. Sr. Manjares said that although the agrarians had applied for an *ejido*, the lumber people had taken steps to have the application applied to an area in the lowlands which is more suitable for cultivation. We were assured that the agrarians would be gone in a few days."

A letter to John from Goodrich in Mexico City, dated April 16, again shifted the focus of attention. Goodrich had verified that it was possible for an individual or an organization (such as Rancho del Cielo, A.C.) to own up to 800 hectares in the cloud forest. A permit from the Ministry of Foreign Relations would be necessary to acquire the property, and the governor of the state of Tamaulipas would have to approve the application.

"Naturally," Goodrich wrote, "we cannot pass on the validity of the present owner's title nor whether the property has been affected by agrarian demands which sometimes lie in the files for years without being published."

In order to start the "investigation," it would be necessary to have the deeds by which the present owner acquired the property, copies of tax receipts, and "whatever information you can get from the local Forestry office as to its supervisory order in connection with the property."

Ned Fritz continued to correspond with Enrique Beltrán. In a letter dated May 27, Ned wrote, "It was good to receive your letter of May 21, and to learn that your board responded well to the idea of preserving the Gomez Farias cloud forest." He encouraged the institute to "move forward on the project."

I received a carbon copy of the letter; it was the last communication I was to receive regarding the above matter, and we have no explanation for what seems to be a cessation of negotiations with Enrique Beltrán.

Marie was a guest of the college on a trip in late August and early September 1969. I received a letter with this statement: "By the way, Pancho says that Arguello owns only the lumber rights up here, not the land."

23

OR Texas Southmost College personnel, the forest surrounding Rancho del Cielo was a living laboratory. Scientists had been there, had investigated much of the region, but much territory remained to be explored, for the forest held many secrets. The entire Sierra de Guatemala, in fact, contained isolated biotic communities that, because of inaccessibility, remained untouched even by the loggers. The local people, who had lived in scattered settlements for generations, probably had explored even the remote places, but their interest was in hunting game or collecting such marketable items as palm fronds.

Early scientific expeditions were for the purpose of collecting and cataloging plant and animal forms, in order to describe the biota of the region. As a consequence, the ecology was defined and the various vegetative zones characterized. Paul Martin's published work, referred to previously, was particularly informative. While providing a panoramic survey of the geology, climate, and vegetation of the region, Martin focused on reptile and amphibian populations. As in instances of plant, bird, and mammal investigations, Martin's work revealed unexpected occurrences and extended the range of certain species. A notable discovery was that of the lungless salamander *Pseudoeurycea belli,* not previously known to occur north of Xilitla, San Luis Potosí. One of five salamander species in the region (and the least common), it is usually found under wet logs. (The species was identified by Charles F. Walker of the University of Michigan from specimens collected by Martin et al. in 1948.)

The work of the forerunners laid a base for further investigation. It was still possible to find species not previously known to the scientific community; for example, a giant slug was found on a college field trip to the upland forests and was named in honor of Barbara Warburton. Other revelations were not of newly discovered species but of the presence of species not hitherto known to occur in the Gómez Farías region, or even in northeastern Mexico. "Mrs. Warburton was very surprised to find *Selaginella pilifera,*" Marie recollected. "She had to order selaginella for the lab in Brownsville, and here it was growing wild on the mountain."

Students were encouraged to pursue graduate research on the mountain. Larry Lof, who much later would become director of the ranch project, suc-

Ornate Hawk-Eagle

ceeding Barbara Warburton, did a study of the ferns—more than 60 different species.

Alfred Richardson, who left a working career to attend Texas Southmost College and eventually earn a doctorate from the University of Texas at Austin, did his work for a master's degree on *Louteridium,* a woody plant genus of the family Acanthaceae, which is peculiar to the New World tropics. The plants in question were growing in rocky terrain in the tropical semi-evergreen forest, just below the cloud forest, a northernmost outpost for the genus.

Alfred was introduced to the mountain by John Hunter and Frank Harrison in 1962. Inspired by their love of nature and the lure of the forest, he turned to botany for a career. Barbara Warburton, his teacher at Texas Southmost, further encouraged him and offered the facilities of the ranch in the pursuit of his project. Our friend Marshall Johnston, by then firmly established in the University of Texas botany department in Austin, assisted Alfred. Both Alfred and Marie collected plant specimens for Marshall and the U.T. herbarium, a major contribution to knowledge of the flora of the region.

To increase the opportunities for scientific study, plans moved ahead for the development of the biological field station. One addition to the campus complex was sorely needed; a cook house and two dormitory cabins were in place, but there was no classroom as such. Although Warburton had acquired a half interest in the Keller cabin, that option was not viable on an ongoing basis.

The college pila having been completed in early 1969, efforts turned to building a structure that could be used as a lecture hall, laboratory, and library, as well as a repository for the various specimens collected in the name of science. A site was selected on the east side of the college clearing at the base of Sam Hill, about midway between the cook house and the Keller cabin. The forest was close by on the east, and the building would face west toward semiopen space. A slope and tree barrier concealed Frank Harrison's place. Tall oak and sweetgum shaded the site.

Barbara Warburton left Brownsville on August 23, 1969, with college employee Bud Crain and a work crew. The cabin would require a week to build, according to Bud. Also on the expedition were some students (including Larry Lof) and a special guest, Marie. Marie recorded in her trip notes for August 24, "The girls cooked and cleaned, and the men put in the floor and frame for one side of the new classroom." The rock foundation had been laid previously. It was this groundwork that Ned Fritz had noticed on his trip to the ranch and which he later referred to as the site of the future "auditorium," an extravagant term for a modest undertaking, one that did not sit well with the college people.

Work was not destined to go smoothly. The lumber purchased from Manjares had not been delivered. This necessitated a trip to Ciudad Victoria to negotiate with Sonny McCollum. Barbara Warburton and Alfredo Muñoz, a student, returned to the ranch at 10:30 P.M., one step ahead of a thunderstorm. The following morning, Alfredo, Larry Lof, and student Juan Pérez set out for Ciudad Victoria, returning in the evening with a load of lumber.

Marie wrote on August 29, "Classroom has been largely finished on the outside. Steps were put up after Bud's fall [possible broken arm] and shutters are being fitted." On September 5, "Larry had finished bookshelves in the new cabin—Harrison Hall."

Harrison Hall was a one-room rectangular building except for a small bedroom and bath at the south end. A narrow back porch and storage area was added some months later. In April 1970, Bob Deshayes fashioned and built, with the aid of Pablo's helper Roberto, a concrete front porch and steps.

Inside, the main room was simply furnished with tables, cabinets, blackboards, an assortment of chairs, and a sink; unfortunately, the sink had no drain. Shelves held preserved specimens such as snakes, vinegarroons, and spiders and a small collection of books and periodicals. Books were prone to mildew, hence few were accumulated.

The big room had several features that made it a popular place for lectures and informal gatherings. Glass windows from old Fort Brown, plus a skylight, provided a light, airy atmosphere. In time, padded benches were built against the walls in the northwest corner, perfect for lounging, and a pot-bellied, wood-burning stove provided a homey touch on winter days.

As the student program for Rancho del Cielo took shape in the late 1960s, Barbara Warburton graciously offered us guest status on student trips. After a while we were spending more time with the college crew than with John Hunter, although we were always welcome at his cabin. Circumstances prevented Marie and me from making trips together on most occasions; as a result, Marie logged more time and shared more adventures with the college.

As guests, we were free to pursue our birding interests, which we shared with the students when their schedule permitted. Marie was particularly helpful when Texas Southmost hosted Pan-American University's Brownsville branch for the field portion of a graduate study program. When not leading bands of wide-eyed lowland Texans through the forest, Marie might be found in the college kitchen making pies from fruit gathered in the orchard.

For us, the major lure of a sojourn with the college people was an opportunity to investigate areas beyond the confines of the cloud forest. Barbara Warburton had an insatiable drive to explore the mountain range, an exercise for the sake of discovery (historical as well as scientific) with the added benefit of keeping track of logging operations.

Had the lumber people not come, it seems unlikely that a road passable by vehicle would have been chiseled out of the mountain, much less a network of logging roads. These roads were maintained as long as timber was available and sawmills were to be supplied. Spurs disappeared under second growth when operations shifted locations, but the few main roads remained open and were used to access remote communities such as La Joya de Salas.

Road conditions rarely discouraged Barbara and her student drivers. A tree down across the right-of-way quickly succumbed to ax and crosscut saw or power saw. Mud holes and rocky roadbeds were routine, hardly a challenge for the all-terrain vehicles. If tires could not maintain traction on wet slopes, the winch was used, truck to truck or truck to tree.

Over the years, Barbara led her charges to probably every locality accessible by vehicle in the central portion of the range. Crucial junctions along the way were marked by yellow paint on roadside tree trunks. If a new logging road appeared, runners were sent ahead to scout the terrain. No matter who might have legal claim to the land, the mountain was the college's living laboratory.

A most intriguing destination was the lost mission, said to have been established by the Spanish somewhere on the mountain in time long past. According to Félix Burgos, there had been a ranch, then a mission, then a road built using the sandstone of the mission. But how to find such a site, assuming that a mission actually had existed? Over the years many a party had looked; none seem to have been satisfied with the results, although Burgos thought he knew the location, and Frank Harrison speculated that he had stumbled upon it once while searching for a cow. Marie was with the college group when they attempted to find the site as described by Burgos.

"There was what appeared to be a stone wall running up- and downhill, but why would they have a wall running up- and downhill? And there was no level place for a mission or anything. And you never are sure these rock formations aren't natural."

The mountain can deceive the most practiced eye. It can hide its wonders from all but the most curious seeker. One July day, Marie wrote, "We went on a field trip up the Mine road to La Perra [El Porvenir] and west toward the cave—but we took the wrong fork in the road and stopped for lunch at a place that looked like water washes through. We looked around and I found a cave hole about 18 inches wide—red mud and rocks [at the entrance] and a bend about six feet below the surface."

The cave would have remained undetected had not a cold breeze emanating from the hole fanned the surrounding vegetation. "You could hear a rushing stream under there," Marie explained to me with a sense of wonder. "It must have been a tremendous cavern."

The mountain is riddled with caves, a subterranean maze the extent of which may never be known. The underground manifests itself in surprising ways. One day a bit of surface land is flat, supporting trees and rocks; pass by a day later and the earth's crust may have given way to open up yet another gaping sinkhole. Collapsing earth, falling trees, and new vegetative growth combine to erase familiar landmarks. Treasured places discovered once may never be found again.

A most ambitious expedition was a truck tour fondly called the across-the-mountain trip, which traversed several favorite highland localities. Each trip was a new adventure with new surprises and discoveries, pleasant or otherwise. An early start was imperative, perhaps while fog still hindered first light, or when the sun sent tentative shafts through the forest canopy on Sam Hill. In any direction from the ranch, the trucks bounced through a narrow corridor, brushing dew-draped branches that sent a shower over those riding in the back of the trucks.

If the trip was to proceed from south to north across the range, we headed south first, toward the Aguacates. By the time we reached Frank Harrison's red gate, we were thoroughly jostled and resigned to a day of more of the same. Then it was down the Aguacates grade, hands firmly gripping whatever appeared stable, feet pushing imaginary brakes, that is, if you hadn't made the trip before.

"It's much more stabilizing to brace your feet and sit there like a sack of potatoes," Marie advised. "You're much less likely to strain something or hit other passengers."

If you choose to stand up, watch for low tree branches.

The trip seemed really to begin at the Aguacates junction, for here we turned right, away from Gómez Farías, and headed uphill to Alta Cima. History, too, began at the Aguacates, for here it was that Murdock Cameron first settled with his family. The steep slopes here were difficult to cultivate, and it is said, by the end of the dry season the Camerons were forced to haul water from the spring at Gómez Farías. Cameron had received a considerable grant from the government (ten kilometers by ten kilometers of mountain land, including the valley called Alta Cima), provided he would settle and develop the land. The family soon moved to Alta Cima. It must have been a major undertaking in those days, but for us it was a short ride up to the head of the narrowing canyon, from tropical mountainside forest to the edge of cloud forest.

Alta Cima is no longer forested. The immigrant Camerons felled the first trees in cutting out a homestead, and the current ejido finished transforming the woodland to cropland and orchard. The original clearing encompassed about 100 hectares. It was called Glen Urquhart Farm in tribute to Cameron's Scottish roots.

Cameron was not satisfied with mediocrity; the house he built was a glorified cabin, and certainly the wonder and envy of anyone who happened to see it. It measured 20 by 40 feet, was two stories, and boasted dormer windows. The logs came from the surrounding forest, and hand-hewn shakes covered the roof.

Barbara had been invited to a reunion of Cameron descendants, held in Hidalgo County, Texas, at which time she learned much Cameron lore from the old-timers, stories she readily shared. She recalled seeing an old photograph that showed the house and the people standing in front: men, both old and young, with bushy beards, wearing long frock coats and bowler hats; top-knotted women in black ground-length dresses. Hired hands were present too, dressed in white, wearing sombreros with tall, thin crowns.

Life at Alta Cima was more than a photograph frozen in a moment of time. Hard labor translated massive stone into fences or walls enclosing the property. A stone cistern was erected beside the house to catch rainwater. Corn, beans, and fruit trees were cultivated. Mrs. Cameron "saw to the fruit trees," according to Dr. Cameron's two sons, who were quite elderly at the time Barbara interviewed them. "Mama arranged for them to be sent from California by rail. They crossed at Eagle Pass [Texas] and came down to Victoria. We picked them up and brought them down here." Fruit of the harvest was carried by mule down to Gómez Farías to barter for supplies. Cattle, also, were driven down the trail to be sold.

The most ambitious undertaking by the early Camerons, it would seem, involved harvesting the black walnut trees from the forest. They were cut and shaped by ax and crosscut saw, then carried down the mountain by mule. Big white mules made up the mule train, according to Barbara's informants. "They hauled those logs to the east, to Xicoténcatl, where they were put on the train and shipped to Tampico, and then to Europe [probably France] for fine furniture-making."

The walnut trade was one means by which the family was able to survive during the early years. Cameron was practicing medicine among the local people, but it was not financially rewarding.

Barbara particularly delighted in relating certain incidents told to her by the old men. "While they were telling me all those things, I saw one look at the other with a twinkle in his eyes, and then they told me this little tale." Her own eyes invariably twinkled at this point.

Seems they had been here [Alta Cima] awhile and the maternal grandmother decided to pay them a visit and came from Canada. And while here she found Dr. Cameron's Protestant Bible, and being a good Catholic, she burned it. And after they told that they just broke into laughter.

And Dr. Cameron called the boys together; the girls didn't count, you understand. He called the boys together and explained that Grandmother did what she thought was right concerning the Protestant Bible. One of the men nudged the other. "Do you remember that Papa put her on the next train back to Canada?"

Another much retold tale concerned Virginia Cameron. "Virginia must have been quite popular in Tampico and had many suitors," Barbara related.

After she came to the mountain, they [her two brothers] were telling about a suitor of hers who rode all the way from Tampico to see her. He got up in the mountains, and as he came up to the house, there was Virginia sitting outside — and not spick-and-span dressy dress — but she was churning, and she was barefooted, and some little piglets were running around the yard. And he was such a dandy that when he saw her like that he just turned around and rode back out. And the men just howled about that; they thought it was the funniest thing that he would ride all that way, then just because she was in the wilds of Mexico, not dressed up as he was accustomed to seeing her in Tampico, that he couldn't take it and left.

By 1912 several of the Cameron children had married and established homesteads within the 7,000 hectares claimed by the family. Virginia Cameron married a McPherson and settled down at what was to be Rancho del Cielo. It is further said that several families from the American colony at Chamal moved into the mountains, settling in the vicinity of Alta Cima and on the ridges above.

In 1910 the colonists at Chamal received news of an armed uprising. There was no immediate impact on the colony, and peace and prosperity continued until Victoriano Huerta forced the resignation of President Francisco Madero and Vice President Suárez on February 19, 1913; three days later both men were assassinated while in military custody.

The Americans remained neutral, yet there was some trouble with both the military and the civilian population, and the settlers were getting nervous. In August the American consul in Tampico advised that women and children be sent to Tampico and the shelter of American battleships there. Those so wishing would be sent to the United States. Some members of the Cameron family went to the lower Rio Grande Valley of Texas, where their descendants live to this day.

Before vacating Alta Cima in 1914, the Camerons arranged for safekeeping of such guns and ammunition as they were unable to carry with them. "They dug a big hole in the mule lot," Barbara stated, "and they buried their guns and drove their mules around and around and around" over the spot to conceal the guns. The Camerons did not return to the mountain but pursued the matter of the land grant, which was not "straightened out" until the 1930s.

By 1915 colonists were returning to Chamal to try to pick up the pieces of their shattered lives, and apparently they were succeeding quite well until the next crisis in the spring of 1916. More on that later.

Alta Cima comes as a surprise. The traveler bounces or trudges up the canyon to emerge suddenly on level terrain. It takes a moment to adjust.

My first impression was of a corn field looking more like a cemetery, green stalks protruding between sunbaked limestone boulders, all stretching away to the tree line. A low boulder-strewn hill loomed over the scene like a mausoleum succumbing to the ravages of time and the elements.

Near the canyon head, in a plot shaded by trees and carpeted by shrubs and weeds, was the old Cameron homestead. The house was burned in a forest fire in the 1920s. Only the pila remains to commemorate the site.

A red clay road meanders through the valley. Farther back, the land is more arable. Corn is the main crop, but fruit trees seem to do well. Nowadays the residents comprise an ejido; they live in small farmhouses scattered about as on an afterthought. A new schoolhouse is, no doubt, the pride of the community.

Peaks, rising to perhaps 5,000 feet, enclose the valley. (Alta Cima is at about 2,800 feet elevation.) At a distance, these peaks and ridges give a deceptively soft, rounded appearance, their rocky surface concealed by vegetation. The forest, in fact, reaches to the very level of the valley and would reclaim the land in time.

The Camerons must have labored long to push back the woodland, and the forest denizens constantly reminded them that they were interlopers. Spider monkeys lurked on the forest edge to raid Cameron crops. Black bears might dine on crops and domestic animals, and the night-marauding jaguars were the terror of livestock. Today the forest may encroach on neglected land, but it does so alone, for its avenging agents are no longer a factor. Monkeys disappeared from the region early in the century, and the large mammals now compose but a token population.

As the canyon we have left splits the otherwise continuous eastern rampart of the sierra, so does the continuum of the second ridge (known from Rancho del Cielo as West Ridge) break down in the Alta Cima area, presenting several lesser peaks and valleys. On our trips across the mountain, the road took us from Alta Cima westward on a series of steep grades.

Barbara Warburton usually called a halt at two overlooks for the benefit of the students, if not the trucks. Only a portion of Alta Cima was visible, in season an incredibly flat patch of green earth hemmed in by forested slopes. Looking east, we could locate the canyon by the almost perpendicular cliff that dominated the south side. Beyond the canyon mouth the Sierra Chiquita stood out against a lowland backstage; this isolated sierra appeared completely wooded, while the well-populated Gómez Farías hogback, much lower in elevation, hid to the right. The vista invariably was presented under multiple layers of cloud disintegrating under the impact of the sun. To the north, Barbara pointed out North Hill and South Hill at Rancho del Cielo, and the Rock Pile, the vertical outcrop at the base of West Ridge.

The road climbed to nearly 5,000 feet before leveling off (a relative term). We could feel the atmospheric difference; the depressing humidity became a bad memory, the air as pure as on the first day of Creation, or thereabouts. The breeze was cool and smelled of pine. Technically speaking, we were still in cloud forest, although at the uppermost level, where conifers indicate the transition to pine-oak forest. This area is referred to as the beech zone (good fodder for wordplay among our coastal students), as that species of tree is present in good numbers.

The road branched. To continue a simplified across-the-mountain trip, we would veer right and proceed northward to Casa Piedras; however, a diversion to San José to the left (south) was a temptation seldom ignored. In this event, Rancho Viejo was the first point of interest; the farm dated back to the Cameron era and later became the ranch of Félix Burgos. The ranch resembled parkland, if a corn field can be worked into the mix. The field was backed by a grove of pines sheltering a modest dwelling. A sheer cliff face stood guard over this pastoral Eden.

A short distance beyond Rancho Viejo a waterfall tumbled over a series of rocky outcrops toward the road, filling pools along the way, one an estimated 70 feet deep. The local people had directed springwater to a roadside holding pond by means of an aqueduct, a series of small hollowed-out logs. The last link in the system was suspended over the drip area by a horizontal pole. As for the waterfall, the flow crossed the roadway and vanished into a rocky bed, to supply some subterranean channel.

San José lies just beyond the waterfall, in another valley sheltering an old settlement — a few houses here and there, the usual small, unpainted frame buildings with sharply slanted roofs of shingles, tin, or even thatch. An assortment of barriers and enclosures made of poles or upright planks failed to restrain cattle, goats, pigs, and fowl, but what caught the eye was a two-story structure, situated on a hillside, that overlooked the entire community.

Stacks of fresh-cut lumber suggested the principal occupation of the villagers. San José had been the site of a sawmill in years past, attested to by the presence of a tiny, rusting steam engine, now vine-clothed, and a derelict lumber truck.

To all appearances the populace at San José was satisfied with its lot, but we wondered if someday they would be roused from their sedentary life style. College personnel had happened upon a color brochure produced by some entrepreneur, which depicted San José as a vacation resort with hotel, chalets, golf course—all the amenities—and accessible by highway and air. After many years, the resort has failed to materialize, and the two-story building would not qualify as a hotel.

Our mountain tours usually turned back north after visiting San José. Were we to continue through San José, we would follow the road westward to La Gloria, then southwestward to El Elefante and Refugio, and finally to the town of Ocampo at the southern terminus of the Sierra de Guatemala.

We were curious about the southern portion of the mountain range, to which the road described above offered the only vehicular access. John Hunter had longed to take that route to Ocampo, but Frank Harrison had dissuaded him; it was dangerous, if not impassable. Later, the college people drove as far as El Elefante. Beyond that point the road appeared to have been abandoned, but that was precisely the challenge that drove Barbara Warburton to every reachable site on the mountain. On one memorable occasion she decreed that a college group take two trucks and explore south of El Elefante. Marie recorded the event in her trip journal.

The man at San José (when we stopped to ask about the road) was having trouble with his diesel engine and asked us to bring him some parts for it. We proceeded to La Gloria and El Elefante, where we gathered Keifer pears and Hawthorne apples which we took home to the ranch for cobbler and such. We spent some time at El Elefante (named after a free-standing rock formation slightly resembling an elephant). We ate lunch there, then proceeded.

The road had not been used in some time and was overgrown—

a few trees down, mostly small, although one about two and a half foot in diameter was broken off about the height of the truck and lay across the road. So we made a road around the base side and proceeded. The road went along a ledge overlooking a beautiful canyon facing west, with a blue-shaded mountain ridge in the background.

All of a sudden Alfredo had the right front wheel off the road. We all piled out and they winched the truck out.

While this was taking place, Marie walked back a short distance and was surprised to see a jagged fissure, about six feet in length and a foot wide at most, in the roadway. Below, through the crack, sunlight shone on the cliff side. Marie continued:

> Then we came across a mud puddle and Alfredo got stuck. We descended on a recent lumber road and went through miles of cloud forest. There were purple achimenes and a new one with yellow throat and red lip.
>
> We came up to a cross road and went to the right. We came into a beautiful valley where there was a small village named Refugio. When we got to the most prosperous-looking home a heavy-set man came out and asked for a ride to Ocampo [20 kilometers distant], and said he had a couple of sacks of beans he wanted to take. Another man came out on the porch and helped him get each sack on his back.

They were large sacks and must have been quite heavy.

The bean crop was a community effort; the people had been waiting two or three weeks to get them to market because trucks were unable to get through to the village. The reason would soon be obvious.

> We proceeded down through beautiful canyons and deciduous forest, and close to the bottom, fields of sesame and sugar cane. The second truck had a flat and while it was being fixed we ate our peanut butter and jelly sandwiches and watched the moon rise over the mountain.
>
> We continued on the wet road through a small settlement with electricity, and on until we came upon two lumber trucks stuck up to the axles in mud. We all got out and Alfredo revved up the motor and flew down the fence line way past the trucks, slipping, sliding and banging away.
>
> Just dark. We slogged through the mud and hoisted our 10-ton

feet into the truck and started off—only to get stuck again. Everybody out. We threw rocks under the wheels and the boys pushed the truck out again.

We arrived at Ocampo about 10 P.M., left the bean man at the buyer's, and went around the square and stopped for a Pepsi. Now we were on pavement. We whizzed on through a canyon to the main highway, on to Gómez Farías, and up to the ranch by 1 A.M. The girls fed us a spaghetti supper and we collapsed.

24

EADING north out of San José, the traditional across-the-mountain trip took us through a pass into another valley ringed by peaks, Casa Piedras. A bare cliff smeared with orange-colored green algae stood at the entrance, a feature Barbara Warburton never failed to point out.

Our vehicle progressed but a short distance into Casa Piedras when we encountered a split-log bridge laid lengthwise across a watercourse where red clay banks bore the scars of erosion. The bridge was scarcely wide enough for the college truck to cross, and a student would walk ahead to guide the driver. Once across the bridge, the crew could enjoy the setting.

Casa Piedras is a mystical place. At about 4,000 feet elevation, and removed from the polluting effects of lowland activities, the air is clean and fresh. Nights in summer are cool, and by noon, when the sun has warmed the earth, mist curtains drop on the cliffs and peaks and work teasingly down to the valley floor; soon all is enveloped in a gray chill.

Old photographs of Casa Piedras show a heavy pine-oak forest, but now the woodland is restricted mainly to borders and slopes. The valley was once a Cameron ranch. On our first visit we saw a few small buildings and other signs of recent habitation. Some years later the structures were gone, the valley deserted, except for a few cows that seemed unconcerned by our intrusion. When we talked with a man who had lived there with his family, and asked why they left, he said, "It is a beautiful place to live, but very difficult to make a living."

The main attraction at Casa Piedras is the waterfall. It originates somewhere high above the valley and tumbles over a maze of boulders and fern-clad rock faces. After a short run into the valley, the stream drops out of sight, but not before leaving pristine pools to tempt the traveler.

Texas Southmost students could not resist climbing up alongside the falls as high as they were able, inspecting the plant life, looking for amphibians, and finally descending to enjoy a long-awaited lunch. Barbara liked to experiment with the menu. A big pot of soup heated over a fire seemed just the right thing for a winter day, but heating a full pot at this altitude was prohibitively time-consuming. Hamburger patties, charcoal-broiled, were

Bumblebee Hummingbird

more practical. (Nowadays, lunch would consist of the ingredients for a custom-made sandwich.)

Casa Piedras was a great place to relax, but we knew that the way north out of the valley could be a driver's nightmare. The road left flat land abruptly and climbed steeply, and its condition varied according to the amount of recent rainfall and the frequency of use. Circumstances permitting, our tour proceeded northward through several miles of pine-oak highland. Eventually we reached La Perra and swung eastward to Julilo, then south to Rancho del Cielo.

Had we been pressed for time, we need not have gone as far as La Perra and Julilo. Four miles out of Casa Piedras, a turn to the right would have taken us down a steep slope to Barbara's Patch, where our leader (while picking dewberries) had her first encounter with poison ivy. This fairly flat basin had been in cultivation from time to time but was partly overgrown now, providing habitat for Brown-throated Wrens, Rufous-capped Warblers, Bumblebee Hummingbirds, and such. A fir attracted the attention of visitors, who expected to find fir species in a more boreal forest and at greater altitudes.

Just beyond the rock-walled confines of Barbara's Patch we burst upon a grand vista. We were on West Ridge looking eastward, the cloud forest spread out below, and Rancho del Cielo a tiny island in a sea of undulating green. Beyond, the easternmost portion of the Sabinas Valley was visible, beyond which scattered mesas bulged from coastal lowlands. About 90 miles distant, surf washed on sand; on a really clear day (which was unlikely) we could fantasize the Gulf of Mexico, but it would only be cloud sculpting the far horizon.

Our road clung to the ledge as it dipped toward the old mine site. Only long-abandoned shafts to show now; the workers' shacks were gone, of course. High-quality barium is embedded in calcite strata, but not in sufficient mass to justify mining. When Ernest McCollum took over logging in the area, a worker told him about the mine and presented samples of ore. It is said that McCollum invested $7,000 to $8,000 in mining equipment but never went up to the mine. After his death, Sonny McCollum brought out some ore but received only $12.50 per ton for it.

Nearby, an ordinary-looking hole at roadside, partly hidden by brush, gave access to the beautiful Mine Cave. Once a favorite destination of the students, it was passed reluctantly now; the entrance had become too treacherous for a descent. The cavern had returned to the silent workings of the ages, its colorful and varied formations secure in their underworld, its chambers inhabited only by creatures that never know the light of day.

From the mine, a steady descent took us to the Julilo–San Pablo road, and thence to Rancho del Cielo.

Before turning off to Barbara's Patch (and time permitting) our tour could have taken a turn westward to visit perhaps the mountain's most delightful spot, Agua Linda. Here is another basin rimmed by peaks, but more confined than others, nurturing a unique intimacy. Agua Linda ("lovely water"), isolated, self-fulfilling, could be aeons apart from human contact. In essence, Agua Linda is wind's gentle touch on pine bough, water whispering secrets along mossy banks, symphony of birdsong in stereo, thunder bouncing cliff to cliff.

This is a place of delight for the birder. A rivulet snakes down a rocky slope, carves a path through needle-carpeted flats. Hummingbirds bathe in tiny waterfalls, and the understory is home to the only colony of Russet Nightingale-Thrushes that we have found on the mountain. We have come to expect the unexpected at Agua Linda; indeed, we have spotted the Black Robin and the Slate-throated Redstart here, both uncommon in this range.

In Frank Harrison's time, this high mountain valley was the property of Everts Storms, purchased from the Cameron estate. Perhaps it had an even earlier post-Indian history, for some contend that Agua Linda is none other than Lonesome Cove, the mountain hideaway of the Chamal people during revolutionary days. The story has become legend.

About mid-May 1916, persecuted by the military and threatened by outlaw bands, the first of many families abandoned their homes in the Chamal Valley and made their way northward across the mountain with pack mules and whatever goods they could carry. The migration continued for three or four weeks, until an estimated 80 persons had taken refuge in Lonesome Cove. There they lived in makeshift houses of some sort. There was enough food to sustain them and abundant water, cold and pure. Wild game was plentiful, although orders were to fire only at tiger, lion, or deer, saving ammunition for defense of the camp, should that become necessary. But no attack was made, and when the rainy season was over, the people made their way to the railroad, thence to the border.

The question remains, is Agua Linda also Lonesome Cove? The latter was reportedly 20 miles from Chamal, and assuming that the primitive trail meandered somewhat, Agua Linda might well have been the destination of the refugees. The reported altitude of Lonesome Cove was 7,500 feet, which exceeds the 6,000-foot reading of the college altimeter at Agua Linda; however, it is doubtful that any valley floor in the range would reach 7,000 feet. The site does meet the criteria of isolation and difficulty of access, with the two trails into the valley easily guarded.

Probably no Texas Southmost student and few faculty members are aware that there was a place called Lonesome Cove, but we have all sensed that Agua Linda is a special place. We leave it with a feeling that something has been given, only to be taken away.

Nowadays old lumber roads, overgrown or otherwise, allow us to reach Agua Linda and other destinations on the mountain. So we scarcely can imagine the hardships the Chamal people endured to reach their safe haven. Although the college crew can expect minor setbacks (flat tires, overheated engines, downed trees), they are usually overcome in time, and the trip resumed. One attempted trip, however, set a standard for adversity. Marie recalls the episode with mixed feelings, but time has allowed good humor to prevail.

Barbara Warburton contended that after a strenuous work trip at the ranch, the students were entitled to a treat in the form of an expedition by truck to some destination of her choice. Accordingly, one August, the morning after an exhausting day of cleaning cabins and cooking, Barbara, Marie, and six students embarked in a single truck for San José.

The trip went well as far as San José, where a cavern near the settlement was explored at leisure. There was one disappointment: the group had looked forward to roasting corn for lunch, but the crop at Rancho Viejo had not progressed to roasting size, so disappointment was swallowed and lunch consumed at the water crossing.

It was too early to head back to the ranch. Barbara turned to Marie. "Would you like to go to Casa Piedras?"

Marie remembers clearly the expression on Barbara's face, the tone of her voice; it was obvious that she fully intended to go to Casa Piedras, had probably planned on it before leaving the ranch.

"I would love to."

Barbara had known Marie long enough not to be surprised by her reply. Adventure and exploration they both embraced.

Casa Piedras was beautiful, Marie remarked, and was thoroughly enjoyed, but Barbara's decision to return to the ranch by the north route proved to be ill-advised.

But first: The log bridge was crossed with extreme caution. It was showing its age; cracks between the logs had widened, and the entire structure seemed to have narrowed. Barbara and Marie stood on the far side, guiding Larry Lof. Barbara had never learned to drive and was in danger of directing the truck over the side when Marie took control, bringing vehicle and driver to a safe landing.

Prospects deteriorated after that. "The road has gone to seed past there," Marie wrote. It apparently was due to a combination of summer rainfall and cessation of truck traffic. The steep climb out of Casa Piedras, always difficult, this time was almost impossible. Rocks had fallen across the roadway, and rushing water had gouged holes in the surface. Everyone except Larry went ahead of the truck, rolling stones away or filling holes with loose rock. At one point Marie noticed that Larry had paused, open-mouthed and wide-eyed in disbelief. From the height advantage of the truck cab, he could see a sizable boulder beyond a rise in the road.

"Larry thought he had met his match," Marie said. "It was six feet long, three feet wide, and three feet thick. We worked with sledgehammers, crowbars, and brute strength." Brute strength may have applied to Jack, whose hobby was body-building; it was hardly applicable to the girls and Mrs. Warburton. Carl, who was on the heavy side, unfortunately had not achieved his bulk by working out. Larry, six-feet-four or so and not skinny, was capable of considerable physical effort and determination.

"I don't see how you ever got it out of the road," I later remarked to Marie.

"Leverage. We moved rocks out from under the low part and wedged rocks under the high part so we could get a chain around it. Then we used the winch to slide it out of the way." It was that simple.

Once the boulder was pushed aside, rocks had to be removed and the road built up before the trip could resume. By that time the group was ready for a respite from their labors, but there was more to come.

The grade was topped, and the road leveled off (as usual, a relative term).

"Just above Indian Spring we found a large tree down across the road. Larry (who hated power saws anyway) couldn't get the power saw to work, so we made a detour around the tree." In order to do so, a smaller tree had to be cut out; it proved to be unfortunate that the stump was not cut closer to the ground.

"Then we started up the bad climb and found another large tree had fallen almost at the top of the grade. We would have had to build the road up (it was badly washed), we didn't have a saw to cut the tree, and it was getting dark fast. So we admitted we were licked and turned around." Turning around was not a simple matter. It was necessary for Larry to back the truck down to the bottom of the grade, the passengers guiding him along the winding roadway.

The retreat proceeded to the bypass created earlier to avoid the first fallen tree. This time the detour, being approached from the opposite direction, did not work as well. Marie remembers a hard jolt as the left rear wheel dropped in front of a rock about two feet high. At the same time, the fresh stump positioned itself before the protective plate at the front of the truck.

The truck was securely wedged between the two obstacles. To make matters worse, full darkness had settled in. It had started raining. Thunder rumbled and rolled, and lightning provided eerie glimpses of a forest ready to claim all intruders.

The only way out of the dilemma was to remove the stump. Being under the front of the truck, the stump was beyond reach of ax strokes. Jack had the idea of cutting the stump out with his pocket knife; he was promptly overruled. As so often happened on subsequent trips, it was Larry who was to bear the brunt of the solution. Prone on his stomach, under the truck, Larry reached out and hacked away at the stump with a machete while others illuminated the target with flashlights. The stump was about eight inches in diameter and did not succumb easily.

Finally Larry emerged from under the truck, triumphant but exhausted. "We gave him my leftover sandwich and some candy. We crawled back in the truck, cold and wet, and started forward again."

The log bridge at Casa Piedras was crossed in due course with the aid of flashlight-wielding passengers, after which all went well, until just before the San José turnoff. Topping a rise, headlights picked out a truck stalled on the grade below. Larry braked the college truck at an awkward angle, and a detachment went forward to determine the situation. The lumbermen had lost the service of their transmission, a common problem with the old trucks. The driver responded rudely to offers of help and stated that they were working to rectify the problem and would have their truck out of the way shortly.

"I'm certain he had no intention of working on the truck that night," Marie told me later. "He was unhappy when we showed up."

The negotiators trudged back uphill and, as there was no room to pass the stalled truck, the crew attempted to find comfortable positions on the slanting seats of the college vehicle. An hour and a quarter later, at 12:45 A.M., the lumbermen got their truck started. "We followed that backfiring truck all the way back to the Aguacates and got to the ranch at 3:30 A.M."

25

OPE for additional land acquisition by the college had reached a low point when John Hunter received a letter from George M. Sutton stating that he had "instructed the manager of two Research Funds in his care" to send a check to Texas Southmost College for $1,000 (each) "to be used for purchase of land contiguous to Rancho Cielo."

"This gives us $4,000," John wrote on March 11, 1970, "which is 50,000 pesos and a respectable sum to start land purchases with."

There were two problems to address: the reaction of the administration of Texas Southmost, and the availability of land. The resolution of either would take time. The remainder of 1970 passed with nothing settled. The year 1971 offered a terrible diversion.

Climatological events in spring and summer of 1970 may be viewed as a precursor to disaster. The dry season, which in the Gómez Farías region begins in late fall and intensifies during spring, exceeded its reputation in 1970 and seemed intent on extending into summer. By late May, John Hunter was calling it the worst dry spell since 1955, when drinking water was hauled up from Gómez Farías to the ranch. The big trees were shedding leaves, carpeting the road as in autumn, and the smaller plants were withering. Finally, the drought was declared broken by good rainfall on June 21, and for a while the wet season encouraged complacency.

Winter came too soon. The mountain had gulped down the rain of summer, and water that had been collected in pila and tank in time of abundance was not soon to be supplemented. Months of drought lay ahead.

We saw trouble on the horizon in late December 1970. Somewhere beyond West Ridge a smoke cloud bulged skyward, a smear of white against blue, bending to the whim of the mountain winds.

Perhaps someone was clearing land and burning, and things got out of control. Visualizing a map of the range, I tried to establish a probable location of the fire. Agua Linda came to mind, a totally unacceptable conclusion. Perhaps it burned even farther west, in montane chaparral where shrubby thickets covered dry ridge flanks, in the region of the rain shadow.

Fires had come periodically to the mountain through the millennia. Lightning was the culprit long before humankind invaded the forest on a mission to clear for crop and lumber. Before exploration, the spread of fire

Ivory-billed Woodcreeper

seemed to be minimized by a moist, canopied environment, but drying came as openings admitted sunlight and drying winds.

Smoke in the lowlands is a familiar sight. Smoke-haze often hangs over the valley of the Río Sabinas as more land is denuded for crops, and in late winter the old cane stalks are burned off in a rush of flame. But we had not witnessed a wildfire in the highlands. I tried to shrug off negative thoughts; perhaps in a few days the fire would burn itself out.

On January 1 we did the across-the-mountain trip, from Alta Cima and San José to Casa Piedras and Barbara's Patch, and down the mine road, without encountering fire—and it had rained lightly at the ranch overnight. Any encouragement we may have nurtured was quickly dispelled by a glance at West Ridge. On January 3 the fire was obviously spreading on a high southwesterly wind. At sunset, the smoke was an ugly yellow smudge defiling the western sky. I departed the ranch on January 5, not to return until late June.

"I feel that Arguello never really put out the fire on his land," Barbara Warburton wrote later, "the one we saw above us on the across-the-mountain trip in January. Fed by unusually high winds and extreme drought, it worked down the mountainside to us and also went west for miles and miles."

According to John Hunter, the fire started in December near La Joya de Salas. By mid-March it had "burned all the way from La Joya to San José to the Aguacates and up the trail as far as Julilo."

By March, fires had progressed down West Ridge into the cloud forest and were pressing against the ranch on three sides. Barbara Warburton and a group of students were at the ranch early in the month when it was apparent that only drastic action would save the property. They cut a *brecha* (firebreak) ten meters wide along the property line. "It just killed me to cut down those gorgeous oaks, maple, sweetgum and even some walnut," Barbara wrote.

Clearing a brecha up- and downhill on rocky terrain was a tremendous task, which fell to the students, Pablo and his helper, and a number of local men hired for the purpose. Not only were trees felled and brush cleared, but also the opened swath was swept as clean as possible of leaves and debris; lacking sufficient brooms, the crew used tree branches. "It seemed like we swept miles of brecha, worked from daylight to dark, and then half the night."

The local people were very much concerned about the possible loss of lives and property, Marie recalled. When the college group reached the ranch they found it occupied by the military and the forestal. They needed the college trucks and drivers to get them to the fires, so they commandeered both. After returning to the ranch the student drivers had the additional responsibility of servicing the trucks for instant use.

The rest of the college people cooked for the soldiers and the forestal as well as for themselves. At the end of the day, covered with soot and dirt from working on the brecha, they just fell into bed exhausted, only to awake before daybreak to start all over again.

One can only imagine the thoughts of the college group on the night the fire burned over North Hill, lying in bed and listening to rock cracking and agave exploding, not knowing if the fire would jump the brecha and possibly destroy the cabins.

"All of North Hill down to the college pila is burned," Barbara's letter continued. "The bird census area up to the amaryllis fields is burned, and the forest is burned on the San Pablo–Gómez Farías road. Most of the fire was grass-fire type, burning out the leaves and rotting logs."

Larry Lof described the situation thusly:

> In the cloud forest, the fire would burn steadily through the underbrush and then leap into the canopy through some of the older hollow trees. These formed chimneys that carried the flames to the top. On many a night, one could hear the whistle and roar as the flames were drawn through these natural flues. Once burning, the fire would smoulder in the stumps for weeks, slowly tracing the roots even below the ground level. On steep slopes, the fire rushed up ferociously, hot enough in places to break the limestone rocks. On the ridges west of Rancho del Cielo, where the pines begin, the fire burned quickly and in a fashion more typical of a great forest fire. At times it would leap from tree to tree in rapid succession. At night the clouds of smoke choked and obscured the air. In the distance was the constant glow of the fire. The vision was apocalyptic.

Efforts to keep the flames from ranch property at the time were successful. Now the fire worked its way down the east slope toward the Río Sabinas. During the Easter period, John Arvin observed the fire from El Cielito on the river, a short distance from Everts Storms' place at Pano Ayuctle. "From

our vantage point on the river it looked as though the flames were climbing into and above the canopy. Each morning the fires would be down to
a smoulder, I suppose from the effects of overnight humidity, but by late
afternoon they would be raging."

John Hunter reported on a trip to the mountain in late April:

> The mountain is unbelievably dry. Our spring has been dry since late
> January. Pablo is able to milk four or five gallons a week out of it with
> a tomato can. Our *pila* has 18 inches of fluid which I would judge is
> 50 percent frog urine, but it still flushes the toilets and I bathe in it.
> The college *pila* is entirely dry and practically no water in the various
> metal tanks.
>
> The oaks and lots of the broad-leaf trees have shed their leaves to
> where they are practically bare. By some way, the maple and sweet-
> gum have put out new, bright green foliage. The fire burned all of the
> undergrowth out, and you never saw so many bare rocks sticking up
> in your life. I see sink-holes that I never knew were there; continuous
> ridge of rocks that I never knew existed.

Yet the fire was unrelenting. On May 6 and 7, as though to wipe out any
complacency on the part of those who had struggled to save the ranch, fire
burned from the college garage over Sam Hill and down to John's gate (all
within the area protected by the brecha), and then burned over the top of
South Hill. It was a dying gasp to a reign of terror; summer rains closed
the chapter. The forest was left to regenerate and its creatures to resume the
cycle of life.

"In the end," Larry Lof wrote in summarizing the fire episode, "only a
few small areas such as the 25 hectares protected by the *brecha* at Rancho
del Cielo remained in their more or less original condition. The important
flora and fauna elements remained—but only just barely. The condition of
the forest had reached its lowest ebb."

Those unfamiliar with nature's resilience might doubt that the forest
would ever recover from its wounds. I first saw the charred terrain in late
June. I remember with sinking spirit the bleached limestone, once covered
with mosses and ferns, and the blackened tree skeletons. Yet there were
pockets untouched by flame, and in even the barest places new growth was
rising from the ashes.

The birds were doing quite well in the clearing, and it was encouraging to find that the census area was not completely devastated; a central area and isolated spots were spared, and most of the trail markers remained in place.

The extent to which wildlife suffered during the period of the fire is unknown. It was Barbara Warburton's opinion that many birds and animals sought sanctuary in the ranch area. In mid-May, John Hunter observed a brocket deer grazing near the college pila. Pablo had seen two fawns. Any observation of this tiny deer is remarkable, as this once-common species has all but vanished from the mountain. Also, Pablo reported a "tiger" cat (jaguar) with two kittens in the area. John gave Pablo orders not to shoot any of the animals.

In May 1972 I received a letter from John Hunter. "I got back to the ranch Saturday P.M. We had five inches of rain last week for total of nine inches so far in May. The forest growth is unbelievable. It looks like late August or September."

The fires having run their course, attention again turned to land acquisition. We were informed that it was the "Meyers land" that was under consideration. It had belonged to Dr. Meyers, who had established the Julilo camp. It encompassed much of the slope east of Rancho del Cielo and dropped to or near the Río Sabinas. According to John, the tract began at the summit of the easternmost ridge (Rancho del Cielo lies less than 300 yards west of the summit) "and follows the summit line for about 3 kilometers down almost to the Aguacates corner. It runs east toward the river for a maximum of about 3½ kilometers or within a mile of the old Everts Storms place. Then it jogs around quite irregularly on the east side and comes back to a point just about opposite the old mud-hole that runs down toward the Aguacates."

Little was known of the area except by the local people, as it was accessible only by foot trail. It sloped from cloud forest to mountainside tropical semievergreen forest to tropical deciduous forest. Most important, human encroachment had been minimal, although an extensive corn field ran downhill within a short walk of the ranch, and Pablo remarked that some coffee was being grown on the lower slopes.

John Hunter was certain that the college would authorize him to purchase the Meyers land. Although they might have preferred a tropical cloud forest area, the tract in question was rough and heavily forested, ideally suited to provide sanctuary for wildlife, perhaps even the Great Curassow, provided there were any of the big birds remaining. In the old days, Frank reported that curassows would come up to the ranch in the fall to feed on acorns. Such had not occurred for many years since.

In a letter dated November 3, 1971, John advised George M. Sutton, "I am happy to report that we have a definite written offer of the 700 hectares tract at 150 pesos per acre. Our committee met this morning and approved the offer and arrangements were arranged for Dr. Oliveira and business manager Hector Hall to go to Victoria this week. They will call on our lawyer, Juan Zorilla, and authorize him to start investigation and approval of the title."

On November 29, 1971, John wrote to us, "Our land deal has been agreed to, and papers are in process of being drawn up by lawyers." We were encouraged to expect immediate results; we should have known better. "It still looks like we are going to get the 700 hectares of land," John wrote on May 5, 1973, "if you don't know how much trouble it is to get a Mexican lawyer off a dead center, you can't understand what I am going through. It is unbelievable how many excuses can be found for delay."

John did not need the stress of a lagging land deal at the time. He had experienced deteriorating health in recent years that would have brought down a man of lesser resolve. John was a diabetic with related problems, but it was a condition of the heart that surfaced in October 1968 that he would not have survived had he been at the ranch. The outcome included a "salt-free starvation diet" and weight loss (down below 300 pounds, the lowest it had been in the last 40 years), not to mention lost opportunities to visit his beloved mountain. About a year later, a pacemaker was installed. By mid-1970, John's weight was down to little over 200 pounds, a dramatic change from when we first met him.

Eventually, the land transaction was consummated, and an official survey of the tract was completed in the fall of 1975. John's letters became infrequent and made no further mention of what came to be called the Sutton tract.

For several years John Hunter had been urging Dr. Sutton to visit Rancho del Cielo, but the latter's schedule had not permitted it. When Sutton did come, it was with a small group from the Oklahoma Zoological Society as guests of the Gorgas Science Society. I was an additional guest, invited I suppose because of my knowledge of birds of the area and my correspondence with Sutton. It was a singular honor to work with an eminent ornithologist and bird artist, especially as he revisited the scenes of earlier expeditions. Sutton's writings had inspired us and created a feel for the country along the Río Sabinas and its creatures.

Barbara Warburton, Larry Lof, and I met the Oklahoma party in Ciudad Mante on February 4, 1976. We traveled north on the Pan-American Highway and turned left on the dirt road leading to Pano Ayuctle, where we had our lunch while sitting on cypress knees. Here Sutton must have been gripped by a bittersweet nostalgia. The cool, now gently flowing waters of the Río Sabinas seemed to whisper of people and deeds interred in memory. Here at Pano Ayuctle, Everts Storms had held court, almost literally, as unofficial legal aide to Frank Harrison and Paul Gellrich and countless people of Chamal, until he succumbed of a possible stroke while bathing in the river. Sutton had first met Frank here in 1939, when Frank came down the mountain to dine with his friend Don Evaristo.

After lunch we crossed the river by a suspension footbridge and entered tropical deciduous forest. We were now on the Sutton tract, the *vedado* (preserve). The trail rambled through the dense woodland that Sutton had been so familiar with in years past (the likes of which was fast disappearing from the region) before emerging at a corn field. A short climb took us into Gómez Farías.

Sutton found Rancho del Cielo hardly recognizable. The college campus was alien, the trails seemed unfamiliar, even Frank Harrison's cook house was completely new to him. "I was beginning to feel that the Rancho del Cielo was really somewhere else," Sutton wrote later, "that Frank had moved without letting me know."

Not until we led the party down a steep trail east of the ranch to our favorite overlook (Larry's Lookout) did Sutton feel, at last, that he had been there before. Surely that magnificent view of the lowlands stirred a host of memories, the Río Sabinas snaking through a patchwork of field and woodland, mesas rising in the haze beyond, the familiar buildup of thunderheads toward the coast. How many before us had stood there, as at the edge of the world! Aeons ago the nomadic Huastecans would have scanned a vista vastly different, but that, too, was an impression of a passing moment.

The Oklahoma group stayed only one full day, hardly enough, I thought, to infuse the ranch into one's bloodstream. That afternoon John Hunter drove up, and we made certain that he had a chance to visit with Sutton. The acquisition of the *vedado* must have given John great comfort, and being with the man responsible was equally satisfying.

The following day Sutton departed Rancho del Cielo for the last time.

Among Frank Harrison's papers was a letter from "Doc Sutton," dated April 28, 1949.

Dear Frank:

Many a time I have thought of you since the wonderful days you gave us at the Rancho del Cielo. I was never more impressed with whole-hearted hospitality. While I was a personal witness to it all I could not believe my eyes; and, now that the experience is farther removed, I still feel I cannot trust my senses. Some experience you've had has made a great man of you, Frank. I swear I'd like to know what it was. Or perhaps it's just a day-by-day, hour-by-hour realization that's dawned upon you that life is truly a continuing thing; that we are all a part of eternity; that the amassing of a fortune or the being regarded by everyone as famous is not the truly important thing. The important thing is *living:* the cramming into each hour all that can be crowded in.

On April 27, 1976, Caroline Hunter addressed a letter to friends of the family: "Since Christmas, John had been exceptionally active. He worked in the yard every morning and several afternoons a week he went to the Elks club to play dominoes. . . . Then early Friday morning, April 2, he left for the cabin in Mexico with three men friends. They reached the cabin in the afternoon and that night John played dominoes and was in good spirits."

Around six o'clock the following morning John went into the bathroom and did not return. He had died of a blood clot.

"John had told many friends that he wanted to die on the mountain. . . . He also wanted to go quickly, so we feel that God was good to him."

Blue-crowned Motmot

26

THE college program at Rancho del Cielo was expanding by 1970. No longer were excursions to the mountain confined to work trips by students of the Gorgas Science Society and college staff. Through arrangements with Pan-American University in Brownsville, field trips were conducted as part of that school's graduate course work. On such trips the ranch was staffed by Gorgas science students or exes in the role of driver, cook, or general handyperson, under the supervision of Barbara Warburton.

With financial assistance from Texas Southmost College limited, students were obligated to raise funds for the ranch, but sales of candy and amaryllis bulbs scarcely brought in enough money to keep the project afloat. There must be other, and perhaps easier, ways to raise money, we thought.

Marie and I could imagine the attraction that the cloud forest and adjacent areas would hold for bird enthusiasts, not to mention those persons with a penchant for botany, hiking, and photography. We expressed our views to Barbara Warburton; she agreed. We would try the guest-tour approach, akin to the ecotour concept. Marie and I would do the organizing; the Gorgas Science Society would provide the facilities and the services; profits would go to the ranch project.

During the Christmas–New Year's period in 1969–1970, we conducted the first bird trip, as they were usually called. The nature tours, as we preferred to call them, continued regularly into the late 1990s, attracting participants from throughout the United States and from Mexico.

Guest trips and other special events posed a problem for the students. With the two dormitory cabins filled with guests, the staff was forced to sleep in the Keller cabin, with overflow at John Hunter's or even Bob's. This necessitated that the cooks walk to the cook cabin before daylight, an exercise not favored by the girls; a bear or a big cat might still be prowling at that hour, and the boys loved to tease with tales of strange nocturnal encounters. Certainly darkness fueled the imagination, rendering familiar sounds unfamiliar, perverting visual images. Should there be heavy fog, one could lose all sense of direction. A new cabin, nearer to the cook house, would minimize the hazards of a walk in the dark.

"Well, we're not going to build any more," Barbara Warburton was quoted as saying after the effort of constructing Harrison Hall.

Barbara was characteristically adamant once she had made a decision, so Marie's statement that "we need a cabin with a fireplace" would seem a useless exercise. However, further discussion chipped away at Barbara's resolve, or it could be that she had seen the wisdom of additional housing from the beginning.

They would build another cabin; it would be on the order of Harrison Hall, but with a fireplace. That overall concept survived only until Mabel's husband, Bob, heard of the plan. Robert Deshayes's architectural exploits were applauded in the Houston area. His offer to design the new building was both flattering and practical. Larry Lof would be in charge of construction. The building would stand on a slight rise at the southwest corner of the college clearing, the other buildings forming an irregular half-circle north and east.

Work on the new project went slowly, influenced and given shape by various heads and hands, and by what lumber was available at a particular time; also, timing was at the mercy of other college schedules. For a while the foundation and chimney (fashioned from rock collected locally) stood alone, a stark reminder of work in progress. The chimney, black and gray, might have been a monument erected by some vanished Indian tribe, the yawning chasm of a fireplace waiting to receive a burnt offering. Some student of medieval history likened the rockwork to the ruins of an ancient castle, or that portion of the castle complex known as the keep. The concept took hold; the building henceforth has been called the Keep.

The basic structure of the Keep was completed by August 1974, with thick stone wall segments freestanding and gaps filled by lumber locally milled. Viewed from outside, the architectural plan was like nothing that had been seen on the mountain: narrow two-story wings at either end of the building, separated by a tin roof on a lower level, slanting toward the front of the building. The upper floors were dormitories, women on the east, men on the west, each with bathroom facilities.

The ground floor featured a large central room, the focal point being the fireplace with its wide stone hearth. Beneath the girls' quarters were two rooms, a bedroom with bath for the director at front and a hallway room at the rear. The latter could be used as a sitting room or library, and it housed a stairway to the girls' quarters. Later, as her sleeping quarters were dark and uncomfortably cold, Barbara Warburton would convert the hallway room to a bedroom and relegate the front room to storage and pantry space, for which it was better suited. (The girls applauded Barbara's decision. Their bath was directly over the front room, and the plumbing was quite noisy, so Barbara was emphatic that there would be no flushing during the night.) A kitchen area was under the boys' quarters, which were reached by stairs partitioned off from the main room.

Thus the first construction phase was complete; later, a porch would be added to the south side (back) of the building. The initial plan for the Keep was to provide not only living quarters but also a place to relax. The large central room (the common area) offered breathing space and recreational possibilities. Also, on student trips, the other buildings need not be opened.

After Barbara Warburton became a partner with Tom Keller, she used his cabin to house the college crew. The arrangement had drawbacks that the Keep would alleviate; therefore, "In the latter part of 1974," Barbara wrote, "I decided we would move into the Keep, finished or not." In October 1975, Larry Lof was dispatched to the ranch to work on the interior of the Keep. Marie and Paula Gómez accompanied him to provide presence and support.

"Larry was unhappy that the building was going to be used by a relatively small group," Marie reported. "It seemed so large, impersonal and pretentious in comparison with the other cabins." Larry kept his thoughts to himself as long as he could—about a week. "Larry and I talked about what the Keep could be used for. It was certainly larger than the cook cabin and would give a lot more space for dining for bird tours and graduate class groups."

Another problem could be solved by moving the main kitchen to the Keep. Then the cook house could be partitioned to accommodate couples, an amenity that the college had been unable to provide.

Barbara came to the ranch later in the month and was approached on the matter. Marie continued, "She did not seem very interested until I reminded her that she would not have to send one of her girl students out to the cook cabin by herself in the dark at 5 A.M. to start the fire in the cook stove—if the kitchen and dining room were moved to the Keep."

Once convinced, Warburton lost no time in ordering the move. Food, dishes, cabinets, stove, refrigerator, and all were transferred to "La Casa

Grande" on October 31. On the following day, "Larry and the boys got the inside of the cook cabin framed up and half done."

Thereafter, the old cook house was referred to as the R and R cabin. Besides three bedroom compartments and a bath, there is space where guests can gather and make hot drinks at any time without disturbing the crew. The front porch is a favorite lounging place after a day in the field; with feet propped on the rail, guests can watch for hummingbirds at the agapanthus blossoms.

As for the Keep, the change has been gratifying, the physical arrangement most convenient. All meals are prepared in the kitchen space, to one side of the central area. Diners are seated along three tables, which occupy most of the large room. When the guests have eaten and departed, the crew reclaims its domain until the next meal.

With the occupation of the Keep, the campus was complete; the Gorgas Science Society could pursue its mission at full efficiency. But would the forest remain a viable resource, could it retain the unique qualities that drew those who would investigate and those who would merely admire nature's treasures?

While the matter of the Sutton *vedado* was being settled and the college was enlarging its program, the agrarian problem continued to fester. In the summer of 1974 the situation threatened to explode. The source of the tension seemed to be the dispute between the agrarians and the lumber people over property rights, but college personnel and friends were drawn in by circumstance.

Barbara Warburton and a student group, with Marie as guest, left for the ranch on July 17. Before reaching Ciudad Victoria, they encountered Bob Hunter, who was returning to Brownsville. On his drive to the ranch from Gómez Farías five days before, Bob reported, he had encountered two trees down, blocking the main road just before the ranch junction. He sawed and moved the trees and proceeded to the ranch. Agrarians had felled the trees, apparently in an effort to oppose the lumber people, who had cut a road along West Ridge near San Pablo to reach a new logging site. Pablo was blamed for cutting the logs, and he had gone to Juan Zorilla in Ciudad Victoria for help.

If Barbara was dismayed by this latest development, she failed to show it; rather, she was determined to settle the matter. A visit to Zorilla was the first step. The crew waited anxiously while Warburton and the lawyer conversed, only to be told that the road in question was public and could not be legally blocked. Details regarding the agrarians' grievances were not discussed then or later.

The next stop for Barbara was the police station at Gómez Farías. After a lengthy absence she emerged with a grimly satisfied expression and three men who were detailed to accompany the college party. If any strategy was planned, it remained a mystery.

It was an uneventful trip to the cloud forest, but with suspense mounting. The site of the controversy was easy to identify; the road had been blocked again. Here the men from Gómez Farías took charge. Ordering Warburton to wait, they sought out the agrarians and negotiations proceeded. The outcome was that the agrarians accepted the college's offer of a chain to put across the road and a padlock, for which the college had a key. "The boys helped the agrarians clear the road," Marie wrote, "and that's all there was to it."

There seemed to be no more particular problems with the squatters until the fall of 1975. On October 20, Marie reported, "Pablo came in tonight and talked with Larry a long time. The engineer from the *ejido* at San Pablo came up this evening. He is from Cd. Victoria. . . . The people living at San Pablo were told that they can stay there and grow crops but can not own the land. Some of the men got mad and left the meeting. Of course they covet the ranch."

"The squatters think they can come in and make a few corn fields and claim the land," Marie reminded me later. "As long as Frank's murderer has been at San Pablo he's stirred up trouble for everybody."

The agrarians seemed to move about as much as the lumber people, and we never knew where we might find a newly cleared field or a dwelling. Most of the activity that we could see took place along the main road through the cloud forest; we could only wonder what was happening away from the road.

We were surprised during a 1979 trip to find a small village along the road just north of the San Pablo clearing. It could not have been there long, but like other settlements it exhibited a timelessness: an ample clearing gouged out of the forest to accommodate small, makeshift houses set on bare red clay, brightened by cultivated flowering plants, dooryards occupied by chickens, pigs, and children.

Paul's Field and later clearings at San Pablo were worked irregularly, one year a corn field, the next a tangle of weeds and bushes. Paul's Field, a natural sink, was comparatively rock free, hence it was more frequently used.

In June 1991, approaching from the south, we found Paul's Field lying fallow, the other cleared tracts a wilderness of weed and exposed rock. Birds and insects combined to dispel a sense of abandonment; they called from the towering oaks and sweetgums that edge the clearing. A Gray Hawk soared high among ever-changing cloud wisps. West Ridge looked dew-fresh, pines clearly delineated along its crest.

The tree border rimming the clearing north of Paul's Field, reduced to low brush some years earlier by ax and machete, had rebounded toward its former status and stature. The brush-loving species, particularly the Olive Sparrow and Rufous-capped Warbler, were gone now. Yellow-green Vireos had claimed the territory, serenading the passerby with their cheery yet tuneless song.

We had planned to move inconspicuously past the settlement, but no barking dog came out to greet us. No curious housewives and clinging children peered from doorways. In fact, there was no settlement at all, no houses — only patches of bare earth being reclaimed by forb and sapling. We did encounter a small, strolling band of pigs or hogs, obviously enjoying their freedom.

Perhaps the former inhabitants of the former village had left the mountain; perhaps not. The ebb and flow of the interlopers was a mystery to those outside the circle. We did know that if they persisted and brought in reinforcements, some years down the road the forest would be decimated, as had the southern portion around Alta Cima. The nutrients that are the forest's life would have seeped through the rocks, beyond recall.

Although the threat of agricultural depletion seemed a distinct possibility in the far future, a more immediate concern was logging. As long as the lumbering interests concentrated on the pines, the cloud forest seemed secure. But the cloud forest had been exploited before. As recently as 1969 the sawmill at La Perra had an order for 10,000 board-feet of maple and was expected to cut in the ranch area.

The logging problem hit close to home in 1974. On a June trip we noticed

a new logging road originating at the brecha and going down Canyon Tableta, east of John Hunter's cabin. Then on a December trip we could hear,
as we stood on the brecha, the crash of ax on tree trunk and the rumble of
trucks. We had not experienced logging activity so close to the ranch.

It had become evident to many interested parties during the 1970s that the
cloud forest was in danger of disappearing. Efforts by private interests to
acquire land for a preserve had failed, partly because of the difficulty of ob-
taining clear title. The Sutton *vedado* was a victory, but it included only a
minor portion of the cloud forest. Elsewhere, lumbering and agricultural
activity ate away at the heart of a unique ecological treasure, one that would
not be replaced if destroyed.

Rancho del Cielo, the biological research station, was deeply committed
to the college program and by necessity directed its efforts in that direction, but in the end it was also instrumental in finding a solution to the
environmental problem.

More than any other entity, the Gorgas Science Society and Gorgas
Science Foundation exposed students to an unfamiliar world and fostered
an appreciation for the interaction of nature with mankind. Student trips,
however, reached only a limited segment of the total population. Since 1970
the bird tours have brought a wider audience to the ranch, wider in a geographical as well as a professional sense. Guests on the nature tours are given
an in-depth introduction to the natural features of the region through a
series of hikes and a one-day trip across the mountain to different vegetation
zones. They listen to talks by Larry Lof (who succeeded Barbara Warburton as director of the project) on history, climatology, archeology, and other
topics pertinent to the mountain and Rancho del Cielo. Not only do guests
gain an appreciation of various biota of the forests, but they also witness
firsthand the labors that college staff and students contribute to keep the
biological field station in operation and moving forward.

Exposure to the general public through the nature tours brought additional financial support to the Gorgas Science Foundation when it was
sorely needed. James George, introduced to the ranch while a tour partici-
pant, became a major contributor to the program. Such outside help made
it possible to buy new trucks as old ones became too worn to repair, buy new
tires, and served a variety of other needs.

Most guests on the bird trips were from north of the border, but some Mexican citizens were curious to know more about Rancho del Cielo. Among them was the conservation-minded Andres Marcelo Sada Zambrano of Monterrey, perhaps Mexico's leading birder. In addition, a friend of Rancho del Cielo from previous years, Laura Alcalá Vargas, joined the tours on several occasions.

Sra. Alcalá had heard of the mountain long before her first trip to Rancho del Cielo in June 1971. In the 1950s, she and her family traveled from Ciudad Victoria to Pano Ayuctle to visit with Everts Storms. Storms, we can be certain, entertained his guests with tales of the mountain and its wonders. After her firsthand experience at Rancho del Cielo, Alcalá was convinced of the uniqueness of the ecosystems in their configuration and geographical location, and of the value of the entire mountain range as a natural resource, not for exploitation but for preservation as a laboratory of life sciences. It was a treasure of which Mexico could be proud.

Alcalá is a charming, gracious, outgoing woman; also, she is persuasive and tenacious in pursuit of that which she perceives as noble and right. The combination can be irresistible. Convinced that the cloud forest and adjacent areas must be saved, she went to work in Ciudad Victoria and Mexico City to contact influential individuals and government officials and urge them to visit Rancho del Cielo. The details of her campaign have not been revealed to us, but we are told that she worked long and tirelessly over a period of years. Larry Lof expressed it well: "There is little doubt that this important and indeed unique region would have been lost without her efforts."

One of Alcalá's first accomplishments, according to Larry Lof, was to persuade the governor of Tamaulipas "to halt lumbering in an area of approximately 1,000 hectarias that comprised the heart of the cloud forest around Rancho del Cielo." In a decree of February 16, 1976, a study was ordered of the possibility of creating a "Parque Nacional" to "conserve the area for future generations . . . as an area unique in the Western Hemisphere." Later, the first moves were made to preserve the area through a nonprofit organization formed by Dr. Gonzalo Halfter (then director of the Instituto de Ecologia), Andres Sada from Monterrey, and Alcalá. "Together," Lof says, "they approached the governor of the state of Tamaulipas, Emilio Martínez Manatou, with the idea. The governor and his entourage visited Rancho del Cielo on May 8, 1981." On July 13, 1985, a major portion of the Sierra de Guatemala was formally declared a biosphere reserve ("reserva de la biosfera"), to be known as El Cielo. It was the first biosphere reserve to be established by a state government rather than the federal government in Mexico City.

El Cielo Biosphere Reserve encompasses 144,530 hectares, or nearly 360,000 acres, and includes the municipalities of Llera, Gómez Farías, Ocampo, and Jaumave. In 1988 administration of the reserve was placed in the hands of the Department of Human Settlements and Public Works and Services, under the office for Urban Development and Ecology of the state of Tamaulipas.

The United Nations Organization has embraced the biosphere in its Man and Biosphere program, at the request of the government of Tamaulipas.

Briefly, the objectives of the biosphere reserve are to preserve plant and animal species, to maintain the biotic communities within the existing natural ecosystems, to sponsor research toward the preservation of the environment and promote the study of ecology, and to promote a balanced development between the environment and the human settlements existing within the reserve.

The zones delineated by the Mexicans differ somewhat from those drawn by Paul Martin (the terms we have used in earlier chapters); they are:

Tropical caducifolia jungle (on the eastern flank of the sierra), which consists of much of Paul Martin's tropical deciduous forest, all tropical semievergreen forest, and some cloud forest.

Mesophyllic mountain forest (or fog forest), which includes much cloud forest and a minor portion of humid pine-oak forest.

Pine-oak forest, which includes probably the remainder of the humid pine-oak forest and all of the dry oak-pine forest, as well as chaparral.

Dwarf oaks and heaths (on the extreme west), which include mainly dry oak-pine forest, plus a little chaparral and thorn forest.

Besides the conceptual demarcation of the reserve into vegetation zones, a practical division was made "to ensure a proper level of conservation and research." There are two nucleus zones. Nucleus I Zone includes more than 70,000 acres of mesophyllic mountain forests and pine-oak forests.

Nucleus II Zone includes nearly 18,000 acres of tropical subcaducifolian forests (Rancho del Cielo is in this zone). Hunters and collectors are permanently barred from nucleus zones in order to preserve plant and animal life. The Buffer Zone includes all remaining acreage of the reserve; here, hunting, fishing, and timber exploitation are restricted.

The biosphere program, in addition to preserving natural areas, offers an opportunity for cooperation between Mexico and foreign entities in biological exploration, a partnership that was not realized earlier in the twentieth century.

Ecological studies were long delayed in Mexico. Apparently the first survey of animal life was conducted by Francisco Hernández, doctor of the court of King Philip II of Spain (1570–1577). Later studies of some importance were done by a royal Spanish expedition at the end of the eighteenth century and a scientific expedition to Mexico during the reign of the Emperor Maximilian.

The often turbulent history of Mexico no doubt inhibited biological exploration, but during later periods of stability foreign investigators began to fill the void. One of the earliest contributions (and undoubtedly the most significant) was by E. A. Goldman and E. W. Nelson for the U.S. Bureau of Biological Survey, who traveled throughout Mexico between 1892 and 1906, describing the flora and fauna and making extensive collections.

The Mexican Revolution put a damper on scientific expeditions for a while, but by the late 1940s activity was accelerating. This was evident in the Gómez Farías region, long inaccessible and unknown to the outsider. The scientists and student interns from major universities in the United States who worked the valley of the Río Sabinas and the Sierra de Guatemala did so with the cooperation of the Mexican government. Although it was necessary to obtain collecting permits from officials of the Dirección General Forestal y de Caza in Mexico City, the foreigners enjoyed freedom of movement and access to the resources of the countryside.

The willingness of Mexican officials to permit outsiders to work in Mexican territory seems to echo an earlier philosophy. During the 1870s and 1880s, a group of advisers to President Porfirio Díaz, influenced by industrialization in Europe, convinced the Mexican government of the virtue of embracing science and technology, as opposed to emphasis on cultural matters. To counteract the nation's shortage in wealth and know-how, and to push economic development, the government encouraged European, North

American, Canadian, and other interests to invest in Mexico, offering land grants and other incentives.

A Mexican national did participate in at least one of the American expeditions in the late 1940s and early 1950s; he was Efraim Hernández. A bulletin (no. 11, 1950) of the Sociedad Botánica de México included the paper "Nota florística de una asociación importante del sureste de Tamaulipas, México" and was credited to A. J. Sharp, E. Hernández X., H. Crum, and W. B. Fox. The English version of the paper, "A Unique Vegetational Area in Tamaulipas," in a bulletin (no. 78) of the Torrey Botanical Club, listed Hernández as the senior author.

Byron Harrell, in his thesis work at Rancho del Cielo, acknowledged aid from Bernardo Villa R. of the Instituto de Biologío, México, D.F.; however, most expeditions were on their own, and their findings were published in the United States. That the work of the North Americans was appreciated is indicated by an invitation to George M. Sutton to exhibit his paintings of Mexican birds in the Palacio de Bellas Artes in Mexico City, a high honor.

Although official participation was minimal, North American scientists found the local people of the Gómez Farías region to be friendly, helpful, and interested in the work of the outsiders, acting as guides and often aiding in securing specimens of plants and animals.

One factor that may have limited participation by Mexican naturalists in investigations during the period mentioned was a lack of biological training, evident in early published works of the twentieth century. Enrique Beltrán was aware of this shortcoming, and in 1934 he introduced a course in wildlife zoology at the Escuela Nacional de Agricultura at Chapingo, designed for inclusion in the forestry curriculum. It was hoped that foresters would be made aware of wildlife problems and perhaps gather data and specimens. Unfortunately, the course was dropped from the curriculum, and in Beltrán's words, "for many years now the foresters in Mexico have had no chance to become oriented in wildlife biology" (from the foreword to *Wildlife of Mexico*, by A. Starker Leopold).

Such agencies as the University of Tamaulipas are reversing the earlier inactivity by Mexican naturalists. Sherri L. Boykin, writing in her thesis "Avian Community Dynamics in Tamaulipas, Mexico" (toward a master of science degree at the University of Wisconsin–Madison, 1987), acknowledged the role of the Universidad Autónoma de Tamaulipas in providing logistical support for her project.

Paul S. Martin made a nostalgic trip to Mexico when he attended the first Simposio de Investigación en la Reserva de la Biosfera "El Cielo," held in Ciudad Victoria in July 1988. Faculty and students from seventeen institutions participated, including the Universidad Autónoma de Tamaulipas, Universidad Autónoma de México, Programa Hombre y Biosfera, and Université Pierre et Marie Curie of Paris, France. The three-day session concerned many aspects of ecology, basic and applied, "that showed the value of the Gómez Farías region as a study site for university students from Mexico City, Tamaulipas, Texas, and many other parts of the region."

A few hundred families remained in the biosphere in the 1990s. Most were in established communities, but some had come into the region with the lumber companies. The latter, no longer able to make a living by cutting timber, turned to farming or selling natural resources. Teaching the residents how to subsist on the land without depleting resources or destroying the forest is a continuing challenge to the biosphere administration and one that is being addressed. Caring for authorized visitors (tourists or study groups) is one means of livelihood for the residents, and modest facilities have been provided within the biosphere reserve for this purpose. Ecotours have been sponsored jointly by the state of Tamaulipas and the Texas Parks and Wildlife Department, and Texas A&M University has sent student researchers into the reserve. Meanwhile, villagers are being trained in ecological matters in the hope that they will be better stewards of the forest.

Thanks to its track record and stated goals, the Gorgas Science Foundation, which was formally incorporated as a nonprofit organization in 1983, is granted permission to continue its program within the reserve. The foundation's mission is "to provide the highest quality educational opportunity, to foster greater awareness and understanding of ecological issues and to encourage conservation of critical natural resources." Rancho del Cielo is a major project of the foundation, but its influence reaches throughout South Texas and beyond.

Formation of the biosphere reserve was a delight and a relief to us, a satisfactory culmination of the labors and sacrifices of dedicated individuals over the years. Although we had little to do with the final outcome, we felt that we had assisted in some measure to see the dreams of John and Frank and Barbara and others materialize. In the end, it was the efforts of the Mexican officials that made the reserve a reality, and because we were not privy to their actions, we can praise them only in general terms.

27

I T was a sunny day in late June 1992 when we left the ranch with the bird-tour crowd. Our principal mission on this occasion was not to entertain the guests; they were quite capable of finding birds for themselves and would be happily lost in their own world of discovery. Our destination was a locality somewhere beyond La Joya de Salas, near the canyon of the macaws. We would pick a suitable spot where John Bax, the cinematographer, would camp out while he caught the Military Macaws on film. John had already made one nature film for the Gorgas Science Foundation, *At a Bend in a Mexican River,* which featured the Río Sabinas lowlands. Now he was working on *El Cielo: Forest in the Clouds.* Macaw Canyon, a secret well kept from the outside world, would provide a climactic episode for the film.

After an early start, we crossed over the wet pine-oak zone in good time and cruised through dry oak-pine woodland until we reached Tierra Colorada. We unloaded the majority of the group and proceeded toward La Joya de Salas with two trucks.

The terrain was familiar, semiopen woodland and shrubby ground cover, canyons and ridges. The birding party would walk this route. They would pick Orange-billed Nightingale-Thrushes and Rufous-sided Towhees from the brush, and search for the diminutive Blue-hooded Euphonia in clumps of mistletoe.

The road changed from red clay to bare, sunbaked rock, and then we dropped into the narrow oak-shaded canyon that we had walked so often, along the dry rock-bound watercourse, where it seemed that no breeze can penetrate. Stifling minutes later the canyon widened, and we were in the valley, flat except for ditches carved by floodwaters. We recalled other times we had run the course, times when it had rained and the white clay was as slick as oiled glass; it was quite dry now. A wilted grass mat covered the valley floor, and on the rocky flanks stunted oaks shaded sparse ground cover. It was the rain-shadow effect.

We looked for the tree where we had enjoyed the sight of *Laelia speciosa,* a beautiful pink orchid that had clustered on a high branch. The tree was there, by the roadside, but the orchids were gone, taken by collectors some years before; nothing remained of the colony.

We passed the expected small farm buildings, fruit trees, and animals,

Military Macaw

all secure within their rock-walled enclosure. The great sinkhole that John Hunter had first shown us was off to the right, in bare, overgrazed pasture. We skirted the little lake (it was full for this early in the season) and passed the tiny lakeside village of La Joya de Salas. Except for one or two men on horseback, we saw no human beings. Had the settlement been deserted? We had been told that La Joya had lost its teacher, and because the people wanted education for their children, they had moved away. At any rate, we felt certain that no one who had known Frank Harrison was still there.

A narrow road through a juniper wood took us to T.S.C. Park. It was years since we had been there, but it could have been yesterday. It was the same wide, open valley with pines scattered about, grassland obviously grazed at regular intervals; indeed, there were horses running free. On long trips, the students had lunched here and run off pent-up energy ("horsed around" is the appropriate term).

We left the road here. John Bax and Alejandro Arizpe, a tour guest, got off the trucks to search for an old lumber road that would lead to the base of the mountain—beyond which we would find Macaw Canyon.

John Bax had been here a few days earlier with a local guide. Now he and the rest of the party had to rely on his memory. We followed, Larry Lof and Juan Pérez driving the Dodge Power Wagons, as John guided us from a more open area into oak and pine woodland, darting first one way and then the other as he looked for clues.

What landmarks John sought we could not imagine. There were no marked trees, no broken branches; one spot looked much like the one we had left. We knew by this time that we were on a typical mountain adventure, the goal determined but the method for reaching it as nebulous as the patches of cumulus crossing the sun. It was a challenge that John Hunter would have relished. Larry's determination, if not his enthusiasm, matched John Hunter's.

John Bax moved about like a man half his age; the trucks followed like puppies after the master. Now and then we seemed to be on the remnant of an old logging road, at other times we bulldozed through brush and saplings that hid any trace of former use.

After an interminable series of false leads and backtracking, the trucks finally came to rest in a small cleared area among oak and second-growth pines. John Bax, appearing satisfied and not at all fatigued, promptly led the party up the adjacent mountain slope, presumably following a trail.

Juan lagged behind to accommodate my slower pace. After a short climb, picking our way around rocks and clumps of brush, we reached a point where the trail took a much steeper angle. I must confess that at this juncture I decided to stop for the sake of self-preservation.

Assured that I would likely survive, Juan disappeared among the rocks while I sought relief from the heat in a shaded spot and on a rock wide enough to alert me to rattlesnakes should one attempt to join me. (It didn't occur to me that I might be sharing the forest with a black bear, nor did one appear.)

Sudden and total aloneness in a strange place is at once freeing and disquieting. It was a situation Marie would have embraced, but Marie was somewhere up the slope, unaware of my defection from the quest, and since Juan's crunching footfalls had receded, I heard no human-produced sound and had no idea how far the others might climb.

Actually, I was not entirely alone. The much-coveted Blue-hooded Euphonia was twittering in some nearby tree. Then I heard a macaw, distant at first, then somewhere near at hand, its raucous "rrrak!" unmistakable. Despite my mental urging, it kept its distance, but I was assured that the canyon was close at hand.

I have vivid memories of Military Macaws gathered in trees below Cycad Point at Rancho del Cielo, we looking down as they flew restlessly back and forth, tree to tree, displaying their bright green and blue plumage and the brilliant red central tail feathers. I remember the flights over the ranch clearing in earlier days, the expectation of distant calls, then a file of magnificent birds, two by two always, unless one had lost its mate.

Later we would view John Bax's film. It was as Marie remembered. She had stood on the rim of the canyon, over the sheer cliff, waiting for the macaws to come to their nest cavities in the rock face below. Soon they came, sweeping in on shallow wingbeat, powerful yet graceful, gliding easily. Marie stood in awe.

Beyond the canyon the mountains fell away in waves, greenish blue, each ridge more haze-dim than the one before, until mountain rim blended with sky. There was no sign of human presence in that vista; surely it was the macaws' own domain. The wind that blew up the canyon and rustled the pines seemed to give assurance; it spoke of ageless time when all macaws flew free, and whispered a hope for the future. Perhaps in this isolated place in the biosphere reserve the species will be able to sustain a population.

Juan came down before the others, and we headed for the trucks. Convinced that I could retrace our steps, I went my own way. It was not a wise move, but I did discover a spring in the mountainside that I correctly assumed provided pure, cool water for the people at La Joya de Salas through a pipeline that dropped downhill. I had lost sight of Juan by now, and had no sense of direction, but we established voice contact, and after pushing aside young pines and side-stepping boulders, I arrived at the trucks.

We unloaded John Bax's equipment. Larry invited Alejandro to stay with John for company and assistance, and we returned the way we had come. This time the trail was easy to follow by reading the signs of our prior passage (flattened saplings, broken branches, and other damage the trucks had inflicted) until we reached the pasture area. We might still be riding about T.S.C. Park had not the water line from the spring set us right. And, yes, we had a flat tire on the far outskirts of the village, but that is hardly worth mentioning.

The hikers were excited about a Bumblebee Hummingbird on its nest overhanging the road. We were willing to let that be the topic of conversation on the ride back. They could see the Military Macaws on film.

We sat on the porch of the Keller-Warburton cabin that evening. It is a great spot to watch birds during the day. Down a gentle slope, past plantings of agapanthus and patches of impatiens gone wild, was John's clearing. The cabin was partially visible behind the loquat tree that had grown to full stature since our first trip to the mountain.

Things were not quite as they were on our first trip. Since John Hunter's passing, the Deshayes had remodeled the cabin. It displayed a fashionable flair, but character had been compromised. It was locked tightly now, and we were told no one had occupied it in recent months. John's orchard, in a depression that made up most of his clearing, was sadly depleted, a few survivors standing forlorn. Of course the old vine-covered hurry house was long gone, replaced by conventional indoor plumbing. Bob Hunter's cabin retained its old look, but it was hidden from view from the Keller porch. Frank's place, had we been able to see it from our perspective, would certainly disappoint. His guest house was mostly intact, but that was about all. The cook house had been completely made over, a sturdy rock house for Pablo's successor, his son Juan. The old walnut tree where the McPherson's log cabin had stood was gone. The amaryllis beds were but a memory resurrected by an occasional eruption of beauty in the spring, and the gladioli were sparse now.

"The wood owl should call soon," Marie said.

Twilight hush had stilled the daytime bird voices. A late Rufescent Tinamou had sent its plaintive whistle from shadowed forest depth, and a robin clucked, chickenlike, along the clearing edge. It was time for the insect chorus, in throbbing, grating cadence. Darkness was well entrenched inside the forest when we heard the Mottled Owl at some distance, the eerie wail greeting nightfall. The resonant hoots followed shortly as the bird left its diurnal retreat. It called for a while, approaching the clearing, then relinquished the night.

Dusk fell heavy on the clearing, the forest rim closing in, the cabin we had known as John's becoming one with shapeless gloom.

"I thought I saw a flash of light in John's window," I remarked.

"You saw a firefly," Marie said. "John would have the window wide open and we could see the light over the table. Frank would be coming down shortly, for a game of canasta."

Fireflies were twinkling throughout the clearing now. A cloud had rolled in unnoticed, except that the insect lights were suddenly muted. Fog helped darkness hide the countenance of the clearing.

"The night is kind," I philosophized. "It erases change. Like we could go back for just . . ."

I knew better.

"We could have a thunder-bumper tonight," Marie said. "Thunderheads were building up before sundown."

Frank Harrison would sit on his cook house doorstep and watch the evening thunderheads form over the lowlands. I knew that Marie would enjoy nature's uninhibited display once more before we left the ranch. We would sleep well with rain pounding on the tin roof.

At the cabins behind us, guests were still up. We heard bits of muffled conversation—rising, falling—and outbursts of laughter. No one walked about tonight; they had done their owling on past nights, playing tapes of owl calls, scanning trees with flashlights. Over at the Keep the students were subdued by fatigue; we heard shutters slam as they closed the building for the night. All were sounds we had heard on many occasions. The script was the same, only the players were different.

Beyond the porch, night had tightened its grip. There would be a moon later if clouds permitted, but for now reality had fled, the universe aroused only by the stirring of life unseen. It might have been any night in millennia past. It would be the same again. Then light breaking in the east, secrets revealed to light. The same setting, only the players different.

Lightning Source UK Ltd.
Milton Keynes UK
UKOW03f2123200614

233774UK00001B/92/P